Dear Reader,

As the hot summer months begin, what better way to be prepared for a day at the beach than with a Harlequin Duets? Remember, when you've finished one story, it's time to check your tan and turn over!

This month offers two wonderful Duets for your entertainment. Long-time reader favorite Victoria Pade brings us *Downhome Darlin'*, a charming and entertaining story of a good girl who's been "good" for too long. Then Liz Ireland, familiar to readers of Harlequin Historicals and Harlequin American Romance, spins a dizzying tale of identical brothers who switch places at a wedding in *The Best Man Switch*.

Popular Cheryl St.John pens a delightful and captivating *pretend* marriage of convenience with *For This Week I Thee Wed*. Next Alyssa Dean writes our second *Real Men* story, *50 Clues He's Mr. Right,* set around the women who work at *Real Men* magazine.

Once again, enjoy Harlequin Duets—the lighter side of love. Double the pleasure. Still no calories.

Happy reading!

Malle V.

Malle Vallik
Senior Editor

P.S. We'd love to [...] in Duets! Drop us a line at:

    Harlequin Duets
    Harlequin Books
    225 Duncan Mill Road
    Don Mills, Ontario
    M3B 3K9 Canada

For This Week I Thee Wed

"Are you married?"

Ryan blinked, his warm brown eyes showing confusion over her abrupt change of subject. "No," he said finally. "Is that relevant to the discussion?"

"Perhaps we can negotiate after all," Francie said.

"Money is not an issue—"

"No, not money. In fact if you agree to this idea, you can keep your money. I'm afraid I've done something—said something—impetuous, and now I don't have any way out of it. Except maybe through you."

"I don't understand."

"I told my grandmother that I'd gotten married."

"What does that have to do with me?"

"I've been cornered into participating at my ten-year reunion. Nana is expecting me. *And* my husband." She paused. "We can make a deal...if you come to Springdale with me as my husband for a week."

50 Clues He's Mr. Right

He'll take out the trash, lass
He'll wash his own clothes, Rose
He'll clean up the dish, Trish
And he vacuums the floor.
He cooks a steak rare, Clair
He knows a fine wine, Vine
He's got lots of class, Cass
He won't feed you a line.
He won't ever be late, Kate
He thinks the opera's a good date.
He's no dummy, honey
He's got his own money.
He's got a great build, Lil
He doesn't assume you're on the Pill
He thinks that you're clever, Heather
And he wants you forever.

HARLEQUIN DUETS

ISBN 0-373-44072-3

FOR THIS WEEK I THEE WED
Copyright © 1999 by Cheryl Ludwigs

50 CLUES HE'S MR. RIGHT
Copyright © 1999 by Patsy McNish

Look us up on-line at: http://www.romance.net

Printed in U.S.A.

CHERYL ST.JOHN

For This Week I Thee Wed

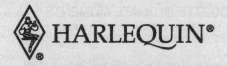

HARLEQUIN®

TORONTO • NEW YORK • LONDON
AMSTERDAM • PARIS • SYDNEY • HAMBURG
STOCKHOLM • ATHENS • TOKYO • MILAN • MADRID
PRAGUE • WARSAW • BUDAPEST • AUCKLAND

Dear Reader,

Opposites really do attract!

After twenty-seven years of marriage, my husband and I have learned to laugh about our differences and to celebrate the very precious and few things we do have in common.

Jay is a man of punctuality—gets up at the same time every morning, goes to bed at the same time every night. He plans his day according to the clock and abhors being late.

I've been known to: forget my children at school, forget the man was coming to install cable before the big game, lose track of what day it is, wonder how old I am...well, you get the picture. The best thing about writing is that I can work according to my impulsive nature.

This amusing contrast is probably why I had such a ball creating Francie and Ryan, two people who couldn't be more different, yet who are inexplicably drawn to each other. I hope you enjoy reading their story even more than I enjoyed writing it! VIVE LA DIFFERENCE!

Cheryl St.John

Books by Cheryl St.John

HARLEQUIN HISTORICALS

SILHOUETTE INTIMATE MOMENTS

1

ONCE AGAIN HER impetuosity had landed her in a jam. Francie Karr-Taylor rifled through a stack of papers on her gigantic wooden desk and picked up the letter for the tenth time that morning. Last week she'd placed the irksome missive on the edge just so, in case her cat took a notion to jump up on the desk and accidentally knock the reminder into the wastebasket. He hadn't.

She'd used the envelope postmarked Springdale, Illinois, as a coaster for the better part of a week, but the return address still remained legible.

No, the letter was still here and she hadn't forgotten about the impulsive promise she'd made, so she guessed she was going to have to give the reunion committee a call. The letter requesting she be the photographer for Springdale's tenth class reunion had arrived months ago, and rashly she'd agreed to participate.

What had she been thinking? She'd known then, just as she knew now, that she wasn't going to be able to attend the class reunion. She was going to have surgery that weekend. Or something else was going to come up. A debilitating sickness maybe. Or perhaps even a death: her own would be convenient.

The intercom buzzed her that someone was downstairs, and she walked distractedly to the panel, the wrinkled letter in her hand. "Yeah?"

"Miss Karr-Taylor, it's Ryan MacNair. I'd like to speak with you for a few minutes, please."

"Who?"

He repeated his name and added, "We spoke a few weeks ago. About the brooch you had appraised? You told me to call back at a more convenient time."

"Oh." She glanced around the cluttered loft where she worked, barely noting the photographs hung on every wall, or even the wet ones drying on a line strung from the bathroom that doubled as a darkroom to the door that led to her sleeping area. The place wasn't going to suddenly become neat and organized, and the time never got more convenient, so she might as well let him in. "Come on up."

She jabbed the button that unlocked the security door and sauntered back to her desk.

How hard could it be to fake her own death? She'd seen it done on TV plenty of times. She could assume a new identity and move her studio to Peoria under a different name.

Francie flopped into her chair and grimaced at her own thoughts. No. Nana needed someone to check up on her every few weeks and make sure the care center was doing a good job. Deserting her dear fragile grandmother was out of the question. It had distressed the old woman enough just thinking Francie wasn't married yet. What a selfish thought. Self-preserving and really clever—but selfish.

How on earth, then, was she going to get out of

this bothersome class reunion? What was she going to tell her grandmother? Nana was the only person in the world she was close to. The only person whose opinion mattered. But Nana didn't agree with Francie's decision to choose a career over a marriage and children. A few months ago, to alleviate the old woman's worry over her being alone, Francie'd told her she'd gotten married.

To a *rich* man.

To a rich man *with kids*.

To a rich *handsome* man with kids.

Holy criminey, how was she going to get out of this one?

A knock sounded on the door.

Francie crossed to open it.

"Hi, Miss Karr-Taylor—"

"Francie."

"Francie. Thank you for seeing me."

She swung the door open wide and ushered the tall dark-haired man in the tailored navy blue suit into her studio. "Would you like a soft drink? The coffee isn't any good anymore."

"No, thank you."

"Well…" She wandered back to her chair and sank into the comfortable cushion, her gaze immediately landing on the letter that still lay on her desk. Darn cat. Darn Nana for thinking a woman couldn't be fulfilled with her career.

"I have an offer for you," MacNair said. He moved a stack of manila envelopes from the seat of the chair opposite her desk to an available spot on the floor and plucked the crease at the knee of his trousers as he sat. "Are you moving out?"

"No, why?"

"Uh, no reason. Do you recall why I'm here?"

Absorbed in her predicament, Francie tapped a fingernail against the edge of the desk. The reunion was less than two weeks away now, and she still hadn't figured out what she was going to do.

"Francie?"

"What? Oh. No, I guess I've forgotten what it was you wanted to see me about."

"The brooch you had appraised at Grambs and Sons last month."

"Right. It was in a box of old junk that I bought at an auction. I thought the stuff would make a great still life. Black and white. Maybe a pair of gloves. Kind of draping out of an old jewelry chest with a piece of old lace beneath it."

"I put the word out to all the jewelers that I was looking for that particular piece," he said. "Grambs called me after you'd been in. That brooch rightfully belongs to my daughter. It's her legacy."

She'd found the perfect pair of old lace gloves. What had she done with them? "Uh-huh."

"It belonged to my grandmother on my father's side. Unfortunately my grandfather's will was contested, and the jewelry went to one of my aunts who only wanted what she could get out of everything. She wouldn't even let my father buy the pieces he wanted, just to be spiteful. I can't even remember why she started the feud with my father. I'm not even sure she does."

"She sounds lovely." Francie picked up a pen and doodled on the letter.

He blinked at her. "She sold it all, and we've been trying to find the pieces to buy them back. My father had intended for that brooch to remain in the family."

Francie's attention drifted to Peyton Armbruster's scrawled signature on the page, and Francie knew she couldn't stall any longer. She either had to come clean…or come up with a husband.

"The brooch was appraised at five hundred dollars," MacNair said. "Miss Karr-Taylor, I'll double that offer."

At his concerned tone, Francie glanced up into his grave features, and finally his words sank into her dilemma-drugged brain. He was as intense about this silly old brooch as she was about taking a husband to the reunion.

For the first time she took a good hard look at Ryan MacNair. His dark hair, bearing a distinguishing widow's peak, was neatly styled and brushed back from a square-jawed face. Dark brows were divided by a V of anxiety that didn't diminish his well-bred features. *He was handsome.*

He had a nice straight nose and an interesting mouth that could probably slide into a knockout smile if he'd loosen his collar and tie and give himself a little air.

His navy suit and cranberry silk tie were of the best quality and taste, and he wore them with ease and panache. *He was rich.* Not her type—if she had a type—but wouldn't he impress the control tops right

off the women back in Springdale? She imagined
Nana looking him up and down.

"You wanted to use the brooch in some photographs," he said. "Have you done that?"

"Are you married?"

He blinked, his warm brown eyes showing confusion over the abrupt change of subject. "I'm divorced," he said finally. "Is that relevant to the discussion?"

Actually a discussion took two people, but she
spared him that reminder, and let the wheels in her
mind whirl with possibilities. "I'm just beginning to
sympathize with your situation, Mr...."

"MacNair."

"Mr. MacNair. I'd certainly feel bad if something
of my grandmother's was sold off against my
wishes."

He nodded, his brow still furrowed. "Then you'll
sell it to me?"

"You want this brooch pretty badly, don't you? It
means a lot to you. And your father."

His carefully guarded expression didn't change.
"Yes."

"So, my decision carries a lot of weight."

"It does," he admitted, though his aggravated expression showed his reluctance to do so.

Francie smoothed the letter, refolded it and placed
it inside the stained and warped envelope. "Perhaps
we can negotiate after all."

"Money is not the issue here. The brooch has sen-
timental value. Five thousand."

"No. Not more money," she said with a flick of

her hand. "In fact, if you agree to this idea, you can keep your money."

His frown deepened. "What idea?"

"I'm in a bind myself. I'm afraid I've done something—said something—*impetuous,* and now I don't have any way out of it. Except maybe through you."

"I don't understand."

"I told my grandmother that I'd gotten married."

"And that's a problem?"

"It wasn't true. It's not true."

"You told her you were married?"

She nodded.

"But you're not married. And you weren't married."

"Right."

"Then why did you tell her that?"

The question was so simple. The answer was so complicated. "Because I'm not."

He stared at her.

"It's a long, boring story," she supplied. "Maybe sometime we'll go over the details, but for now I'll just say I had my reasons."

"So you lied. And now this lie is causing you a problem."

"Oh, yeah." She stood and walked restlessly to the row of windows and gazed, unseeing, down on the street.

"What does that have to do with me?"

She turned back. "I've been cornered into participating in the tenth reunion celebration in my hometown. Nana is expecting me. *And* she's expecting me to bring a husband."

With a wary expression, he waited for her to speak.

"You can have the brooch…"

He leaned forward in the chair, waiting for the other shoe to drop.

"…if you come to Springdale with me as my husband for a week."

He stood. "I suspected you were going to say that, but I didn't believe you would. That's the most absurd thing I've ever heard."

"Well, hey, it was worth a try." She gave a half-hearted wave. Shoulders slumped, she hugged her upper arms and turned back to the window. "I saw something about escort services on *Dateline* the other night. Do we have any of those around here?"

Ryan studied her small frame in profile against the window, her words sinking in and shocking him once again. "You can't go to one of those places!"

"Why not?"

"You don't know anything about them. You could place yourself in serious danger."

"I am in some serious danger, here, Mac."

He straightened his shoulders at the flip nickname. "You're simply in an embarrassing situation because you lied. You have only yourself to blame."

"I'm not blaming anyone. I'm trying to come up with a solution."

"Why don't you tell your grandmother the truth?"

She turned back, a hint of irritation in her blue eyes. "Because she'd only make my life miserable until I *really* found someone to marry, and I'm not willing to do that. I guess we don't have anything more to talk about."

"What about the brooch? An arrangement? I'm sure we can come up with something—"

"Those were the terms, Mac. If you want the pin, you need to pose as my husband. It's only one week out of your whole life. If that's too much of a sacrifice, well…"

"Lady, I've never heard anything so unprofessional and unethical in my life. Real people just don't go around doing these kinds of things. That only happens in the movies."

"Sure they do. Negotiations take place on Capitol Hill every day."

"Honest negotiations."

"*You* think."

He didn't know if it was her irreverent attitude or the fact that she held him over a barrel that irked him. Ryan reflected back on the only heirloom he had to hand down to his daughter and held himself in check. His grandfather had had that piece of jewelry made for his grandmother as a wedding present.

He intended for Alanna to have that brooch, and had been sick over its loss for the past year. When Ryan had received the call from the appraiser and learned that the piece of jewelry had fallen into the hands of a young woman, he'd decided to appeal to her sense of fairness.

How could he ever have imagined that the woman would be a zany, flippant photographer with more nerve than sense? She didn't operate on his wavelength. He didn't think she operated on anyone's wavelength but her own.

"Bartering was the first type of selling around," she added. "Our country was founded with trades."

Artists. He'd dealt with his share in his position at the museum. He could deal with this one.

But a week in Springdale pretending to be her husband? The demand was preposterous. Outrageous.

It was also his only option.

"I don't have anyone to take care of my children for an entire week." It was as good of an excuse an any, and it was the truth.

She inched toward him like a dog sniffing a steak. "Children?"

"Yes. I've never left them for that long. I keep my business trips to just a day or two. My housekeeper fills in during that time, but—"

"How old are they?" she asked, circling him. "Girls? Boys?"

"Twelve and nine. A girl and a boy."

She stepped close, her blue eyes lit with a determined fire he didn't trust. "That's perfect. They can come along!"

"What do you mean?"

"I need kids, too! Oh, this is great. Now I won't have to do something drastic."

"What? What could be more drastic than this scheme you've concocted?"

"I'll make the plane reservations, don't worry about that."

"Hold it. I can't just pull up and take off for a week. I have a job. My children have school."

"A week out won't hurt them." She perched on the edge of her desk, sending a stack of papers sliding across the top and onto the floor, and grinned a naughty grin. "This is great."

"Now wait a minute," he said, stopping her gush of pleasure with an upraised palm. He leaned down to collect the papers she'd knocked off and shuffle them into a semineat pile. "I never said I'd do this. I can't just take a week off to play some game of house. And I can't subject my children to it, either." He tried to find a place to lay the papers, and finally shoved them into her hands. "What kind of father would drag his children along and ask them to participate in something so dishonest?"

Carelessly she dropped the stack of papers on the already laden desktop behind her. "A father who wants my brooch?"

Her irritating confidence got under his skin. "I can't ask my kids to lie. I've always taught them honesty."

"I guess we could say they're at boarding school."

Ryan's mind had remained three steps behind hers since this meeting had begun. He gave himself a mental shake. "What about the logic of all this? What did you tell your grandmother that your husband's name was? Who would I be expected to be?"

"I don't think I actually gave you a name. I told her I go by Karr-Taylor because that's the name I've established in my career. Plenty of women don't take their husbands' names. Don't tell me you're a chauvinist."

Ryan blinked. "No! I'm not—what does being a chauvinist have to do with it, anyway? It would never work."

The woman was enough to drive a sane man nuts.

Hopping off the desk, she sat in her chair, rifled though the papers and books and produced a Rolodex. "Fine. You know the way out."

She flipped index cards, pulling a few out and setting them aside.

"What are you doing?"

"Finding someone else to do it. I don't know why I didn't think of this before. Of course they may not have kids. We'll use the boarding school story."

Ryan stood watching her peruse the cards with a pencil between her teeth. His logical mind grappled with what was happening. She had no intention of selling him the brooch unless he went along.

He had an ultimatum.

He could walk out and disappoint his father and his daughter.

Or he could grit his teeth and go along with her outrageous mandate for one week. One week. How difficult would that be?

He could get the time off. He'd gone over his planner just that morning and knew what lay ahead. The next few weeks were going to involve intensive cleaning and painting in preparation for the summer and fall exhibits, and he could afford to take the time off. There was only a week of school left before summer vacation, and then what? He had no one to care for his daughter and son for a week.

He had been promising to take them on a vacation and teach Alex to swim. He never got enough time with them.

What would he tell them?

The truth. He'd never done anything less.

They would see how important this was—he'd have to stress that he didn't condone the masquerade, but that he'd had no choice—and they'd understand. His daughter had lost so much already. She wasn't going to lose her legacy if he could help it.

Francie had picked up the receiver and was dialing.

He took a step forward. "Is there a pool in Springdale?"

"There's one in the hotel, I think."

"All right," he said.

She paused and glanced up. "All right?"

"All right," he repeated. "I'll do it."

A delighted grin spread across her features, and she slid the receiver back into place. "The kids, too?"

He nodded grimly.

"All right!"

"When exactly is this…event?"

She gave him the dates. "It'll be fun, Mac. You'll see. We'll wow 'em."

"My name is Ryan."

"Right. I'll make the flight arrangements and call you with the itinerary. What are the kids' names?"

"Alanna and Alex."

"Good choices. We won't have to change them."

"I'm so glad you approve."

"We'll leave a day early," she went on, apparently oblivious to his sarcasm, "because we need clothes for the oldies dance, and there are some great consignment and thrift stores in Springdale."

"Oldies dance?"

"Yeah, you know…bobby socks, bell bottoms,

ducktails. The theme is a mixture of fifties, sixties and seventies. The Partridge Family, Frankie and Annette, styles like those. You'd make a great Ricky Nelson. Who do you think I could be? Shelley Fabares, maybe?''

A disturbing knot of indigestion settled in Ryan's stomach. A week with this woman. One solid week. But it was one week versus his daughter's legacy.

He hoped he had the stamina to live through it.

2

A BATTERED SUITCASE in each hand, the strap of a travel-worn camera case slung across her chest like an ammo belt, Francie hurried through O'Hare airport toward the agreed meeting place. Ryan MacNair, dressed in sand-colored summer trousers and a neatly pressed linen sport shirt, waited impatiently beside two dark-haired children.

"You're late," he stated, a look of displeasure creasing his brow.

She dropped her mismatched suitcases on a nearby cart. "Well, White Rabbit, I had to take Stanley to a friend's."

He ignored her jest, moving her cases from the stranger's cart, and placing them on top of his steel gray leather luggage. "Stanley?"

She adjusted her purse and camera bag on her shoulder. "My cat."

"You knew you'd have to do that two weeks ago, couldn't you have left a little earlier?"

She looked up at him. "What's the big deal? We're not late. The plane doesn't leave for another twenty-five minutes."

"That's cutting it close. We still have to check our luggage and find our seats."

"Okay, okay, don't pop a blood vessel, Mac. Are you going to introduce me to our children?"

He set his mouth in a straight line and nodded at the kids beside him. "This is Alex."

"Hi," the boy said. He had neatly trimmed hair and wore an outfit much like his father's. He resembled MacNair, except that his eyes were a friendly gray-blue.

"Hi, Alex." Francie stuck out her hand and he placed his small one into it for a shake.

"And Alanna," MacNair added.

"Hi, Alanna." Francie reached forward again, but the dark-haired girl deliberately kept both hands on the handles of the designer carryon she held.

Her assessing eyes, the same deep brown as her father's, swept Francie from head to foot. "I'm really going to have to use my acting skills," she said with a sidelong smirk. "No mother of mine would be caught dead in those clothes."

Francie glanced down at the lightweight slacks and top she'd bought for the trip, then pretended to study the area leading to the terminals. "Do the fashion police have a checkpoint set up again? Darn!"

Alanna glanced uncertainly in the direction Francie had indicated, then back, her eyes narrowing suspiciously.

"Let's check our bags." MacNair ended the strained moment and gestured to an attendant who wheeled the cart toward the baggage check.

The line moved quickly, and they hurried down the corridor, through the metal detectors, and had only a five-minute wait before boarding their plane. MacNair gave Francie the window seat and sat on the aisle, directly across from his children.

"What's there to *do* at this Springdale place, anyway?" Alanna asked.

"We'll be staying at a nice hotel," Francie offered, leaning in front of MacNair to speak to his daughter. "You guys'll find stuff to do. We'll go thrift store shopping tomorrow, getting ready for the dance."

Alanna's nose almost skimmed the ceiling of the plane. "*Thrift stores?* What does that mean?"

At the stiffening of MacNair's posture, Francie realized she'd pressed her thigh against his and that if she turned her face slightly, her eyes would be level with his mouth. She recognized the expensive spicy scent of his soap.

She deliberately focused on the conversation with his daughter. "You know, consignment shops, Salvation Army, stuff like that."

The girl gaped. "You don't mean *used* clothing? That's disgusting! You won't actually *wear* someone's old clothes, will you?"

Alex watched the verbal exchange as though he had a front row seat at Wimbledon.

"I don't know where else we'd find outfits for the dance," Francie said, vividly conscious of the man scrutinizing her at close range. "I doubt your dad has anything in his closet left over from his high school days in the seventies." She turned, and sure enough, his sensuous-looking mouth was mere inches away. "Do you?"

"Junior high," he stated, his lips softly forming the words.

"Really." An enveloping warmth cloaked her, and she quickly settled back in her seat. "Hard to imagine."

"What is?"

"Well, I'm trying to picture you stuffing other guys into lockers and hiding Playmates under your mattress."

"I never did those things."

"No kidding." She pretended surprise and cast him another glance. "You belonged to the German club and were class valedictorian."

"Do you think you know everything?"

"Which part's wrong?"

He averted his face. "It was the chess club."

"Well, see? I know more about you already." She grinned and leaned forward slightly, this time careful not to touch him.

"I think I'm going to be sick," Alanna said.

Alarm crossed MacNair's face. He turned toward his daughter. "Are you air sick?"

"I think it was either the thrift store talk or the fact that you and I are having a conversation," Francie said for his ears alone. She reached into the pocket on the seat ahead of her, found the blue bag and tossed it across the aisle.

Alex caught it with a grin and handed it to his sister.

She gave Francie a haughty stare, stuffed the bag into the pocket ahead of her and turned her gaze out the window.

MacNair looked relieved that it had been a false alarm.

"You know she really is perfect," Francie said, settling back. "Those snooty looks are great." Feeling MacNair's gaze again, she turned. "What?"

He simply shook his head and pulled a folder and a laptop computer from his briefcase.

She studied his profile surreptitiously, noting his classic good looks and impeccable grooming. He could easily be the Armani poster boy.

He plucked a pair of gold-rimmed glasses from inside his case and slid them on. They did nothing to diminish his refined good looks. In fact they added a touch of sophistication. "Do you wear those often?"

"When I read. Is my vision going to be a problem?"

"No. I, uh, just wondered. You look very nice in them. Wear them all the time if you like."

"Well, now that I have your permission to wear my glasses, I feel so much better. Does this shirt meet your approval?"

Her gaze skittered across his broad chest in the lightweight shirt. "It does."

He opened the Franklin planner she'd suspected he carried, and turned his attention back to his work.

Francie closed her eyes. She'd stayed up too late, packing and trying to find mates for earrings, and she could use a nap before they arrived in Springdale. She wanted to be rested tomorrow when she saw the look on Nana's face. Ryan MacNair was a major coup on her part. A self-satisfied smile turned up the corners of her lips. Her old high school acquaintances would be pretty impressed themselves. She couldn't wait.

"I almost forgot."

She opened her eyes. "What?"

He slid a minute white envelope from his pocket and shook something shiny into his palm, then extended it.

Francie stared at the modest gold band. "What's this?"

"Your grandmother will think it's odd if you aren't wearing a wedding ring. I guessed at the size."

Still she stared. "Where did you get it?"

"I bought it."

"You bought me a wedding ring?"

"Just put the thing on your finger. Gold is a good investment."

Hesitantly Francie took the ring from his palm and slipped it on her finger. It went on easily.

Ryan turned back to his blinking cursor, as if dismissing her. This time when she closed her eyes, all she could think of was the weight of the gold band on her finger. She should have thought of it herself. Maybe MacNair wasn't as unimaginative as she'd thought. Nah, he couldn't be.

She smiled a satisfied smile and relaxed. She really couldn't wait.

RYAN STOOD NEAR a pillar with Alanna and Alex while Francie handled the room registration with her credit card. From the expression on the desk clerk's face, Ryan could tell he wasn't the only one who wondered if it would be more gratifying to kiss her or place her on a plane headed for a distant country.

Why had the thought of kissing her entered his

head? She must have him more rattled than he thought. He buried that image deep.

Minutes later she hurried toward them, her shoulder-length dark blond hair swaying and her pert energy drawing admiring glances. He had to pull his gaze from her curvy figure to pay attention to her chatter about the registration process. She doled out three plastic card keys. "Room 512," she said.

Ryan gestured to a bellboy standing nearby and gave him the room number.

"We could've gotten the luggage ourselves, couldn't we?" she asked, leaning into him again, and Ryan didn't know a woman who felt softer in all the right places.

"That's what the bellhops are here for." He led them to an elevator, and stood a safe distance from her.

"Seems kind of silly, paying them to carry our suitcases when we're perfectly capable," she said with a shrug.

Alanna rolled her eyes.

"Francie! That's you, isn't it?"

Ryan turned at the cry. A pencil-thin young woman with a man and boy in tow, hurried toward the elevators. Her hair was cut in a sleek short bob that made her neck appear all the scrawnier.

"Peyton," Francie said, and Ryan couldn't tell if the look on her face was dread or pleasure. "I've been looking forward to seeing you."

The woman she'd called Peyton stopped a foot from Francie and leaned into a mock embrace, kissing the air by her cheek. "Donald, come see Francie. And we get to meet the husband we've heard about."

She turned and cast an assessing glance on Ryan's hair and clothing. One penciled eyebrow rose. *"Well...!"*

Her stocky husband stepped forward and extended a fleshy hand. "Don Armbruster."

"Ryan MacNair." He adjusted his briefcase and shook the man's hand.

"And this is Donald Junior," Peyton said, gesturing to the chubby boy of about ten or eleven just as the bell dinged and the elevator doors whooshed open.

The two families stepped into the elevator and the doors slid shut. The atmosphere grew claustrophobic.

"These are *our* children," Francie announced proudly. "Alanna and Alex."

Peyton gave them the once-over. "How old are they?"

Francie's gaze flew to Ryan's as if trying to recall the information. "Uhh."

Alanna, never one to appreciate being talked about as though she weren't present, piped up and saved her. "I'm twelve. My brother's nine."

"These are *your* children, then," Peyton said to Ryan.

"Yes," Francie said quickly. "But they're like my own. Aren't you, dears?"

Alex accepted the arm that Francie threw around his shoulders and gazed up with mingled surprise and pleasure on his face.

"When are we going to shop for my new bathing

suit, Mom?'' Alanna asked in a syrupy sweet voice. ''I want to try out the pool right away.''

''We'll go shopping as soon as we're settled into our room,'' Francie replied without blinking an eye. ''That is if Daddy's not too tired.''

Still keeping a hold on Alex, she slid her arm around Ryan's waist and leaned into him, this time, her breast pressing against his chest. Their thin layers of clothing weren't enough to prevent his body from taking notice at the same time his brain grappled with her words. *Daddy?*

''You're not too tired, are you, *Daddy?*'' his daughter asked, downright devilment lacing her words. She'd never called him Daddy in her entire life.

Ryan focused on ignoring Francie's warm curves pressed along his side. ''No, *Pumpkin,* I can't wait to shop with you girls.''

Alex looked from his sister to his father and back up at the woman enfolding them in a hug, a look of total puzzlement on his young face.

''Isn't that sweet?'' Peyton asked. She looked from Francie to Ryan and her gaze slid assessingly across his features. ''I don't believe I've heard what you do, Ryan.''

''Executive arts administrator for the Shepperd Museum in Chicago,'' Francie replied for him, and to his ears it sounded like boasting.

Peyton's green eyes narrowed as though she were calculating how much he earned at a job like that. ''Donald's a financial analyst with the Daily Corporation.''

"Is that a local company?" he asked, turning to Donald, and praying for the salvation of reaching their floor. In order to look at the man, he had to turn his head, placing Francie's fresh-smelling hair directly beneath his nose. The scent, combined with the pressure of her supple body, stirred his long-dormant hormones to life.

"His office is local," Peyton answered for him, "but the company is international. Donald has an M.B.A. and a law degree."

The bell rang, saving him from hearing any further bragging, and Ryan ushered Francie and the children from the elevator.

"We'll see you soon," Peyton threatened, waggling long red-tipped fingers.

Alanna and Alex hurried ahead, searching for the room number.

Ryan moved away from Francie as quickly as possible. He shook his head helplessly. "This whole thing is already out of hand. I can't imagine why I agreed to this."

"Because you love me," she replied with a teasing grin. "Remember?"

"Do you need to play this thing to the hilt in front of your friends? I thought this was all for your grandmother."

"This is a small town," she replied more seriously. "Nana has already told the nurses and the nurses have spread the news around. That's how my 'friends' heard it. It has to look real."

"It sounded like someone should have been keeping score while you two sparred over whose husband was more prosperous.''

Francie waved an unconcerned hand at him. His daughter had the room unlocked, and she and Alex were inspecting the television and the balcony.

''You guys did just great back there,'' Francie said, including all three in her praise.

Alanna perched on the edge of one of the double beds. ''Let's go get my bathing suit.''

''That was a slick one,'' Francie said, admitting she'd been duped. The look on Peyton's face when she'd sized up MacNair had been worth a dozen bathing suits, but she didn't plan to tell the girl that. Not for the first time, Alanna's confident words didn't meld with the way she hunched her shoulders forward, and Francie thought it a curious posture for a girl so slim and lovely.

''As soon as the luggage comes, we'll hang up our clothes and head out. Lunch first, then shopping. How's that sound?''

''Yeah, how's that sound, *Daddy?*'' Alanna asked.

MacNair frowned at Francie. ''I can't wait.''

ALANNA HADN'T allowed her near the dressing room door, so Francie had no idea how the suit she'd forked over eighty bucks for looked on the girl. She appeared with a faded T-shirt covering the suit, and the four of them grabbed towels and took off for the elevator.

Beneath an enormous skylight, tables and chairs surrounded the pool area, a small restaurant advertising drinks and the hours for breakfast and lunch. On two sides and above, hotel rooms opened onto balconies.

Alanna immediately perched on the edge of the pool, dangling her legs in the water. Alex sat several feet away. MacNair kicked off his deck shoes and walked toward the board. He looked as good in modest trunks as he did in a three-piece suit. Nah. Better.

He had a handsome amount of dark hair on his well-formed chest and legs, and a nice flat stomach. Francie kept her perusal covert, and observed his impressive dive into the deep end. He swam to the edge and came up beside his son.

She removed her terry robe and thongs and met his eyes as she approached the edge. He slicked his hair back and watched, undeniable attraction revealed in his dark eyes. She was no Cindy Crawford, but she knew she had an adequate shape. She plunged into the water.

"Coming?" she called to Alanna.

The girl glanced self-consciously at a couple of other swimmers with a toddler at the opposite end, and slipped into the water without removing the T-shirt.

Francie cast MacNair an inquisitive glance, but he'd swam to where Alex sat, and was encouraging him to leave the side.

"Wanna race?" Francie asked Alanna.

The girl shrugged.

Francie left her and swam several laps.

Reluctantly Alanna joined her and kept up.

Finally Francie paused in about four feet of water

to catch her breath. Ryan was holding Alex in the water.

"Look, Francie," Alex said. "I can stick my head under."

He proceeded to demonstrate.

She laughed. "Don't you get water up your nose?"

He laughed. "Nah. Ya just gotta blow out. My dad's showing me."

"Ask your dad if he can stand on his head underwater."

"Can you, Dad?"

To Francie's amazement, MacNair accepted the challenge. He left Alex on the side and dipped under, his feet appearing above the surface for an impressive length of time. He somersaulted and came up sputtering.

Francie had to laugh aloud at the man. This certainly wasn't the same guy who'd appeared at her door so serious and stuffy. Right now he didn't act like the uptight man who resented her infringing on his time and had seemed so wholeheartedly disapproving of her.

"That's cool, Dad!" Alex cried.

"Want to try it?"

Alex shook his head.

"Okay, we'll practice your back float, then."

Alanna swam over and encouraged her brother.

Francie stood watching him with his kids for a few minutes, puzzling over the difference in the man. The revelation came to her immediately: His love for his children loosened him up and made him seem more human.

Her attention became distracted by two women entering the pool area in long brightly colored caftans. They carried frosted drinks to a nearby table.

With a little start of surprise, Francie recognized Becka Crow and Shari Donegan. Before the women had a chance to see she'd discovered their arrival, Francie quickly sliced through the few feet of water separating them, and slipped her arm around MacNair's shoulders from behind.

Sleek skin slid against Ryan's legs and shoulders, and those soft, ample breasts, covered by a thin layer of spandex, pressed into his back. He'd already been unable to ignore the fact that Francie had a soft, round figure, unlike women who thought anemically skinny was stylish. As a man he appreciated that.

He immediately experienced more difficulty breathing than he had after a full thirty seconds on his head underwater. "I have a fun idea," she said near his ear, loud enough for Alanna and Alex to hear, yet sending a shiver across his shoulders. "Let's play war!"

"How do you do that?" Alex asked.

"You get on Alanna's shoulders. I get on your dad's shoulders and we try to knock each other off."

"You can't knock me off," Alex said, terror in his eyes. "I can't swim yet."

"That doesn't sound very fair, anyway," Alanna complained. "I think Alex should get on your shoulders and I should get on Dad's."

"We'll switch off," Francie agreed. "And I promise I won't knock you off, Alex. You can take your best shots at me. Go under,'' Francie said to Ryan, ''so I can get on.''

At her insistent pressure on his arms, he sank under the water. She slid onto his shoulders, her sleek legs hanging down his chest, and he stood.

He grasped her supple calves to keep her balanced.

Alanna and Alex had to go to the side, and ended up with Alex squealing and Alanna screaming for him to let go of her hair.

Ryan couldn't help a laugh.

Alex did his best to knock Francie from her roost, but Ryan had no trouble keeping his footing. Alanna insisted they trade partners.

They played the game that way for a while, and finally, Alanna begged to stop.

''You're the best,'' Francie whispered in his ear, sliding her water-slick body alongside his, and flattening her palm against his chest in an intimate caress.

His physical reaction to her nearness was immediate and potent. He placed his hand on her wrist as if to pull it away, but the pleading look in her blue eyes halted him. She blinked, water dripping from her lashes.

Over her shoulder, a movement and a bright flash of color caught his eye. Two women watched them intently. Realization dawned. His gaze skittered back to hers. ''Friends of yours?''

''Becka and Shari,'' she said softly.

Unnerved, he didn't know why her acting out her part should insult him. That's what they were here for. This whole thing was a charade.

If she wanted a performance, he'd give her one. "Let's give them the whole show, then."

Impulsively he hooked his arm around her waist and pulled her flush against him. Her eyes opened wide in surprise, but she came along easily, both arms draping over his shoulders.

Her skin glowed with the same health and vitality that oozed from her personality. Though her eyes were wide and filled with doubt, her lips parted ever so slightly, and Ryan dipped his head and kissed them full on—a healthy, this-is-just-a-promise-for-later kiss that he should have known better than to initiate.

Because she kissed him back. And she was good at it. Too good. There wasn't enough fabric or space between them to keep his response a secret, and he released her. Her craziness was rubbing off. That was the kiss he'd thought of giving her earlier, and under any other circumstances he'd have had enough sense to keep it just a fleeting thought.

Francie loosened her arms from his neck and drifted back a couple of feet in the water, staring...her heart pounding.

They'd had an eyeful, old Becka and Shari. She fully expected to see steam rise off the water. Old Mac could kiss, she'd say that for him.

When her thoughts came into focus, she looked over to see Alanna and Alex staring, Alex's expression amused, Alanna's horrified.

"Are you hungry?" Ryan asked them, as though they hadn't just witnessed their father soundly kiss a near stranger.

They nodded.

"Let's go before we sprout gills." He hoisted himself on the edge and walked away, water sluicing down his muscular body. The kids scrambled out behind him, both glancing back at Francie.

Still slightly dazed, Francie swam to a ladder and climbed out. MacNair held a towel out to her. She stepped forward and hesitated, wondering if he planned to continue the charade, and not knowing how she'd keep her cool if he did. She hadn't expected that kiss to feel so real, or for either of their reactions to be so intense.

But he turned his attention to helping Alex find his vinyl thongs and saved her the worry.

Alanna fixed her with a frigid glare, and Francie knew whatever points she'd gained in the pool play, she'd lost when she and the girl's father had locked lips. She gave her a tentative smile, and Alanna cut her stare away abruptly.

After they'd dried, donned their robes and headed for the exit, she reached for Ryan's arm.

"We don't have to pretend when nobody's watching," he said, drawing back from her touch.

Francie glanced over to see the table where the women had been sitting empty. She shouldn't have felt disappointed or shut out. This was only a charade.

Ryan MacNair didn't have to touch her or even be nice to her when they were alone. The touchy-feely game they'd played in the pool had been for the benefit of their observers, and for no other reason. That kiss had meant nothing to him. To either one of them.

That fact gave her small comfort.

Unexpectedly Francie found herself hoping they'd find themselves watched a lot over the next week, *and* she found herself not giving a hoot why she wished it.

3

"THAT WAS THE worst pizza I've ever had," Alanna complained as they let themselves back into the room after a late supper.

"There are only three pizza places in town," Francie apologized. "That's the one we went to when I was in school."

"I think they're still using the same batch of dough for the crust." Alanna flopped herself on one of the beds.

"I thought it was good," Alex said.

Francie smiled at the boy. He was so eager to get along and see everyone happy, it made Francie feel bad to see how hard he tried only to have his sister complain about everything.

"We'll try the buffet in the hotel dining room tomorrow, how's that?" Ryan asked.

Alanna shrugged. "Whatever."

"Sure," Alex agreed. He opened a cabinet, found the remote and flicked on the television. "Cool! We have cable!"

Immediately Ryan crossed to the cabinet, found a cable guide and thumbed through it. "Don't change any channels until I come back." He went into the bathroom and closed the door.

Francie watched him with puzzlement. It was fine if the man liked to read in the bathroom, but why had he instructed Alex not to change channels?

"He's calling the desk to see if there are any bad channels," Alex explained with a grin as he settled cross-legged on the other bed nearest the bathroom.

"Bad channels," Francie repeated.

"Hel-lo!" Alanna said, snottily. "R-rated? Stuff us kids aren't supposed to see?"

"Oh." Francie went to one of her bags and unpacked her toiletries.

Ryan returned. "Okay, Alex. Go ahead."

Alex grinned at Francie and flipped through channels. She returned his amused smile, went into the bathroom, washed and moisturized her face and brushed her teeth.

When she returned, the family had settled, Alex and Ryan on one bed, Alanna on the other, watching a movie with a dog and cat finding their way home. She made herself comfortable on the other side of the bed where Alanna sat.

"Wait a minute," the girl said a few minutes later. "I'm not going to sleep with *her*."

Ryan looked over, staring at his daughter. "Honey, there isn't—"

"No! I don't want to sleep with her."

"There's no other place for you to sleep," her father reasoned.

"I don't care. I don't like her, and I'm not going to sleep with her. You shouldn't try to make me."

"Maybe they have rollaways," Francie said. She picked up the phone near the bed and dialed the desk.

A minute later, she rested the receiver back in its cradle. "They're all rented out already. We should have called earlier. They'll call us if they get one returned."

"This wasn't my idea," Alanna continued. "Let her sleep on the floor."

Ryan's face actually reddened, and he avoided Francie's gaze. "You're being rude, Alanna. There's no reason why this arrangement can't work out. We—"

"No," Francie interrupted. "She's right. She shouldn't have to sleep with me if she feels so strongly about it. I'll sleep on the floor tonight. I saw some extra blankets in the closet. I can make a pad."

"If anyone sleeps on the floor, it will be Alanna," Ryan said firmly, no room for more argument in his tone. "*You* can sleep on the floor, miss."

"Fine." Her dark eyes shot daggers at Francie. "Just as long as I don't have to be next to her."

"I can sleep on the floor, Dad," Alex offered.

"No. Alanna will."

That was that.

They watched the rest of the movie, Alex laughing from time to time, Alanna shooting Francie a frosty glare every time she knew her dad wasn't looking.

When the movie was over, Ryan announced bedtime, then flicked to a news channel and lowered the volume. Alex used the bathroom and snuggled right down. "Night, Francie."

"Night, hon," she said softly. She made Alanna's pallet on the floor and gave her the extra pillow off the bed while the girl was in the bathroom. Alanna returned in a long T-shirt nightie, deliberately rearranged everything Francie had just done and laid down with her face turned away.

Francie used the bathroom to change into her T-shirt and the shorts she'd decided to wear since she had to cross in front of Ryan to get back to her bed. She slid under the covers and halfheartedly watched the news. Her eyelids grew heavy. Packing and flying had zapped her energy.

"Will the lamp disturb you?" Ryan asked softly, glancing at her over the top of his glasses.

He'd opened his laptop and briefcase while she'd been in the bathroom, and sat with his back propped against the headboard.

"No."

"Do you have a schedule for the week? I'd like to enter the times on my calendar."

"Yeah, they sent me one. It's in my bag somewhere. I'll find it for you in the morning."

He looked as if he wanted to say something else. Though Alex appeared soundly asleep, Alanna might still be listening, so Ryan turned back to whatever he'd been doing.

So far Alanna was the only wrench in the works. And yet, she'd put on a perfect performance in front of Peyton that morning. Francie could only hope that she'd contain her surliness to the room, as she had until now.

She hoped, too, that Alanna's obvious contempt for the whole situation wasn't going to change Ryan's mind about going through with this week. They were here now, and he'd given his word.

But they'd only made it through the first day.

RYAN SURVEYED THE double sink and counter in the bathroom with dismay. His shaving kit sat in one corner, the kids' toothbrushes and toothpaste beside it, while Francie's paraphernalia had been strung from one side to the other with the same haphazard carelessness that characterized her reasoning.

There were cleansers and toners, a bag of makeup, a bag of sample-size toiletries, a blow-dryer, brushes, combs, hair bands and cologne. He made a spot for his razor and shaving cream and proceeded to shave.

The shower stall looked the same: a sleek purple razor, shampoo and conditioner, body cleanser, and a loofah sponge. Her scent hung everywhere, that exotic, erotic smell he'd noticed from the first time he'd been close to her. Shaking his head, he unwrapped the hotel soap and showered.

Dried and dressed, he found the family waiting for him. "Can we have breakfast in the hotel, Dad?" Alex asked. "They have a place by the pool. Me and Alanna just went and saw it."

He raised a brow at Francie, and she gave him an agreeable nod. She wore a pair of belted white shorts with a peach-colored cotton shirt tucked into them, and a pair of clunky suede sandals. The feminine scents from her shower still lingered in the room. One side of her freshly washed and dried hair had been tucked behind her ear, and the other swept across her cheek as she grabbed her purse and camera case from the unmade bed. She could have passed for a teenager.

The car rental agency was just across the street from the hotel, so after breakfast by the pool they walked.

"Francie!" the man at the counter cried, when he saw her. She pulled her sunglasses up on her head and walked to the counter. "Digger?"

"Nobody calls me Digger anymore." He laughed.

"Uhh," she said, as though she had to think about it. "Tom, is it?"

He grinned. "Yeah. It's great to see you! This week is going to be so much fun."

"I'm looking forward to it. I reserved a car."

"This your husband?"

Francie turned and gestured for Ryan to step forward. "Yes, this is Ryan MacNair. Tom Wallace."

Ryan shook the man's hand. "Tom."

"Okay, let me find you on the computer. Do you have a confirmation number?"

"Yes." She opened her purse and dug through the contents. Ryan watched, wondering how she managed to find anything in the disorganized jumble. "It's here somewhere."

He and Tom exchanged a look over her head. Alanna rolled her eyes and took a seat on a plastic chair. Alex found a gum machine and asked for change. Ryan handed him a coin.

"Here it is." She produced the familiar envelope stained with coffee rings.

"Okay." Tom pulled up her account and asked for their driver's licenses. They each placed one on the counter, and Francie turned to Ryan, a look of alarm on her face.

He frowned a question at her.

She rolled her eyes and turned to watch Tom. He took her license first, entered the data into the computer and then picked up Ryan's. "She doesn't use your name?" he asked with a raised brow.

"I'd already made a name for myself with my photography business," she replied quickly, as though she'd been anticipating the question. "It was a business decision."

She looked pleased with her quick reply, and Ryan noticed she draped the hand with the wedding ring over the top of her purse.

"You don't have the same address, either?" Tom asked.

Her gaze flew to Ryan's, and he held his passive expression. This was her show. Let her write the lines.

"We, uh, we just moved," she said. "He hasn't had his license renewed yet."

"New house?" the man asked.

"Yes," Ryan said.

"Condo," she replied at the same time.

Tom glanced from one to the other. "A house or a condo?"

"Well, it's a condo, but it's so spacious, it's like a house," she said.

"I've always wondered," Tom said. "Do you have to do your own lawn work on those condo deals?"

"Ask her," Ryan replied.

She stabbed him with a glare, then smiled at the man behind the counter. "He doesn't have to, but he likes to so much that the groundskeeper lets him help."

Tom offered insurance and took Francie's credit card. She signed the receipt. "You can come over and do mine if you like taking care of lawns so well."

"I don't think I'll have time," Ryan replied as if he thought it was a clever joke.

Tom handed Ryan the keys. "Stall ninety-one on the east side of the lot. Don't forget to fill it with gas before you bring it back, otherwise they charge you an arm and a leg. We're meeting for drinks at Quigley's at eight tonight. Can you come?"

"We'll sure try," Ryan replied. "Thanks." He held the door for Francie and his children to file past.

They located the rental car and Francie directed as Ryan drove to the Thrift Store.

"This place smells," Alanna complained as soon as they set foot inside. Dramatically she pulled the neck of her shirt up and covered her nose and mouth.

"Now, we have to decide on our characters," Francie told Ryan. "Look! Here are love beads. Who would have worn love beads?" She held up a strand of multicolored beads she'd spotted on a jewelry rack. "This is going to be more difficult than I thought. Alex, get us a shopping cart, will you, sweetie?"

His son ran obligingly to bring back a wobbly cart, and presented it to Francie as if it were a gift. She smiled and thanked him, and his features nearly glowed. Ryan recognized his need for a woman's attention. He'd been so small when his mother had abandoned him, and Mrs. Nelson was kind and efficient, but she was hardly a warm, nurturing replacement for a mother.

He hoped it hadn't been a terrible mistake bringing

his son on this trip. A week with Francie wasn't going to fill the gap in the child's life, and growing attached to her could be detrimental when the agreement was fulfilled.

"Check this out." Francie laughed, showing him an orange flowered synthetic shirt with a long, pointed collar.

"That's awful," he replied.

"Yes, but it's Greg Brady all the way."

"Who?"

"'The Brady Bunch,' Dad," Alex piped up.

"We could find a pair of bell-bottoms and some round-toed shoes, and you'd be all set. You could wear a curly wig to look like a 'fro."

"No wig," he replied firmly.

"We could be the Brady parents and Alanna and Alex could pick two of the kids."

"There aren't enough of us for the kids," Alex said, getting into the spirit.

She agreed and moved on through the racks. "You're right. Not macho enough for you, Mac. This could take most of the week just deciding on our costumes."

Ryan and Alanna exchanged a look of dread.

She stopped in her tracks. "But then…"

"What?" Alex asked.

"There's always the *Grease* theme."

"What's that?"

"The play the high school drama class is presenting. It's a movie, too. You've seen it, Ryan."

Forty minutes later, they exited the store with three bags of clothing, jewelry and shoes.

"I'm not wearing those stinky clothes," Alanna said.

"We'll wash them all," Francie said. "They'll smell just like your own clothes. I have to drop this leather jacket off at the cleaners."

"I think I have that smell in my head," she complained.

"I think it was in your head to start with," Francie said under her breath, but Ryan caught it, and so did Alanna, because she snorted and flung herself into the car.

Alanna's temperament didn't improve as the morning progressed. His daughter was never easy to get along with, but this petulant side was one Ryan hadn't seen with such prevalence before now. Yes, Francie was irritating, but Ryan was making the best of the week for Alanna's sake, and she could certainly try harder to do the same. He'd talk to her later when they had a few minutes alone.

For now, Francie had taken the keys from his hand and slipped behind the steering wheel. She pulled out of the parking lot and into traffic. If she drove the way she did everything else, they were in big trouble.

She talked to Alex over her shoulder. She changed lanes as if they were in the Indy 500.

"Do we have air bags?" Alanna asked from the back.

Ryan turned enough to assure himself both offspring had their seat belts buckled.

They pulled up in front of a spacious well-manicured lawn, and she parked, scraping the bumper on the concrete stopper and backing up.

"Bring me here to mow, did you?"

She grinned. "No. This is where Nana is. I brought you here to meet her." They got out of the car. "Remember, kids, it's important that we make a good impression and play convincing parts for my grandmother. This is all for her."

"No," Alanna argued. "This is all for me and my great-grandma's brooch."

"That's right," Ryan told her. "And in order to get that brooch, we have to go along with this."

"If she was a decent person, she'd have given it to us," she said with a sneer in Francie's direction.

"Excuse us for a minute, please," he said to Francie, and took his daughter by the hand.

He led her to the shade of an ancient weeping willow near the curb. "Alanna, she didn't have to agree to give it to us at all. But she did. And we want it, so we're going through with this. Is that understood?"

She looked away and answered quietly, "Yes, sir."

"Now, I expect your behavior and your attitude to improve immediately."

"I don't like her, Dad. I don't want to be around her."

"You don't have to like her. I can't make you like her. But you do have to be civil. That means polite. This is our vacation…can we please not have it ruined?"

"This isn't a real vacation. Other kids' parents take them to Disneyland."

Her words stabbed him with guilt. He studied the daughter he loved so much and who was slipping away from him. He had only himself to blame. "I'm sorry. I know this isn't your idea of fun, and I will do better in the future. For now this is the week we have to spend, so let's not make each other miserable.''

"Why do we have to spend it with her?"

"You know why. We agreed to treat this as a vacation knowing we'd get Great-Grandma's brooch for you at the end. And we're going to make the best of it. Understood?"

She nodded.

"Now, show this grandmother of Francie's what a lovely girl you are, okay? For me?"

"Okay."

He hugged her. She pulled away, and they joined Francie and Alex, already engaged in a conversation with two white-haired men seated on the cement bench beside a fountain. One of them pointed at Ryan and Alanna with his cane. "This your daddy now?"

"That's him," Alex said with pride.

"Well, no wonder you're such a fine lookin' young fella. Your daddy is, too. Is he a hard worker? I worked in a mill most of my life. Was a farmhand when I was your age. Are you Duane Sweeney's boy?"

"No, sir," Ryan replied.

"Raised turkeys, he did."

"Ah."

"Come on," Francie whispered, and waved goodbye to the men.

It took a while for Francie to track down her grandmother. The white-haired woman was sitting in the shade of a long side porch in a wheelchair.

"Nana!" Francie cried, and knelt to give her a hug.

"Francesca?" she asked, reaching for her hand and looking into her face.

Francesca? Ryan had to grin. Francie suited her much better.

"Francesca, you look so pretty." She fingered Francie's hair.

"Look, Nana, you get to meet my husband and our kids."

Francie's grandmother cast faded blue eyes his direction. Her skin was a mass of wrinkles, and her frame feeble-looking, but her eyes were bright. "Jim? I finally get to meet you. Francesca told me all about you."

Jim? Francie took on a startled expression, met his eyes with a shrug, then looked back.

"Pleased to meet you, ma'am." He crouched so he'd be eye level with her, and extended a hand.

She took it in her papery-dry one, and patted his fingers.

"So, you're the one, huh?" Her alert gaze inspected his face as though she could read all there was to know of him.

"Yes, ma'am."

"She said you were handsome. And rich." She cackled, and the laugh surprised him. "I can see you're handsome. What about the rich part?"

"I make a good living, Mrs...." He looked up at Francie, surprised to see a blush staining her cheeks.

"Taylor," Francie supplied.

"Mrs. Taylor."

"None of that crap. Call me Nana. That's what Francesca calls me."

"All right, Nana."

"Here are Alanna and Alex," Francie said, taking Alex's hand and stepping forward with him.

"You look like your daddy," Nana said to him. "'Cept your eyes. Whose eyes did you get?"

"My mama's," he replied.

"She abandoned us," Alanna said bluntly, and humiliation clawed its way up Ryan's cheeks. "She left us when we were babies."

He'd only told Francie that he was divorced. He hadn't told her the sordid details. He didn't meet her eyes.

"Some people ain't cut out to be parents," Nana said. "Too bad God don't see that ahead o' time and keep 'em from havin' young ones, ain't it?"

"I'm very grateful for my children," Ryan replied automatically. "I'm glad their mother had them."

Nana's eyes narrowed. She gave him the once-over and a grin creased her aged features. "I think I like you, Jim."

"Nana, his name is Ryan. Ryan MacNair."

"You told me you married a Jim."

"You must have gotten it mixed up."

"I don't get mixed up. I'm old, not stupid."

"Does this chair go fast?" Alex asked, looking the wheelchair over.

"When I can get someone to push me," she replied. "Push me, Jim," she said. "Don't ever have nobody to push me where I want to go."

"Where would you like to go?" he asked.

"To the garden. And down by the fountain. Did you see any ducks down there?"

"I did," Alex said.

Nana's eyes twinkled at Alex. "Hop on," she said, patting her lap.

He looked up at his dad.

Ryan looked at Francie, and she nodded.

"Okay, but only down to the fountain. We don't want you putting Nana's legs to sleep."

Ryan pushed the wheelchair, balking at Alex's cries to go faster. Alanna followed without speaking.

At the sound of a high-speed shutter, Ryan glanced to find Francie snapping away with a state-of-the-art Nikon. "*That's* the camera you carry in that beaten-up case?"

She zoomed in for a close-up of his face as they passed beneath the shade of a tree, then lowered the camera. "There's nothing wrong with this case. It's been a lot of places with me. It's sort of an old friend."

"It was her daddy's," Nana supplied.

She'd never mentioned her parents. Ryan wondered if they were dead. He and Francie sat on the concrete bench surrounding the fountain, Nana's wheelchair between them. Alex balanced on a short fence nearby and Alanna found a spot in the shade.

Francie took pictures.

"I wanna put my feet in," Nana announced.

"In the water?" Francie asked.

"'Course in the water. Take my shoes off."

Ryan glanced at Francie and then around them. How would they handle this?

Immediately Francie placed the camera in the bag and knelt to remove her grandmother's shoes.

"Francie, you can't do that," he objected.

"Why not?"

"What if someone sees?"

"Her feet? So what?"

"Well, it—it might not be good for her. She might catch cold."

"It's seventy-five degrees, in case you haven't noticed."

Their gazes locked.

"She's an old lady," she whispered. "She has few pleasures left, and I aim to see that she gets this small one." She set the last shoe and sock aside, and stood from her crouched position. She was barely bigger than the old woman.

"Move aside," he ordered.

She looked at him, then obliged. He gathered Nana up effortlessly and turned to sit her on the concrete, her feet dangling in the water.

She sighed and laughed out loud. "I do like you, Jim."

He sat beside her. "I like you, too, Nana."

"You got a grandma?" she asked.

"Had a wonderful one," he replied.

"What about your mother?"

"She's gone, too."

"No wonder you needed a woman in your life. Francesca's a whole lotta woman in a small package."

He'd noticed.

"Look, kids!" she called. "There's goldfish nibbling at my toes!"

"Can I do it, too, Dad?" Alex asked, excitedly.

Francie slipped off her sandals, helped Alex with his Nikes, and the two of them sat side by side on the other side of Nana, giggling as the fish brushed against their feet. The gold band on Francie's finger glittered in the sunlight and the sight sent an odd sensation pinging through his chest.

"Come on, Jim," Nana said with a cackling laugh. "Put your feet in the water."

"Come on, Dad, it's cool!"

Ryan glanced from the old woman to his son, and finally allowed his gaze to light on Francie. Her lips held a smile, and her blue eyes a dare.

He slid off his leather sandals, rolled up his pant legs and lowered one foot into the cool water. "You didn't say it was cold."

"Ain't cold," Nana declared. "It's refreshin'."

Ryan grinned and plunged the other foot in. He turned and observed his daughter, her haughty facade keeping her from enjoying their company, or the day, or this week away from home. But from time to time, she glanced over, and once he thought he saw her hide a smile. Maybe this week was going to do her more good than harm, after all.

Maybe it was going to do them all some good.

4

"ARE YOU SURE it's okay?" Francie asked as they closed the door and headed for the elevator.

"Alanna's twelve years old. She's very responsible. They'll watch TV for a while and fall asleep."

She glanced back. "I left the number for Quigley's near the phone."

"They won't call. They'll be just fine."

"We can call them after an hour and make sure everything's okay," she suggested.

"If you want to," he agreed and ushered her into the elevator.

Francie studied his closely shaven jaw while he watched the numbers above the doors. They'd just spent two days and one night together, and she knew little more about him than she had before. Except what the kids had revealed.

"Your wife abandoned Alanna and Alex?" she asked hesitantly.

A muscle in his firm jaw twitched. "We're not friends," he said pointedly.

"You're right. Sorry." With a stab of hurt his suitably chastising words shouldn't have caused, she glanced up at the numbers he watched so intently.

Silence stretched between them. She would have to

be more careful not to cross any boundaries that bent his nose out of joint. He didn't have to discuss his life with her. He didn't owe her anything. What he was doing this week was enough.

They walked to the car, and Francie pulled the key from her purse.

"Allow me." He plucked it from her fingers.

"Do you have a problem with my driving?"

"The less stress, the better, all right?" He unlocked the doors and drove in silence. At a stoplight he asked, "This the street?"

"Yes. It's just behind that sign there."

He parked the car and glanced at her.

"It's going to be just fine," she assured him. "These people have no way of knowing we're not exactly what we say we are."

"I'll take my cues from you," he replied.

They got out of the car and entered the dimly lit lounge. Francie smoothed her wraparound jungle print skirt, a fluttering of nerves in her stomach, and swept a glance across the interior. It was show time. They had to make these people believe they were married. Where had the assurance she'd just exhibited for Ryan flown?

"There they are," she said, spotting a few familiar faces. She took his hand and led him forward. Several voices called greetings. Becka Crow and Peyton Armbruster were seated together chatting, and Peyton scooted over to make room to pull in two chairs.

"Have you met Francie's husband?" Peyton asked Becka.

"Not yet," the young woman replied.

"Everyone, this is Ryan," Francie said.

A chorus of voices welcomed him.

"Newlyweds," a female drawled. "Isn't that precious?"

Francie turned on a smile for Shari Donegan.

"When were you married?" she asked.

"Six months ago," Ryan said at the same time Francie came up with a reply.

"Valentine's Day," she answered.

They glanced at each other, but apparently the others didn't notice February had only been five months ago.

"Valentine's Day! How romantic," Shari said. "Whose idea was that?"

Wisely Francie bit her lip this time. Ryan must have done the same because a blatant silence followed. Finally she turned to look at him.

"It was my idea," he said, meeting her gaze steadily. "She thinks she has all the good ideas, but I have my share, too."

"Yes, you do," she agreed.

"We were beginning to wonder if Francie would ever find a husband," Peyton said.

Anger warmed Francie's cheeks. "Apparently everyone else has been more concerned about my marital status than I have. I have a fulfilling career and I support myself nicely. What do I need a husband for?"

The stares she garnered revealed she'd just stuck her foot in her mouth. She glanced around for a waitress.

"Apparently Ryan showed you something you

need a husband for,'' Becka said, joining the conversation with a suggestive tone.

The others laughed.

"You don't need a husband for that, either," Francie said quickly.

Becka's husband, J.J., chuckled.

"Was your biological clock ticking?" Peyton asked with a grin.

Francie frowned at her. "No! I'm not going to have children."

The others exchanged glances.

Becka giggled. "Remember, guys, this is Francie. If she had a biological clock, it would be set for another time zone."

Laughter rose around them.

Ryan didn't appeared amused. He straightened in his chair. "What Francie means is Alanna and Alex are a handful. In a few more years they'll be grown, and we'll have all our time just for each other. That's why we decided not to have more kids."

He looped his arm around her shoulder, and something inside her warmed at his quick defense. He'd behaved just like a real loving husband would have.

A waitress arrived. "What can I get you?"

"A Coke, please," Francie said.

Ryan named a prized Chicago beer.

"Sorry. Don't have it."

"Killian's Red then," he said, and the waitress left.

"So, you were married before?" Peyton asked, leaning toward Ryan.

"I've been divorced for almost eight years," he replied.

"Goodness, you must have been Chicago's most eligible bachelor when Francie caught you."

"I don't know about that."

"Oh, you're modest. Where did you do your graduate work?"

"Stanford for an M.B.A. and an art history."

"A double masters?" Peyton asked with both brows raised, probably sorry she'd asked now.

He nodded.

"Have you given Francie exposure?" Peyton asked. "As a local artist, I mean?"

"That's a good idea." Thoughtfully he turned to Francie. "Come to think of it, I've seen some of your photographs displayed around the city. How come we've never done a show at the museum?"

"I tried to interest the museum in my old Chicago photos last year and didn't reach first base," she said. "Didn't fit in with the ancient artifacts themes, or something."

"Your photos would be perfect for the bicentennial celebration coming up this fall. We can work out an offer. Give my office a call when we get back. We'll set up a show."

The surrounding silence grew deafening. The jukebox played a song for the third time. Francie glanced up quickly.

"You have to call his office for an appointment?" Becka asked, voicing the question on all their faces.

Francie's cheeks warmed again. She faced the women, but cuddled into Ryan's side. "As if work is on my mind when this sexy guy comes home. If you had to compete with his job for his attention, would you talk business when he finally got there?''

The men snickered.

Ryan leaned down and placed a gentle kiss on her lips, then drew her snugly to his side. Her lips tingled from the unexpected contact. Against her shoulder, his heart beat steadily. The waitress brought their drinks, and Ryan paid.

It was the first time he'd paid for anything on this trip, since she felt responsible, so she planned to pay him back later.

He took a drink of the Irish beer without pouring it into the glass the waitress had brought. Don Armbruster leaned across the table, and started a conversation. Francie sat in the shelter of Ryan's arm, recognizing the oddity of the scene. No man had ever held her so possessively in public. No man had ever kissed her so purposefully. She wouldn't have allowed it. But Ryan was playing his part as her husband. And for some bizarre reason, she was almost enjoying it.

She imagined the possibility of a man who loved her enough to come to her defense, a man who found it natural to express his tender feelings with a kiss. As the others talked, she glanced from one face to the next. Envy tinged the faces of the women. She gave each of them a self-satisfied smile.

They thought she was in the first bloom of new love, probably imagined her and Ryan having hot sex once or twice a night. They'd all been married for years, and no doubt the initial flame had faded to an ember. She glanced at balding, squatty Don Armbruster and tried to picture him and pencil-neck Peyton locked in a passionate clinch. A giggled escaped her. She covered her mouth with her hand. "I should go call the kids now."

"Got change, honey?"

She stood. "Yes, I do, sweetie. Will you miss me?"

"You know I will." He slid his warm hand up the back of her thigh in a suggestive caress. Francie's heart skipped one beat too many, and her breath stuck in her throat. "Hurry back," he said huskily.

Oh, he was playing this game to the hilt. She hadn't thought he had it in him. Or was he deliberately taunting her when he knew she couldn't do anything about it or risk exposing the truth to their audience?

"You know I will," she repeated, using his words as suggestively as he had. With one hand on his shoulder, she leaned down. Recognition flared in his dark eyes. His lips parted slightly in anticipation, and he met her mouth with his. He raised a hand to her neck and kissed her back as if they were lovers!

His lips were warm and pliant and tasted yeasty. The tips of their tongues touched, but his remained impassive, as though he were waiting...hoping... Heat curled right through Francie's chest and slipped lower.

Her mind registered the catcalls on either side of them, and she came to her senses and pulled away.

He gave her a smile that the others would see as a sexual implication. She would herself, if she didn't know better. It was deviltry, pure and simple.

Heart hammering, she made her way to a phone in the hallway near the rest rooms. She'd have to check her face after this call. She couldn't have any lipstick remaining, and her cheeks were probably as flushed as a case of hives.

It took her a couple of minutes to sort through the paper clips and coins on the bottom of her purse and come up with correct change.

She dialed and the phone rang twice.

"Hello?"

The woman's voice startled Francie. "Oh! I'm sorry, I must have the wrong number."

"No, no," the heavily accented voice replied. "Are you seeking the MacNairs?"

"Yes. Who *is* this?"

"This is Señora Miguel from housekeeping. I am attending young master MacNair until his parents can be located."

"What? Where is his sister? Put Alanna on, please."

"Miss Alanna is not here. The staff is searching for her now."

Francie listened to a couple more disjointed sentences before slamming down the receiver and running back to the table.

"We have to go!"

"What's wrong?" Ryan asked, setting down his beer.

"Alanna's not there. Alex said she's been missing since he went to the bathroom shortly after we left. He got scared and called the desk. They have a housekeeper with him until we get there."

Ryan stood. "Why didn't they call us? We left the number."

She shook her head. "I don't know."

The others settled up their tabs and rose to leave, too.

Ryan drove the rental as fast as he dared, his heart thudding, and his mind conjuring up images he couldn't let himself dwell on.

"It's going to be all right," Francie said to him. "This is just some mistake, and we're going to find her. She'll probably be back when we get there."

"I know, I know," he said, his voice unsteady. "You just hear such awful things. I mean, on the news every day."

"This is nothing like that," she reassured him. "There is a simple explanation."

He parked with a screech of tires, and they ran from the car to the hotel. They arrived at the desk out of breath. "I'm Ryan MacNair," he said. "What's going on?"

The young man standing behind the counter turned to exit a door and appeared in the lobby with them in seconds. "Your son called the desk earlier. He said your daughter was not in the room, and that he didn't know where she'd gone. We think he waited about an hour before he called. He thought she'd gone to the pool and would be back soon, but then, I guess he went looking for her himself and couldn't find her.

"I went and searched your room first, myself, thinking she might be playing a prank on her brother. We've had every available person searching the hotel and the surrounding streets since then. They meet back here every fifteen minutes for a check in. So far nothing."

Ryan ran a hand through his always impeccable hair, setting the waves in disarray. "I guess I need to see my son."

Francie thanked the assistant manager and followed.

The elevator took forever to arrive. Once inside, they stared at each other. He cut his glance toward the door and flexed his fingers impatiently. Finally the elevator reached their floor. Ryan was out the door and down the hall before she could catch her breath.

He had his plastic key out and the door open without waiting for her. She arrived to see Alex get up from the bed and run to his father. "I'm s-sorry, Dad. I didn't know what to do. I d-don't know what happened to her."

Ryan sat on the end of a bed and took Alex in his lap. He stroked his dark hair. "It's all right, son. Everything's going to be all right. Can you tell me exactly what happened?"

The tearful story sounded just as the manager had relayed it. Alex had gone into the bathroom and returned to find Alanna missing. He'd searched the room for her, thinking she was teasing, and then he'd become worried. After a while, he'd grown scared and ventured down to the pool area.

After that he'd come back and called the desk.

"Why didn't you call us?" Ryan asked.

"I forgot about that number," Alex wailed. "I picked up the phone and the man at the counter answered."

Ryan patted his back. "That's all right. You did just fine, and we're here now."

The dark-haired housekeeper stood. "I will help the others now. We will find your *niña*."

"Thank you," Francie said to her. The woman let herself out quietly.

"I have to go help, too," Ryan said, grimly.

Francie understood it was harder to wait here and do nothing. "Alex and I will stay together and wait for her to return."

"You didn't do anything wrong," Ryan said carefully, looking his son in the eye. "It was very smart of you to call the desk and ask for help." He got up and left the room.

Francie glanced at the clock and noted that it was after ten-thirty. She pulled back the covers on Ryan and Alex's bed, sat, and patted the mattress. "Come lie down. I'll sit with you."

"I'm scared," he sniffled.

"It's okay to be scared," she told him.

He padded to the bed and crawled between the sheets. Francie tucked him in and snuggled on top of the covers beside him. He seemed so small and helpless. What an enormous responsibility children were. She'd always known she wasn't cut out to be a mother, just as her parents weren't cut out to be parents. She had her career, and she hadn't time nor energy to maintain the physical and emotional well-being of another human being.

"When I was little, I had a dog for when I was scared," he said.

"A real dog or a stuffed dog?"

"A stuffed dog. But he was as good as a real dog."

"I bet he was. Where is he now?"

"Home. I don't take him with me places anymore. That's for babies."

"Well, you're sure not a baby."

"I cried."

"Everybody cries sometimes, Alex."

"They do?"

"Sure."

"When did you cry?"

Francie remembered only too well what it was like to be an alone and frightened child. "I cried when my mother left me."

"Your mother left you, too?"

She'd known he would grasp her story. It was something she had never shared with anyone else, but Alex was different. "My mother and my father left me."

"Both of them? Why'd they do that?"

"Oh," she said, brushing his hair back from his forehead. "They had careers. They were photojournalists."

"What's that?"

"They took pictures for newspapers and magazines. They were out of the country a lot. It was hard for them to keep me with them. So they left me with Nana."

"How old were you?"

"I was ready to start junior high. That was a problem, too. They never stayed in one place long enough for me to go to school."

"But you love Nana, don't you?"

"I love her very much. She took care of me and loved me and gave me a home. That's why I took her name. My parents' name was Karr, but I added Taylor onto it, because she was my real parent.

"But I'd only seen her a few times when my parents left me with her. I'd been moved from place to place and stayed with too many people to ever become attached to anyone."

"I don't remember my mother leaving," Alex said.

"Do you wish you could remember her?"

"Sometimes. Sometimes I hate her."

"It's okay to be mad at her," she told him. "But don't stay mad at her. You'll only hurt yourself."

"That's what my dad says."

"Well, listen to your dad. He's a smart guy."

"I know."

He snuggled closer. "I get mad at Alanna, too, but I love her. I don't want anything bad to happen to her."

"I know you love her," she said softly.

In seconds he was sound asleep.

Francie paced the floor for another half hour until she heard a commotion in the hall. She hurried out, closing the door behind her so Alex wouldn't be awakened.

Alanna's voice carried down the corridor, and relief swept through Francie as if it were a warm current. Ryan had his daughter by the arm. A few of the people who'd been at Quigley's followed them, including Becka and Shari, their husbands, and Tom Wallace from the rental place.

"Oh, thank God," Francie said, hurrying forward. "Why on earth you would pull such a fool stunt and scare me half to death is more than I'll ever understand," Ryan said angrily.

At the passion in his tone, Francie stopped her forward motion.

"Look at all these people you've put out," he went on. "The entire hotel staff has been searching for you."

"I don't care!" she shouted. "I told you I didn't want to come here. This hotel stinks! I didn't want to come because of *her!* You never spend any time with me, and when we finally go somewhere, it's to a stupid reunion in a stupid little town, all because of her!" Tears streamed down Alanna's cheeks, and the hurt and anger in her voice made it shake. "And that *stupid* woman has spoiled everything! *Everything!* I hate her!"

Ryan glanced up and saw Francie standing outside the room. He looked back at the half-dozen hotel patrons and staff who had heard Alanna's outburst. Francie noted Becka's and Shari's aghast expressions, and the embarrassment on the faces of the men.

Francie forced her feet into action. She walked right past Alanna and Ryan without a word, and stopped in front of the others. "Thank you, everyone, for your concern. We appreciate your help."

"We'll see you tomorrow, Francie," Shari said.

Subdued good-nights sounded, and the group moved to the elevator. She didn't even want to speculate as to what they were whispering about.

Francie walked back past Ryan and Alanna and stopped with her hand on the doorknob. "Do you have your key?"

Ryan moved behind her. Without saying a word about her locking herself out, he unlocked the door and ushered her in. She went into the bathroom, washed her face and returned. "I'll be down by the pool for a while."

"Francie—" he began.

"You two need some time alone together. Please wake up Alex and tell him his sister's safe."

A stricken look crossed Alanna's face. Francie knew she wasn't afraid of her father. He was angry, but he was a kind and gentle man. Alanna must have just realized the panic she had inflicted on her brother.

Without a backward glance, Francie left the MacNair family to themselves.

5

AN HOUR LATER, sitting at one of the small tables near the pool, Francie swirled the melting ice in her Coke and contemplated going back to the room. She'd watched couples and families returning to the rooms above, those whose doors opened onto the balconies.

It seemed everyone was paired off and grouped together. The entire civilized population moved in twos and fours and fives. She'd always considered herself self-sufficient, never lonely. Not until now, anyway. It was this town and the people she'd gone to school with and her grandmother that were making her feel this way. They'd pointed her out as an oddity for as long as she could remember.

Oh, Nana didn't mean to. She had good intentions. She just thought every woman should have a husband whether or not she needed or wanted one.

And the dating fiascoes... Idly Francie stopped the straw with her index finger and dribbled watery cola back into the glass. She'd tried her best to put those high school dates out of her mind. Rarely had she clicked with a guy, and if she had, something had come up to spoil the relationship.

Like Ted Chapman. Their interests had been fairly well matched, and he hadn't minded Nana's constant checks on their whereabouts; he'd even tolerated Francie's passion to take pictures everywhere they went.

The iguana had been the end of that.

Francie'd bought it at a carnival. She planned to place it in the neighbor kids' sandbox and take photos. Ted had hated it and refused to allow it in his car. She'd walked, the iguana tucked under her arm.

The pictures hadn't been outstanding. Nana hated it, too, so Francie'd sold the lizard to a pet store. Ted had never called again.

Whatever had made her think of that? She needed to get some sleep. She'd forgotten the room key again, and Ryan and the kids might be sleeping. Maybe she could get an extra one at the desk. The entire hotel staff knew her by now; ID wouldn't be a problem.

The window where she'd purchased her soft drink had closed, and the lights in the small restaurant turned out one by one. A lone swimmer, an older gentleman, sliced through the water.

"Francie?"

"Oh!" She jerked her arm back at the touch, and cola shot out of the straw across Ryan's shirtfront. Recognizing him, Francie stood. "Oh, I'm sorry. You startled me."

"It's all right." He accepted the damp napkin she offered and dabbed at the spots ineffectually. "You've been gone a long time."

"You needed time with your daughter."

He gestured for her to sit again, and she did.

"Are they both okay?"

"Yes. They're fine. She's in deep trouble, but she's asleep now." He sat in the chair opposite her and placed his forearms on the table. He watched the man swimming for a few minutes. "I'm sorry about the things she said—especially in front of everyone."

"You don't have to apologize for her."

"She will apologize, too."

"Don't make her do that, Ryan. She hates me enough already."

He tipped his head as though he were uncomfortable with her words or the situation. In the glow of the soft lights that lit the pool, she studied his handsome features.

"It's okay," she reiterated. "You can't force her to like someone she doesn't want to."

He fixed his dark eyes on her face. "Her rudeness is unacceptable."

"She has enough to deal with at this age without me adding to her problems," she said.

"She added to her own problems," he said. "She should not have left Alex alone in that room. She knows that." His tired eyes and grim mouth revealed the extent of his exhaustion.

"Where was she?" she asked.

"She hid in one of the conference rooms in the dark."

"She did it for attention, you know."

"That's the wrong way to get attention."

"Kids don't think about that." She shifted in her chair. "They're hurting and they just do things. Her resentment of me and the time I've taken from your family is justified." Francie glanced away and then back. "I do things without thinking them all the way through, too, so I know how ideas seem good at first, then get kind of out of hand."

"You're defending her."

She gave him a crooked smile and placed her hand on his. "Yeah. Don't punish her on my account, okay?"

He glanced at her hand on his. She pulled it away self-consciously.

"Okay," he said finally.

She smiled.

The lone swimmer splashed out of the water. They glanced up as he dried off and left.

Silence stretched between them.

"Their mother just left," he said. "Packed up and took off."

The subject surprised her. Especially after his reaction that afternoon when she'd questioned him about Alex's comments. "You were right earlier. You don't have to tell me."

"I know I don't. But it's part of who Alanna is. And why she does some of the things she does."

Francie nodded her understanding. "You had no warning that your wife was going to leave?"

"I knew she was unhappy. She did okay with Alanna when she was a baby. Left her with sitters a lot. Alex was an accident, and she was unhappy from the minute she knew he was on the way. She was in such denial, I couldn't even get her to the doctor until she was five months along. She slept all the time while she was pregnant." He wadded the napkin into a tiny ball.

"I thought it was just her condition, you know, that she'd get over it. But she got more and more depressed."

Francie listened without saying anything, hearing the frustration he tried to keep from his tone.

"She became self-absorbed," he said. "They needed her, but she didn't want to do anything or go anywhere. I insisted she see a doctor, and she was better for a while as long as she took her medication. But she didn't want to take it, and she'd slide back into her melancholy."

"That must have been awful," she sympathized.

"I came home one day to find her gone. She hadn't even called the sitter. Alex had lain in his bed all day, wet and crying. I found Alanna in our bed. She must have cried herself to sleep. She wasn't even three yet."

"Oh, Ryan, that's awful," Francie said, blinking back tears and swallowing a lump in her throat. She knew his intent in telling her hadn't been to gain her pity.

"I was used to taking care of them with the help of sitters by then," he said. "When I realized she wasn't coming home, I hired a live-in nanny. Her name was Chris, and she loved the kids. She stayed with us until she got married a few years ago. Since the kids were older, I just hired a housekeeper."

"It's fortunate you could afford to hire help."

"Fortunate?" he said, looking up with a frown.

"I wasn't making light of your situation. I just meant that a good many men wouldn't have had the means to keep the children with them, and do as well as you did for them. A lot of men wouldn't have wanted to try without a woman to do most of it.''

"I did the best I could,'' he said.

"I know that. You've done a great job with them.'' He raised a brow.

"I mean it. All teenagers act like that. Worse.''

"I guess.'' He shrugged, and leaned back, glancing across the now deserted pool. "I don't know why I told you all that. It's not something I talk about.''

"It helps me understand the kids better,'' she said.

His dark eyes came back to her face. "And why would you want to understand them?''

"Well...'' She looked at her hands. "I don't. But now I'll know to be wary of Alanna when we're in public situations.''

His gaze warmed her, and she refused to look up. She should have known better than to take an interest in hearing about his wife. She didn't need this man to become a real person to her. He was just a means to get her through the week and keep Nana happy. If she were to think of him in any other manner, she would have to wonder what kind of a woman would walk out on this guy.

He was the perfect catch Nana had believed she'd needed.

And she would have to wonder how hard all this was on him.

Once again she'd been impulsive, and once again, she was seeing repercussions. When would she learn? She caught herself twisting the wedding band on her finger and dropped her hands self-consciously.

"Don't you think we'd better head back?" he asked after several minutes.

She stood, and together they walked down a corridor to the elevator. The deserted lobby provided no distractions, so they watched the numbers above the door. The elevator arrived, and he ushered her in.

Francie glanced at his spotted shirtfront, then at his face. The image of kissing him so boldly at Quigley's that evening rose up in her mind and amazed her, embarrassed her. In front of her old classmates and as long as it was a performance, they'd both been daring and uninhibited. Alone and confined like this, they awkwardly avoided each other's eyes.

The elevator stopped, and they walked to the room. Ryan inserted his card. The image of doing this with him under different circumstances flashed before her. She couldn't help wondering what it would be like to stay in a hotel room with Ryan MacNair...without his children along...with a different plan in mind.

Cheeks uncomfortably warm, she entered ahead of him and hurried about her nightly routine. She glanced at both of the kids in the dark, Alex settled in the bed, Alanna on the floor. Unexpected tears came to her eyes at the reminder of how much the insecure girl resented her.

Francie climbed into bed and listened to the sounds of Ryan turning off the bathroom light and getting into bed. Even if the entire population were paired off, she could still be herself. Francie Karr-Taylor was satisfied with her life just the way it was. Wasn't she?

"IT SAID ON THAT poster that today was a roller-skating party!" Alex shouted.

"Is that right?" Ryan's deep velvet voice interrupted Francie's sleep. "I still haven't seen the schedule."

She rolled over to see him being bounced awake as Alex jumped enthusiastically on their bed.

"Sit down, Alex," he commanded gently.

The boy sat by aiming his feet in the air and dropping on his behind. Ryan grunted with the impact of seventy pounds of child against his hip.

Alex discovered Francie awake and bounded from their bed to hers. "You're awake!"

"It's not easy to sleep through your morning calisthenics," his father said. Francie avoided looking at his bare chest and shoulders above the sheet.

"When are we gonna roller-skate?" the boy asked, his gray-blue eyes wide with excitement.

"That's not until tonight," she replied. "I have the schedule in my purse. I think it's at six-thirty. I thought I'd visit Nana today. You guys can do whatever you'd like."

"I want to visit Nana, too!" Alex cried. "We can go, too, can't we, Dad?"

Ryan sat up and scratched his head, and Francie stifled a giggle at his tousled head of hair. "What would you like to do, Alanna?" he asked.

Francie turned to see the girl sitting in one of the wing chairs, her knees up under her nightgown. She shrugged. "We can go see her if Alex wants to."

Her guilt over frightening Alex the night before was apparent in her congenial reply.

"We could do a little shopping this morning," Francie suggested, hoping to catch Alanna's interest and lighten the mood that had been created the night before.

Alanna met her eyes, but replied only, "Whatever."

They took turns showering and dressing, ate breakfast by the pool again and again Ryan insisted on driving. Francie directed him to the mall.

"Alanna and I will meet you back here in an hour," she said.

Alanna's expression revealed displeasure, but she said nothing.

Ryan glanced from one to the other and nodded.

"Come on, Dad. Let's go to the baseball card shop." Alex grabbed his father's hand and dragged him away.

Alanna gazed down the mall as though she were bored already.

"Anything special you want?" Francie asked. "A haircut? A dress?"

Alanna shook her head.

"Well, let's just look then." She led her into a department store. Alanna didn't want to try the perfumes or sample the lotions. They passed the purses and the girl said, "You should get one of those, so you're not always hunting through your purse, holding everyone up."

Francie glanced at the organizer she'd pointed to. "That's a good idea."

After a few minutes, she selected one and wrote a check for it. They remained at the counter where Francie dumped out the contents of her old purse and stored them neatly in the compartmentalized bag.

A photo wallet lay flopped open to a picture of two adults and a toddler.

"Who's that?" Alanna asked.

Francie glanced at it. "My parents and me."

"Are they dead?"

"They are now."

"Alex told me what you said about them."

"It's not a secret."

"Did you ever think they didn't love you?"

The question caught Francie off guard, but it had seemed sincere. "Sometimes. Nana said they loved me. But I wondered why they didn't love me enough to keep me with them."

"Parents are supposed to take care of you," Alanna said.

Francie had finished loading her purse, and tossed the old one into a wastebasket behind the counter. "Yes, they are. So I guess it makes a kid wonder if there's something wrong with them if their parents run out, huh?"

Alanna still held the miniature album. She closed it and handed it to Francie. "It wasn't your fault," the girl said. "The problem was theirs."

The adult-sounding comment brought Francie's brow up.

"That's what the counselors told me," Alanna said with a dismissive shrug.

"They were right." Francie led her toward the clothing. "But it doesn't make up for the years that I didn't have a parent like everyone else."

Alanna gave her a noncommittal shrug.

Francie found the lingerie department. "I need a few things here. How about you?"

Alanna glanced around in dismay, her cheeks reddening.

Francie had finally figured out that Alanna's slouching posture was caused by embarrassment over her developing body. The girl's father obviously hadn't thought to consider her maturing figure when he'd bought her school clothes.

Francie sought out the salesperson, a friendly grayhaired woman who smelled of expensive powdery perfume. "Will you measure us and bring us a few bras to try on?" she asked.

Alanna looked at her with shock written plainly across her face. "You'll never see this lady again," Francie whispered.

The woman led them into separate dressing rooms.

Twenty-five minutes later, Alanna joined her, her face flushed beet red, but her posture straighter. "I can't believe you made me do that."

"I don't think seven bras apiece is too many," Francie said. "Do you?"

Alanna rolled her eyes and followed Francie toward the shoes.

NANA WAS OVERJOYED to see the children again. This time they joined her in the day room, where the residents gathered to watch television and play games. The room had a wall of windows and sliding doors, giving it an open and airy feeling. Francie opened the box of chocolates she and Alanna had purchased, and the confection enticed several visitors, including nurses, past their table. Nana licked chocolate from her fingers and grinned with delight.

Alex had immediately climbed into Nana's lap. She hugged him soundly and showed him how to see what kind of center the candy had by poking a hole in the bottom of the chocolate.

"Tell me how you met my granddaughter, Jim."

Ryan glanced at Francie in immediate dismay.

She shrugged.

"Well, I—I had asked all of the jewelers in the Chicago area to notify me if they bought or appraised a certain piece of jewelry I was looking for." He explained about his grandmother's brooch. "Your granddaughter acquired the piece at an auction and had it appraised. I sought her out to buy the piece for Alanna."

Nana patted Ryan's hand. "That's a lovely story. And when you saw her, did you know you loved her right away?"

Ryan glanced from Nana's weathered face to Francie's ivory-complexioned one. "I knew she was unlike anyone I'd ever met before."

Nana cackled. "That's the truth, isn't it? How'd you convince her to give up her single life she values so much?"

"I'm irresistible," he replied.

Even Francie had to laugh at that one.

"Let's go see the ducks," Alex suggested.

"Push us, Jim," Nana directed.

"Is Alex getting too heavy for you?" he asked.

"I'll tell him when he is," she replied in her no-nonsense tone.

Ryan, getting used to responding to his new name, glanced at Alanna, but she didn't seem jealous of the attention Nana bestowed on the boy. In fact she carried herself a little straighter today for some odd reason. And he didn't think it was the new pair of shoes. She seemed less angry, or perhaps what he was seeing was repentance; in any case the lack of hostility came as a relief.

After a lengthy walk, they wheeled Nana to her room. The facility and the old woman's surroundings were impressive. This home must cost a pretty penny, and he wondered how much of the cost Francie provided. It was obvious that the old woman meant everything to her.

Alex had taken to her from the start, and seeing the two of them together pleased and worried Ryan at the same time. Alex knew this was a show. After this week he wouldn't see Francie's grandmother again.

That, too, was one of those things Francie had spoken of that had seemed like a good idea at the time. Now, all the details he hadn't considered were cropping up.

Alex was starved for the attention of these two women. But growing attached to either one of them would only cause heartache later on. Watching his son with Francie and her grandmother had a painful effect on Ryan's chest. The sight pointed out vividly how much the boy had missed having a woman around to spoil and coddle and love him. It pointed out, too, how sadly lacking all their lives were.

And he was partly to blame for it. He worked long

hours and had depended on Chris, and then Mrs. Nelson, to meet the kids' needs. He'd had to provide for them, though. His job granted enough for them to live comfortably and have things many other children didn't have.

"Who are these pictures of, Nana?" Alex asked, looking over the woman's possessions.

"Those are my children."

"Who are your children?"

"Francesca's father was my child. I have another son, too."

"Oh." Alex studied the photographs. "Where is he?"

"He lives in Anchorage. He's a professor."

"Is that far?"

"Yes, it's far," Alanna said. "It's in Alaska."

"Oh. Does he come here?"

"Not very often. He calls me sometimes. Francesca is the one who comes to visit me."

Ryan listened with half an ear. He had been trying to fool himself, but something about this week and these women made him take a long, hard look at reality. Time at home with his children had always pointed out the glaring absence of their mother. It had been more painful to stay at home with them than to work long hours.

He was as much at fault for deserting them as their mother had been.

6

I'LL JUST WATCH," Ryan said, trying to edge his way to the tables behind a waist-high barrier around the skating-rink floor.

"No, Dad, you gotta skate with us," Alex cried, pulling on his arm. "It won't be fun without you."

Guilt over his revelation that afternoon still ate at him. He could probably count on one hand the number of times in the last year he'd done things with his kids. And this was supposed to be their vacation time. So what if he made a fool of himself? "All right."

Alex whooped and ran ahead to the rental counter. Alanna followed more sedately. But Francie. Francie had a grin on her face and a spring in her step that he didn't like one bit.

Skates rented and laced, Francie and his children rolled across the carpet toward the highly polished floor. As a body, they turned and looked back at him expectantly.

"Dad?" Alanna said.

Hanging on to the table, he stood.

"You've *never* done this before?" Francie asked.

He shook his head and reached for the wall, making his way slowly, awkwardly, toward the opening into the room that yawned, in his imagination, as wide and incomprehensible as a black hole.

"Not exactly a chess club activity, eh, Mac?"

He ignored her. Many of her classmates and their families had arrived and were rolling around the rink like pros. At least nobody was paying any attention to his clumsy progress.

"I'll stand here and watch a minute," he said.

"Okay. We'll come back for ya." Alex and his sister and Francie moved into the flow of skaters. Francie skated as fearlessly and purposefully as she did everything else, weaving in and out of the crowd, turning to take pictures of Alex and Alanna behind her. She skated forward, backward, without a care or a pause.

She rolled past Ryan, a smile on her pretty face, her soft-looking hair flying behind, the ever-present camera strap around her neck. Alex passed next, and Alanna followed. After several times around they returned, smiles lighting their faces. "Okay, come on."

"Maybe I'd better stay up here on the carpet," he said, already shaky on his feet.

"Come on, you'll get the hang of it," Francie coaxed.

Hanging onto the wall, he sidestepped his way to the floor. Several skaters whooshed by, and he let them pass before venturing farther.

"Take my hand," Francie offered.

He raised a brow.

"Come on. Trust me."

"I've seen your driving, remember?"

She was a dangerous person to trust, he knew, but

clinging to any tenuous lifeline seemed imperative at this moment. He grasped her hand.

"We'll just stay here close to the wall for a while," she promised.

"Thank you." His feet wanted to go in different directions, rolling back and forth in a seesaw motion. "This is harder than it looks."

"You have to work your skates," she said, "don't let them work you. Walk into it, like this."

"I think I should stay on the carpet."

"You can't skate on the carpet. Now take a few sliding strides forward."

He did as she instructed and made a little progress.

"There you go—confidence is the key."

He was skating now, away from the wall, but still clinging to her hand. They made it halfway around the rink before he lost his balance and had to grab the wall.

"You're doing great," she said.

"Look, Dad!" Alex came up from behind and skated past, a wide grin splitting his face.

Ryan gained a little momentum, getting into the flow of the skaters with Francie's help. "You can let go now," he said.

She did.

They made another half turn around the rink. Now it felt as if he was going way too fast. "How do you stop?" he called.

"You slow down and then use the toe stop," she called. "But don't try it until—"

He tipped his toe forward and the rubber stopped his foot cold. The rest of his body propelled forward, and he splatted on the wooden floor with a resounding *thwack*.

"Of course, that's another way to stop." Francie glided to a stop beside him. "You all right?"

"I'm just fine," he said, sitting up. His palms stung and his teeth felt numb.

"Oh, you've skinned your chin," she said, sympathetically.

"I'm lucky I didn't break my leg and an arm and loose my teeth," he grumbled.

Alanna and Alex each skated to a smooth stop beside him. "Awesome landing, Dad!" Alex cried.

"Are you all right?" Alanna asked.

"Did everybody in the place see it?" he asked, now crawling to the wall.

"No, not everyone," Francie denied.

He kneaded his palm. "Did you get a picture in case someone missed it?"

"It *was* pretty loud," Alex argued, and Francie cast a wide-eyed look meant to stifle him. "But I don't think everybody saw it," he added quickly.

"No, there might have been *someone* in the bathroom," Ryan said dryly.

Alanna giggled, and he looked up in surprise.

"Sorry, Dad. I couldn't help it. I've just never seen you so...so..." At a loss for words, she shrugged.

He brushed his palms together.

Laughter erupted. Ryan glanced toward the tables on the other side of the barrier where Don Armbruster, Becka, J.J. and Shari sat like a row of judges and held up napkins with numbers from zero to nine scribbled on them.

"Very funny," he muttered. "Does Armbruster have a pair of skates on?"

"Dad?" Alanna said.

"What?"

"You'll never have to see these people again after this week."

He glanced up to see her grinning, a look of pure enjoyment on her young face. What was a little humiliation compared to giving his children the joy they deserved? "That's true enough, I guess."

She and Francie exchanged a look he didn't comprehend.

Hoping to regain at least a small measure of dignity, he got to his feet and stood against the wall.

"Let me get a washie out of my bag for your chin," Francie said. "I know right where they are." She skated off and returned in a flash to dab his chin. "Does it hurt?"

"Not much. You really did know where it was."

"You have to get back on the horse that threw you, you know," she said, her blue eyes wide and serious.

"Come on, Alex, they got free hot dogs over here!" Donald Armbruster Junior called to Alex, and Alex skated toward the refreshment stand.

Francie and Alanna urged Ryan back into the flow of skaters, and by the time they were ready for a break, he was skating on his own and proud of himself for only falling down two more times.

They joined the other adults at the tables and watched the kids for a while. Ryan removed his skates and, grateful for the solid footing, bought a round of colas.

"Hi, Francie." A slender man with thinning fair hair and a toothy smile greeted her.

"Ted. I hadn't seen you yet. Did you just get in town?"

"Yeah. I'm living in Rockford. Drove over for the rest of the week."

Francie seemed almost reserved when she spoke to the man, not like her gregarious manner with everyone else, arousing Ryan's curiosity.

"Ted, this is my husband, Ryan MacNair. Ryan, Ted Chapman."

"Hi, Ted." Ryan shook his hand.

Peyton spotted them and came over to stand beside their table, too. "Hello, Ted, how are you? Is Marian with you?"

"I'm divorced," he said simply.

"Oh," she said, clucking sadly. "There are just so many domestic problems everywhere you turn. So many dysfunctional families." She looked right at Francie, the implication plain. She patted Ryan's arm. "Hang in there, darling."

She moved off, leaving Francie glaring.

Ryan took her hand and rubbed his thumb across the backs of her fingers. She closed her eyes, briefly, then gave him a smile.

"Still taking pictures?" Ted asked Francie.

She nodded.

"Taken any good iguana shots lately?"

"No, not lately."

Shari Donegan discovered Ted and drew him into a conversation with her and Becka's husband.

"Iguana shots?" Ryan asked later, as they got into the car and buckled their seat belts.

She gave him a quick version of the lizard story. Francie must have seemed as odd to Ted back then as she had to Ryan the first time he'd met her.

"Dad?" his daughter said softly from the back seat.

"What, Alanna?"

"You and Francie can meet the others tonight. I will stay with Alex. You can trust me."

Her words touched his father's heart. "I do trust you, Alanna. Thank you for the offer. Would you like to go, Francie?"

She looked over at him in surprise. "Actually I wouldn't. Why don't we take the kids to a movie?"

She no longer seemed so odd to him. He understood that she felt out of place with her old classmates. The only reason she'd come to Springdale was to ease her grandmother's worries by convincing everyone she was happily married. "I'd like that," he said.

And he discovered he meant it.

THE KIDS TALKED them into a late swim after the movie. Francie cut through the water vigorously. She'd be exhausted when they got back to the room. She'd been enjoying her swim immensely when the Armbrusters showed up, followed by several other families.

"Hey, Alex," Donald Junior called. "I got some Gummi Bears!"

Alex climbed the ladder and joined Donald at a table.

"Dad, there's a show I wanted to see tonight. Is it okay if I go up to the room and watch it?" Alanna asked.

"Let me walk you up," he said.

Francie was talking with Becka when Ryan returned and slipped into the water beside her. "Did you get her settled?" she asked.

"She's fine. She was just tired."

"Girls that age need time alone," Francie said.

"You mean it's not unusual for her to want to spend so much time alone in her room?"

"Not at all," Becka agreed.

From behind, Ryan placed his arms around Francie's waist and pulled her back against him in the water. "Stay here," he whispered.

Her bare back brushed the hair on his chest, and the backs of her legs came against his thighs. Enough was enough when it came to this showing off business, but something kept her where he'd pulled her.

Becka pushed away and swam off, as if leaving them to their private cuddle.

"I know that man," he said into her ear, and a shiver of pleasure ran across her shoulder.

"What man?"

"That one. Up there."

She glanced up and caught sight of the man in dark trousers and a sport shirt letting himself into one of the rooms on the balcony above.

"Of all the places to run into someone I know," he muttered.

"How fast can you grow a beard?"

"I've never grown one."

"It was a joke, Mac. Who is he?"

"He's a historian. Owns an enormous Abe Lincoln collection." His low voice rumbled in his chest against her back. "We've had it on display at the museum."

"What's he doing here?" she asked rhetorically.

"Making my life more insane," he replied.

"He didn't see you."

"No." The man had gone in and closed the door. "Let's go."

She swam to the side with him, and they got out and towel-dried. He held her terry-cloth robe open for her to slip into. Francie caught Shari's expression as she watched them leave. She smiled a satisfied smile and waved.

Ryan got Alex and they took the elevator to their room, another day put to bed.

THE FOLLOWING EVENING was Springdale High School's production of *Grease*. The couples met for dinner preceding the event, filling a banquet room in a local restaurant.

The salad dressing passed while Ryan visited the rest room with Alex.

"What kind does Ryan like?" Lisa Richards asked from the chair on the opposite side of Ryan's empty one. She held the tray, ready to spoon dressing and pass it on.

"Uh." Francie racked her brain for what kind of

dressing she'd seen him order if any, and couldn't remember.

Lisa waited.

Her husband and, farther down, the Armbrusters waited.

Francie glanced in the direction of the rest rooms, praying he'd be coming.

She glanced at Alanna, but the girl deliberately kept her eyes on her own plate and offered no help.

"He'll eat anything—except blue cheese," she added, just in case he hated it.

Shrugging, Lisa spooned something on Ryan's salad and passed the tray.

On the other side of the table Alanna chose dressing for Alex and spared Francie that decision. "Thanks a lot, girlfriend," Francie said barely loud enough for Alanna to hear.

"Making me buy underwear didn't make you my friend," she said with her usual haughty flair.

Francie had thought they'd made a little progress, but obviously she'd been fooling herself. Alanna didn't like her, and she had no intention of trying. Francie could handle that.

Ryan and Alex finally returned.

"All this has to be costing quite a bit," Ryan said softly from beside her. "You've been paying for meals and activities, not to mention the hotel and the plane fare." He reached inside his jacket and withdrew a slip of paper.

She cut her tomato slice. "What's that?"

"A list of the meals and expenses. Some of them I'm not sure of because you've taken care of everything. I know you bought Alanna something at the mall, because I saw the bags, but she won't say.''

"It was part of the deal, remember? I'm getting what I wanted.'' She took the paper from his fingers and wadded it into a ball.

He gave her a puzzled look, but something more lurked behind those dark eyes.

"What?'' she asked.

"*Are* you getting what you wanted?'' he asked.

She had no idea what he was getting at. "Is this really the time and place for this discussion?''

"Let me pay for dinner this time. My kids have been having a good time.''

Oh, yeah, Alanna was having the time of her life. "What about you?''

"What do you mean?''

"Have you been miserable?''

"You shouldn't have to pay for all the entertainment is what I'm saying.''

"No, Mac, what you're doing is avoiding the question.''

"Is this really the time and place for this discussion?'' he asked, using her own words in retaliation.

Francie couldn't help a grin. "You're not such a stuffed shirt, after all, you know that?''

"And you're—never mind.''

"No. Go ahead.''

"You're the ditzy blonde I suspected was in there all along.''

"Thank you.''

"You're welcome.''

He took a bite of his salad. "What is this?''

"Looks like Thousand Island."

"My favorite."

"Really?"

"No. I like blue cheese."

"Figures. They were in a hurry, and I didn't know your preference."

"So, where do you live in Chicago?" Lisa asked from Ryan's other side.

Peyton's long neck stretched as she strained to hear his reply.

He glanced at Francie, and she quickly stuffed a bite of salad into her mouth and gestured for him to reply.

"One of the North Shore suburbs," he replied. "Winnetka. It's on the lake."

Even Francie's eyes widened. The area he indicated was one of pricey estates with private beaches.

"Wasn't the house they filmed in *Home Alone* in Winnetka?" Lisa's husband, Robert asked. "I only know that because my brother lives in Lincoln Park, and he mentioned it."

Ryan didn't seem to know, but Alanna confirmed Robert's question.

"So, how long does it take you to get to work?" Shari asked from the other side of the table, and Francie hadn't even realized she was listening.

She placed a tomato slice into her mouth and chewed slowly.

"About thirty-five minutes taking Lake Shore Drive," Ryan replied. "But the drive along the lake is so pretty that even in traffic, we don't mind."

Francie leaned into him to whisper, "Do you have

a map in your pocket, too? You could show them that."

He ignored her jibe.

"I thought your studio was in your home," Shari said. "That's what I'd heard, anyway."

"Oh, it is," Francie said, finally having to answer. "I drive into the city for business. And, of course, for pleasure."

"What's your favorite restaurant?" Lisa asked. "We'll have to try it out when we visit Robert's brother."

"The 95th," Francie replied. She'd never been there, but she'd seen the advertisements for the plush, glass-enclosed restaurant lounge at the top of the Hancock Building.

"They have the best Thousand Island dressing," Ryan commented from beside her.

Francie covered her lips with her napkin to hide a smile.

"Take your kids to the zoo, too," Alanna piped up, and Lisa showed interest. "There's all kinds of animals and paddleboats to rent. *Daddy* takes us all the time."

A disturbed look crossed Ryan's face. "I was thinking we could go when we get back home," he said to his daughter.

Doubt clouded her features as if she were asking, "For real?"

"Would you like that, Alanna?"

A blush tinged her cheeks. "Yes."

"It's a date then," he said, and Francie heard the promise in his tone.

Alanna glanced at Alex, and then gave her father a hesitant smile.

By theater time, Alanna and Alex had bonded with the other children and sat in a cluster near the front.

"Alanna seems to have found a friend," Francie commented, watching her chatter with a girl about the same age.

"Looks that way," Ryan replied.

They had about a twenty-minute wait until the production began.

"You don't think she'll say anything, do you?" Francie asked, leaning to whisper. "I mean about us. Something that could get back to that girl's parents?"

"I don't think so. I made it clear to them that the secret must be kept in order to keep the bargain. She doesn't have anything of her mother's. The brooch is important to her, even as young as she is. Maybe more so because Nikki left her."

"Was that her name?"

He nodded. A few minutes later, he said, "I think I owe you."

"You paid for dinner."

"No, not that. For this week. For opening my eyes. I was hiding in my work, avoiding my kids without knowing it or realizing why. It hurts to know that part of Alanna's fantasy in this game we're playing includes trips to the zoo. It's a normal family thing, but she had to make it up."

"You've never taken her?"

He shook his head regretfully. "No. She went with her school once."

"You'll fix that," Francie said.

He turned his attention to the curtained stage.

His stuffy workaholic demeanor was a cover-up for a lot of pain and uncertainty. Underneath that Armani suit beat the heart of a loving father and a man with as many hopes and dreams as the next guy. The thought of how he'd been hurt disturbed Francie in a way she wouldn't have expected.

Once again, Francie regretted peeling back the layers and discovering the man beneath them. She couldn't afford for Ryan MacNair to become a real person to her. He was a means to pacify and please her grandmother, and nothing more.

The lights dimmed, and anticipatory silence filled the theater. The scent of his unique aftershave drifted to her. His warmth emanated along her side. Her gaze dropped to his hand on his knee in the darkness, and for some unexplainable reason her heart tripped a little faster.

Yes, he was a real man. A handsome, rich, complicated man whose presence rocked her already precarious thinking. But he wasn't for her. The kind of life that involved a family wasn't for her. She'd made her decision years ago, a decision to absorb herself in her career. She'd risked a lot and given up too much to change her way of thinking now.

She was not the wife and mother type.

And until now that had never bothered her.

7

FRANCIE LOVED THE high schoolers' rendition of *Grease*. She clapped and cheered, and praised each one of the performers during the refreshment time in the gym afterward.

"*This* is where you went to high school?" Alanna said, looking around with a lack of appreciation. She'd appeared wearing a vivid fire engine red shade of lipstick and enough mascara to fill all the cracks along Interstate 94.

Francie glanced around the small gymnasium that had once seemed so huge and intimidating during basketball games and Friday night sock hops. "This is it."

"Where did you get that makeup, Alanna?" her father asked, in a horrified tone.

"Some of us girls put it on in the bathroom," she replied.

"You shouldn't use other people's cosmetics."

Francie gave Alanna a knowing girl look, and rolled her eyes.

"Besides, it makes you look like a hooker," he added.

"What's a hooker?" Alex asked, just coming up beside Francie.

"Never mind," Ryan said. "But you don't need to look like one, Alanna."

"You treat me like a baby, Dad," Alanna said, her cheeks turning pink. She glanced around. "I'm old enough to wear makeup."

"No, you're not old enough to wear makeup. You're twelve."

"Maybe if your lipstick was a soft shade of pink. That would be pretty," Francie said to Alanna, and to Ryan, "And then you wouldn't mind, so much, would you? I have some in my bag."

Alanna turned on her. "I don't need your help. I can talk to my father without you butting in, can't I? You're not my mother."

"I'll handle this," Ryan said to Francie, his tone soft but stern enough to let her know she'd been dismissed.

Alex slipped his hand into Francie's, whether for his own comfort or for hers, she didn't know. She grasped it gratefully. Unexpected tears smarted behind her eyes, and she blinked, turning away, castigating herself for getting involved in the father-daughter encounter. Their argument was none of her business.

But she hated to see Alanna embarrassed when her self-esteem was so obviously fragile. She led Alex to the punch table and the teenager standing behind the bowl filled a clear plastic cup for each of them.

"It was a cool show, wasn't it?" Alex asked.

She nodded. "I liked it a lot."

"Maybe someday I can be in a play like that."

"You can if you want to."

"Will you come watch me?"

Francie's guard had been temporarily lowered, and his earnest young gaze zinged an arrow to her heart. It was the first mention anyone had made of a relationship continuing after this week. Their understanding had been that this would be their one and only time together, and when the week was over, they'd gratefully go their separate ways as though they'd never met.

Francie studied Alex's solemn young face, his narrow chin and the sprinkling of freckles across his nose.

That would be impossible.

"When that time comes, and you still want me there, you ask your father. If it's all right with him, I'll come."

"Cool!" he said and grinned. "Maybe Nana can come, too."

Tears sprang to her eyes again. Nana would not be around when Alex reached high school. Francie would have enough trouble facing that when the time came. "Maybe," she said.

The crowd dispersed a few minutes later, and the somber foursome walked to the rental car. Alex was the only one who spoke as they rode to the hotel, his enthusiasm over the play still high.

"I'll be up later," Francie said, leaving them at the elevator. She bought a blended drink at the window and sat beside the pool, nursing it and her bruised feelings.

If this was what parenthood was all about, she was better off than she'd even dreamed. Why had Nana ever wished this on her? Being self-reliant was better than being stuck with an egotistical man and mouthy children.

No, thank you. Her career decision suited her just fine. Nobody told her what to do. No one demanded her time and attention. She and Stanley got along just fine together. Stanley only required feeding and litter box changing. He didn't wear clothes to grow out of and he never smarted off.

Lisa and Robert and a few others had left early and were using the pool. Idly Francie watched the couple. They'd separated themselves from the rest and were nestled in the shallow end of the pool, speaking with their heads together.

After a few minutes, they called good-night and walked up the stairs to the balcony above, Robert's arm around her shoulders.

No show. The real thing.

The statistics were more convincing, however. Considering Peyton and Becka and Ted Chapman, as well as being on the fringes of the MacNair family, convinced her she'd chosen right.

A week of marriage was long enough for her, thank you very much.

The hour grew late, and Francie had grown tired. She waited for the elevator. It arrived, and the doors opened. She faced a surprised Ryan, who was just preparing to step out.

She entered, and he stepped back in.

She leaned around him to press the button, and noted he'd removed the suit jacket and tie and unbuttoned the top two buttons of his shirt. He still smelled great.

"You all right?" he asked.

"Fine. Why wouldn't I be?"

"I'm sorry about earlier. I was terse with you."

"You were perfectly right. How you discipline your daughter is none of my business."

"I wasn't disciplining her."

"Okay. You were criticizing her."

"I wasn't criticizing her. I'm her father. She's twelve years old."

"As you've pointed out to all of us."

His exasperation was evident in his tense posture. He gestured with one hand. "Look, it's tough being a parent, cut me a little slack, will you?"

She crossed her arms and leaned back into the wide metal handrail. "Sure. All you need."

"Francie." He stepped forward and cupped her elbows.

She raised a hand instinctively, and placed her fingertips against his shirtfront. It was warm, and beneath it his heart beat steadily. "I was wrong. You *are* a stuffed shirt. You're uptight and rigid with yourself and with your kids, and you don't know how to cut loose."

"I skated," he said defensively.

She raised one eyebrow. "What you did can't really be called skating." At his wounded look, she cut him the slack he'd requested. "Okay, you skated," she agreed. She took her hand from his chest and tapped her temple. "But up here, Mac, your inhibitions are more than social restraint."

"So, I don't blab my every thought like you do—"

"I don't!"

"You do."

"You're just repressed."

"Oh, and what is the cause of this psychological repression, Dr. Francesca? Is it Freudian? Jungian perhaps? Maybe if I wasn't sexually frustrated, I'd pull out all the stops and run wild."

"Shut up."

He did. For about ten seconds. The elevator came to a stop, and behind Ryan the doors opened. "I said I was sorry," he tried again.

"Yes, you did. Now move out of the way." She tried to step around him, but he blocked her. In the brief glimpse she had of the hallway, she spotted Becka Crow carrying an ice bucket.

"I forgive you," she said.

His expression smoothed out.

She stepped against him, wrapped her arms around his neck and kissed him with a groan, as though she couldn't wait until they got to their room.

He caught her around the waist, and balanced them, his response more shock than passion.

That changed in a heartbeat. She sensed the joining of their lips change to a mutual exploration. His taste created a hunger for more.

He wrapped one arm across her back and drew her flush against him. She slanted her head, and aligned their mouths more perfectly. His tongue dipped out to test her inner lip, surprising her with the warm tactile sensation. She inhaled sharply, breathing him in, using every sense she possessed to enjoy this kiss, forgetting Becka in the hallway, forgetting everything but the confusion he created in her head and her heart.

He pulled back slightly, pleasure and apprehension dueling for prominence in his dark eyes. She placed a hand on each side of his strong neck and caressed the warm flesh. The hand on her back slid a little lower.

"What are you doing?" he asked, his voice a low grate.

She remembered what she'd been doing. "Forgiving you," she replied against his lips. "Isn't this how married people make up?"

Behind him the elevator doors closed again, but the compartment didn't move. The isolation wrapped around them like a sleek, tantalizing secret.

Becka could no longer see them. Francie didn't have to continue the kiss for her benefit. But when Ryan's head moved toward hers and his lips descended again, Becka was nowhere in Francie's thoughts.

For a repressed fellow, Ryan sure kissed like there was no tomorrow. His unrestrained kisses made the earth move, and she clutched his shoulders to keep from falling. The glorious pressure of his lips sent a tingling through her body, and she pressed herself more closely against him.

"Francie," he groaned against her lips, not quite an endearment, not really resistance. And he shifted her to the back wall of the elevator, and braced his arms on either side of her head, his forearms against the interior as though he needed the steadying support.

His teeth found her ear and nibbled it at the same time she threaded the fingers of one hand through his hair. His breath in her ear created havoc with her senses. Her fingers and toes felt numb.

He kissed her ear, her neck, her jaw, her cheek...and paused at her lips.

Their eyes met for the briefest of moments, and she read the unfettered desire in the depths of his. She was flattered that he desired her, frightened that she felt the same.

He kissed her again, openmouthed this time, a possessive, mind-drugging sort of kiss that stole her breath and her sense and swept her mind free of all thought except him and this enticing embrace.

Ryan pressed her against the wall, the wide handrail arching her hips toward him. He feathered his hands down her sides and back up.

His touch gave Francie a jolt of pleasure and excitement that nearly buckled her knees.

A sound broke through her passion-dazed senses. She paused and listened. Clapping—as in applause. A few giggles thrown in.

Francie grasped Ryan's upper arms and pushed him away. His eyes registered confusion, and finally comprehension. He ran a hand through his hair and turned to look over his shoulder at the crowd outside the elevator.

They'd returned to the first floor lobby, and the doors stood open. Several of the reunion attendees, in wet bathing suits and robes, applauded them.

"*That* was a perfect ten, MacNair," Robert Richards announced.

"Lucky for you he kisses better than he skates, eh, Francie?" someone else kidded.

Another couple, hotel guests Francie had never seen before, stared in abashment.

"Shall we wait for the next elevator?" one of the men asked, a grin on his face.

"No," Ryan said, and gestured for the group to enter.

They did so, still tittering.

Francie stared straight ahead, her heart pounding, embarrassment spreading tingling fire across her cheeks.

A few of the passengers disembarked a floor ahead of theirs. The elevator arrived on five, and they got out amidst a few good-natured jibes.

The doors closed. Francie walked several feet before leaning her forehead against the wall.

He stood behind her, but she tasted him on her lips, smelled him on her skin and her clothing.

"You all right?" he asked.

"I'm all right. I've been kissed before." *Not like that. Goodness, not like that!* She had been rude. She didn't mean to be, words just came out that way. "I'm sorry," she said. "I'm just embarrassed."

"You've even kissed *me* before," he said.

"I know, but that was for show," she said, still not turning to look at him. "Becka was in the hall when we reached our floor."

"I might have known you weren't just a forgiving soul."

"No, no," she said hastily. "It didn't end up that way."

"What did it end up like?"

"You know...you were there."

He chuckled.

She turned around. "You're laughing!"

"You're funny. I confess! You're really funny."

"I wasn't trying to be."

"That's when you're the funniest."

His hair stood in finger-combed waves, and his shirt had been pulled from the waistband of his trousers. He had a five-o'clock shadow, the sight of which made her cheeks tingle. His arresting mouth drew her attention. Her heart dipped and her legs lost strength again. "Have you had enough laughs for one night, Mac?"

His gaze traveled her face and hair as hers had his. "We're both tired," he said.

Tired, she thought. But wide-awake. "I'll be visiting my grandmother tomorrow," she said. "You're welcome to come or not, whichever you prefer."

"I'll do what the kids want to do," he replied. He dug in his pocket and came out with the plastic card for the door. He paused, just before inserting it into the slot. "Good night, Francie. Sweet dreams."

She met his eyes. "Good night."

THEY SPENT THE morning with Nana, who asked Francie to play the piano for her in the dayroom.

"Oh, Nana, you know I'm not very good," Francie objected. "Those lessons were years and years ago, and I haven't practiced since."

"Alanna can play," Alex announced.

All eyes turned to the girl.

"You can play?" Nana asked, a smile creasing her already wrinkled features.

Alanna nodded.

"You don't have to," Francie assured her, not wanting to pressure or humiliate her.

"I like to play," Alanna said simply.

She went to the upright piano, and they gathered chairs nearby. Alanna discovered sheet music in the bench, but nothing familiar. She tried a few of the hymns and the old songs. The piano was in tune and in good condition.

"Do your practice pieces," her father suggested. "You don't need music for those."

She began a piece Francie vaguely remembered hearing before. "What is it?" she asked.

"Mozart," Ryan replied.

The notes flowed in fluid progression, some played lightly, others with intensity and concentration. Other residents came to sit and listen. A few of the nurses wandered in.

"How long has she been playing?" Francie asked quietly.

"Since she was five."

"She's wonderful."

He nodded. "She has a gift."

Nana watched and listened with rapt pleasure, her face glowing.

The piece trailed off and everyone in the dayroom applauded. Alanna nodded to her audience, and smiled brightly, a smile Francie had never seen her wear before, and she led right into another composition.

Francie glanced over at Ryan midway through and noticed the sheen glistening in his eyes.

"I've missed a lot of her recitals," he said thickly. "Or I've been late."

She wanted to reach over and take his hand, but she didn't. She couldn't. They weren't friends. They weren't anything. Not even after that kiss last night.

"I'll be at all of them from now on, and I'll be early," he said, and she knew it was a promise he made to himself, one that he would keep.

She admired his devotion to his children. He'd done something commendable, made more of a commitment than many parents ever did. What kind of person had his wife been to leave him? Francie couldn't bring herself to think too harshly of her. Perhaps she'd been like Francie, just not cut out for children and marriage and the whole commitment thing, and she'd realized it too late.

Thank God Francie had known from early in her life that she was not parent material. She hadn't messed up anybody's life or walked out on any children. She'd never left a child thinking they were unloved and unwanted.

Oh, but she might have. She might have if placed in the same set of circumstances.

Alanna's song ended. Francie joined the others in applauding her.

"I'm tired, Francesca," her grandmother said.

"I'll take you to your room, so you can rest." Francie excused them and wheeled Nana to her room and helped her into bed.

"Jim's a good man," Nana said softly.

Francie nodded.

"He loves those kids so much," she said with a smile. "It just does my heart good to see such a good father."

"Mine, too," Francie admitted.

"He loves you very much, too," Nana said, her eyes twinkling. "I see it in his eyes every time he looks at you." Francie tucked the spread around her. "Don't be so afraid, Francesca," she said.

"I'm not afraid, Nana," she denied.

"Yes, you are. You're afraid to love him too much. But you can't love anybody too much. Especially not him. And not his kids."

Flustered, Francie kissed her cheek.

"Remember that."

"I will." She gave her a smile and located the MacNairs waiting for her by the fountain.

"Is Nana all right?" Alex asked.

"She's fine. Just tired."

Satisfied, he took her hand and they strolled to the car.

Francie pondered her grandmother's words. Ryan didn't love her. Nana was seeing what she believed to be true. He desired Francie; she had no doubts about that, but he couldn't love her. She was a career woman with no time for emotional investments.

She smiled, remembering Nana thinking she was afraid to love "Jim" too much. She didn't love him at all, and she didn't plan to. As appealing as being with him was, as heady and liberating as his kisses were, she had no plans that included loving Ryan MacNair.

"I'll drive, okay?" he asked. He wore his sunglasses, preventing her from seeing amusement if it danced in his eyes as she suspected.

She shrugged, and got in on the passenger side, allowing only a momentary glance at his features. She placed her right hand over her left in her lap, hiding the gold ring. No, no plans whatsoever that included feelings for this man. Why then, did she repeatedly need to remind herself?

RYAN HADN'T WALKED or thought straight since their encounter in the elevator the night before. Looking at the surface, he and Francie had nothing in common. They were as opposite as two people could be. But if he hadn't spent these last days with her, he'd never have known the lack of truth in that superficial assessment.

She'd drawn him out of his safe habitat, away from the distractions that kept him from seeing exactly what he was doing to himself and to his children by thinking all he had to provide for them was a nice house and good schools and designer clothing.

He watched Francie help Alex with his slicked-back pompadour for the dance, and once again recognized the boy's hunger for love and attention. He gave Francie bashful smiles and complimented her on her slinky black pants, leather jacket and high heels.

"You look just like Sandy!" Alex cried, meaning Olivia Newton-John's character in the movie they'd had to rent twice and Alex had watched again that morning. "Do I really look like Danny Zuko?"

"You're a T-Bird if I ever saw one," Francie said

and gave him a hug. "And look at your sister, she's a regular Pink Lady."

Alanna grinned, pleased as punch with this present situation because she got to wear as much makeup as she wanted. This was, after all, a costume dance. She twirled around, and her poodle skirt flared in a circle.

Alex grinned at his dad. "Dad, you have to try to look tougher if you're gonna be a Scorpion."

"I'll try to get into character," Ryan replied. "Will I have to beat anyone up?"

"Not unless that Chapman guy tries to put the moves on Francie again," Alanna said with a smirk. "She's supposed to be your wife, after all."

"Ted Chapman?" he asked. "What did he do?"

"She's exaggerating," Francie said. "He just stood a little close after the play last night."

"Tell him he blew his chance when he freaked out over the iguana," he said, and realized his vernacular sounded like something Francie or Alanna would say.

Francie burst into laughter. "Did you say that?"

"I said it." He grinned. "Can't be too 'stuffed' in this shirt."

She perused the form-fitting black T-shirt she'd cut the sleeves from, and gave him an appreciative wink. "Guess not. Seems you're loosening up, Mac. So don't plan to tell me you can't dance."

"I can dance."

"He goes to fund-raisers all the time," Alanna said. "They have dinners and orchestras."

Francie shot him an amused glance. "Not *that* kind of dancing."

"Dancing like in *Grease,* Dad," Alex said and demonstrated a twist.

"You won't get me doing that, so forget whatever you're thinking right now," Ryan stated adamantly.

Francie loaded a new roll of film into her camera, smiling to herself.

She glanced around, checking the lighting and the most interesting visual aspects of the enormous room. Springdale High School's gymnasium had been transformed into a bygone era, using the sets from the play and hundreds of balloons.

A cash bar had been set up in the cafeteria window, punch and snacks on tables along the walls.

"They must have worked all day at this," she said aloud.

Ryan leaned his head back to observe the multicolored balloons suspended from ceiling beams. "Be glad you're the reunion photographer and not the cleanup committee."

"Tom Wallace and I were talking. We're going to ask the old yearbook committee to put together an album using the pictures I've taken and articles written by several of us."

"You've been enjoying yourself, haven't you?"

She glanced over. "I guess I have. And I guess I'm surprised."

"Why is that?"

"I'm sure it's been obvious to you that these weren't exactly my best friends."

"Who were your best friends?"

She shrugged. "Didn't have any."

"Why not?"

"Springdale was even smaller back then. It's a close-knit sort of town. When I came to live with Nana, I was an outsider."

Not many had arrived yet, so they had their choice of tables. Ryan selected one and Francie placed her scuffed camera case on it. "So that changed?" he asked.

"No." She seated herself and glanced around. "I stayed an outsider. But I've never been a wallflower, so they had to deal with me."

He leaned against the edge of the table.

"I think that's why I love taking photographs so much," she said thoughtfully. "That's when it became important to me."

"Why?"

"Well..." She wanted to express it to him, and wasn't sure how. "I love taking photographs of all kinds of things, but I especially love the shots of people. I love to capture and study their faces. Candid shots are the best. The subjects seem like friends later."

She wasn't doing a very good job. He probably thought she was nuts.

"There's nothing judgmental about a picture," he said.

She smiled. He understood better than she thought.

"They're safe," he said. "You can't hurt them and they can't hurt you."

She looked away.

"Sort of like working all the time was safe for me."

She looked back at him, not liking what she'd revealed to both of them.

"Francie! Oh, my gosh, that's darling!" Becka cried, examining Francie's outfit, and ending the conversation that had grown far too serious. "You're a perfect Sandy!"

She and J.J. were hippies, with their hair crimped, bare feet and threadbare bell-bottoms.

J.J. let out a hoot, and they all turned to observe the Armbrusters' arrival. Don had dyed and slicked his hair, pasted on sideburns and wore a white glittery Elvis suit that emphasized his short legs and neck; a wide gold belt was lashed around the girth of his belly.

Peyton, his extreme opposite, had outfitted herself in a dark beehive wig that made her appear six feet tall and six inches wide. Her black eyeliner was the tip-off that she was supposed to be Priscilla. Francie stifled the giggles that welled up in her throat.

J.J. didn't hold his amusement back, however, and Becka slammed her elbow into his ribs.

Tom Wallace and his wife showed up as Sonny and Cher. Francie had a ball snapping posed and candid photos of each arrival.

The band appeared, and the music began, a combination of fifties, sixties and seventies hits that had the crowd cheering and dancing wildly.

Sometime later, Francie found Ryan still at the table with Lisa and Robert.

"Out of film?" Ryan asked.

"Never. Came for you."

"Don't you think Danny'll be jealous?"

She grinned, placed her camera on the table and took his hand. "You're cutting loose more every day, Mac."

"Don't be surprised if I waltz."

"Don't worry, I won't."

She pulled him onto the dance floor just as the music changed and "Blue Moon" echoed from the speakers.

They exchanged a glance and he took her into his arms quite naturally. Francie raised one arm behind his neck, and he held her other hand. He led gracefully, the heat of their bodies touching where her jacket gaped in the front.

This closeness did something wacky to her pulse. Though he worked hard at being standoffish, Ryan was one of the most intense men she'd ever known. If he ever focused all that fiery drive and energy on her alone, she'd probably melt into a puddle.

Francie glanced at the other couples, some with partners other than their spouses, others actually dancing in intimate embraces. What would it feel like if she'd danced with him a hundred times? What if he really was her husband? Would the excitement of being this close to him have worn off?

"Do you think it's possible to keep the romance alive in a marriage?" she asked.

"Why do you ask?"

"Have you seen how some of them have been looking at us this week? They think we're newly wed and hot for each other, and they're envious."

He glanced over and spotted Tom Wallace and his

wife locked in an embrace. "Some of them seem to have done it."

"Some," she agreed, remembering Lisa and Robert leaving the pool the other night. "But what about the others, like Peyton?"

"Peyton married Don for his degrees and his job potential, not the chemistry between them."

"You're right. And Becka and J.J. got married directly out of high school. She had a baby that very summer, and I assume that was their reason for marrying."

"Must have been chemistry there to start with."

She shrugged. "Hormones don't make a marriage."

"You can't analyze a half a dozen marriages and come up with sound statistics," he said.

"Why not?"

"There are more than a few reasons for marrying, and hundreds more why marriages don't work out. If two people are committed, they can keep the fires burning."

She shook her head. "I've seen too many people sorry for the choices they've made."

"Are you talking about your own parents?"

"Maybe."

"Or maybe you were thinking about my marriage."

She shrugged again, noncommittally.

Gratefully the music changed, and along with it the mood. Francie kept Ryan on the dance floor, and he held his own among the throng of nostalgic dancers.

Francie had a ball.

Ryan MacNair had turned out to be a good sport. She'd never in a million years have imagined he had it in him to join the celebration, even participating in the contests and the partner-switching games.

By the end of the evening, she realized he'd not only kept his word by coming to the reunion and all its various activities, but he'd shown everyone that Francie Karr-Taylor had made a great choice in a husband and that they were a match unequaled.

Any reports that got back to Nana would be glowing ones. She owed Nana's present peace of mind to him.

Alanna and Alex fell asleep in the car on the drive to the hotel. "Where did you and Nana live?" Ryan asked.

"Want me to show you?"

"Sure."

She directed him to the neighborhood where Nana's old house stood, and they pulled up in front.

"Who lives there now?"

"I don't know the people." She pointed to the basketball hoop above the garage door. "They obviously have kids."

"Would you like to see the inside again?"

She shook her head. "I'm sure they've remodeled and changed things. I like to remember it the way it was."

They studied the house for a few minutes longer, and then Ryan drove to the hotel.

HE HAD TROUBLE sleeping that night. The more he was around Francie, the more sense she made, and that was scary. Yes, she had a chameleonlike nature, and could adapt to situations seemingly effortlessly. Her fabrications were like self-preservation skills she had created.

Yet he knew she'd never lied to him. When he asked her a question, he got a straightforward answer. Seeing her day after day in real situations, she was not at all like he'd thought at first. She loved her grandmother above anything else and had concocted this scheme to placate her.

Finally Ryan got out of bed, hoping a shower would relax him. He stood under the warm water, letting it buffet the muscles of his neck and shoulders, and entertained thoughts of seeing Francie after this week was over. In a million years, he'd never have imagined himself being drawn to her, enjoying her company, but he admitted to himself now that he liked being with her. Her humor and her zest for life was contagious. She made him feel younger some-how, almost as though life had passed him by until she'd pointed it out to him.

Ryan dried, momentarily studying his reflection in the foggy mirror. What did she see when she looked at him? A stuffy businessman grown old before his time? He didn't know how or when he'd come to this point, but he knew he wanted to change the direction he'd been headed. Finally he stretched back out on the bed and drifted into a restless sleep.

Francie awakened them early. She'd gone to the lobby for coffee, juice and rolls, and opened the drapes, allowing bright sunshine to spill across the beds and Alanna's pallet.

"Good morning, MacNairs!" she called.

Ryan opened one eye and blinked at the red digits on the clock radio. Behind him, Alex bounced to his usual morning attention with a flurry of covers and bedsprings.

"This had better be important," Alanna said, sitting up groggily.

"It is. Here, have your juice and coffee to wake up." Francie poured and served.

"Wow, breakfast in bed," Alex said cheerfully. "Cool!"

Alanna went into the bathroom and returned to sit in one of the chairs.

"I have something for you," Francie said finally.

Ryan hadn't lost all his good sense yet, because he remained skeptical of her ideas and offerings. "What is it?"

"It's for Alanna, actually, but it will mean a lot to you, too." She went to her organizer and pulled out a gaily wrapped little box.

Alanna took it from her without a change in her sullen expression.

"Go ahead," Francie urged. "Open it."

Alanna glanced at her dad, who nodded. She sat down her juice and used both hands to untie the ribbon and peel back the foil wrapping paper.

She revealed a silver box.

Francie gestured for her to continue.

Alanna glanced at Ryan again before taking the lid from the box. His daughter stared at the contents with a blank expression. "What does this mean?" she asked finally.

"What is it?" he asked.

Alanna left her chair to come over to the bed and show him the contents.

Nestled on a bed of cotton lay the gold-and-garnet brooch he hadn't seen for years; his grandmother's brooch.

8

RYAN LOOKED AT her in confusion. Her smile seemed a little strained, or maybe he read uncertainty in the tightness around her mouth. "What does this mean?"

She backed up to the edge of her unmade bed and sat. "It's a gift. For Alanna. For all of you. It was really unfair of me to ask you to go along with this. It was selfish. I wish I'd just given you the brooch in the first place."

Ryan didn't know what to say. Alanna wore a stunned expression, and Alex looked confused.

"It was unkind of me to use up your vacation time together." Francie stood and jerked up the bedcovers, found a pair of earrings on the nightstand and placed them in her ears without looking at him. "You still have this weekend." She went to her suitcase, withdrew folded papers and carried them back.

He looked at the plane tickets she handed him.

"But there's still the picnic," Alex said, jumping up to retrieve the schedule. "And the thing on Sunday." Disappointment laced his tone, and the almost panicked look on his face gave Ryan a sick feeling in his stomach.

"I can tell everyone that one of you kids got sick.

Or that you had other plans for the weekend already.
I'll think of something.''

"I've no doubt you could think of something.''
Ryan studied the tickets. But why go? Why quit now?

"Thanks for everything this week,'' she continued
briskly. "I'm sorry I made you do this.'' She grabbed
her bag, and paused before Alex as though she wanted
to say more, as if she'd like to scoop him into her
arms. But she walked to the door, her posture straight.
"Enjoy your weekend together. Please.''

Ryan stared at the door, then at his children's faces.
Alex looked ready to cry.

Francie closed the door behind her, regretting so
many things she didn't know where or who to start
apologizing to. She'd made the decision during the
night to give them the brooch as an offering of repentance. The MacNair family could still salvage a
couple of days together.

Feeling good about this decision, yet sick at heart
at the thought of them leaving and her not seeing
them again, she bought coffee and sat by the pool.
She'd give them an hour. That way she wouldn't have
to witness their departure. All through the night she'd
struggled with not only her conscience, but in making
a decision on the kindest and easiest way to end this
for everybody's sakes.

She'd been awake when Ryan had climbed from
bed and taken a shower. He'd been right to remain
protective of his children. He'd been right about
nearly everything. Maybe he'd even been right that
she should never have lied to Nana about a husband.
Maybe. But thinking it was so lent Nana a peace and

comfort that made her remaining days easier. Francie didn't regret that.

She only regretted she'd involved a truly good man and his children in her scheme. And she'd known she needed to bring it to an end before anyone was truly hurt. Giving Alanna the brooch was the honorable thing to do, the thing she should have done first.

Belatedly she noticed the gold band she still wore. She would return it when she got back to Chicago.

After only thirty minutes, hurried footsteps sounded behind her. A small hand fell on her shoulder, and she glanced up at Alex.

"Alex! Is everything all right?" He'd come to say goodbye, no doubt, something she'd hoped to avoid.

Alanna and Ryan appeared behind him, and they seated themselves at the table.

Francie glanced at each of them. "Are you going?"

"We're going," Ryan said.

The dull ache in her stomach intensified. Why hadn't they just gone on without a big scene?

"To the picnic!" Alex added.

Butterflies fluttered in her chest. She hadn't even wanted to hope. "You're staying?"

"We discussed it as a family," Ryan said. "And we all agreed to stay."

Francie let her surprised glance slide to Alanna. *She* had wanted to stay? The girl made no comment. Francie gave her a timorous smile.

"We made a list of pros and cons," Ryan said and unfolded a slip of paper.

"Oh, and I can't guess whose idea that was," she said in a wry tone.

He grinned and stuffed it back into his pocket.

"Let's get our breakfast here, Dad." With a nod, Alex indicated the restaurant a few feet away.

"You had the rolls Francie brought for breakfast."

"Then let's call this brunch," the boy said.

Ryan pulled out his wallet. "Go ahead and get something."

"Coming?" Alex said to his sister.

Together the two entered the restaurant.

Ryan moved to sit in the chair at Francie's right, and leaned his elbows on the table. "We didn't do something wrong here, did we?"

She tipped her head to study him. His deep brown eyes were filled with uncertainty and concern.

"By staying?" he clarified. "Did you want us to go?"

Had she wanted them to go? It might have been easier to break it off sooner rather than later. Surprisingly enough, she enjoyed Ryan's company. Alex, of course, was lovable and fun to be with. And even though Alanna merely tolerated her and cracked scathing remarks, Francie didn't mind having her around.

No, she hadn't really wanted them to leave. The thought of having their company for the picnic and baccalaureate gave her profound pleasure. Her mock family unit had lent her security during this week's activities. She'd felt more accepted and more a part of things than she ever had in the past. And she didn't resent that fact as she should.

"No, I didn't really want you to go," she admitted honestly, hating the little catch in her voice. "I wanted to be fair to you, though. I got to feeling guilty about the time I'd taken you away from your kids."

His intense expression relaxed, and he flattened his hands on the tabletop. Francie couldn't help noticing his long fingers, the dusting of dark hair on their backs. "It's not like that. This week has shown me the importance of spending time with my children. I have you to thank for that."

She shook her head, still not looking up.

His hand moved toward her, and her heart skipped a foolish beat. Reaching across the tabletop, he took her hand. "It's true."

Francie looked down at his thumb as it brushed back and forth across the backs of her fingers, grazing the wedding band with each sweep. Warmth shot along her arm and created a soft fluttering in her chest. She studied his ringless fingers and his gold watch, rather than raise her gaze to his. "Have you changed your mind about what a demented idea this was?" she asked.

"No. I still think it's nuts."

She looked up then, and grinned. "Alanna really voted to stay for the weekend?"

Tiny lines fanned out from the corners of his eyes in his grin. "She did."

"And there were a lot more pros than cons on the list?"

"There were."

Spending the rest of the weekend together was a reckless thing to do, considering the way she was feeling about his touch on her hand. But for some insane reason, she didn't want to get off this emotionally crazy roller-coaster ride just yet.

"Hi, guys." Lisa sat a tray on Francie's other side and seated herself. Robert appeared next. Ryan and Francie exchanged a look of regret that their privacy had been interrupted, and morning greetings were exchanged.

Alex and Alanna returned with their food, and Ryan released Francie's hand to help Alex get settled.

"Ryan MacNair!" a male voice called behind Francie.

Ryan glanced up, and his expression alerted Francie to a problem. She turned as the man approached their table.

Ryan stood and extended his hand. "Ralph."

The shorter man shook it. "Do you have business in Springdale?"

"No, I'm here purely for pleasure."

The man's gaze darted from Francie to Lisa and Robert.

Francie recognized the man Ryan had spotted on the balcony before pulling her back against him in the pool. The historian with the Abe Lincoln collection.

"It's my wife's tenth class reunion," Ryan said, and Francie's hearing stuck on his use of the word "wife." "This is Francie," he said, "and these are my children, Alanna and Alex. These are our friends, the Richardses. This is Ralph Hanscom, a professor from the University of Illinois."

Lisa and Robert nodded and went about their meal.

"I didn't realize you were married," Ralph said. "You must keep her all to yourself."

"I guess the subject never came up in our business dealings," Ryan replied. "Are you married?"

"Oh, yes. I have a grandson who is two years old."

"No!" Ryan said.

Francie raised her cup of cold coffee to hide her smile. Ryan had just lied every bit as effectively as she had from the beginning. But he'd adroitly managed to turn the topic of conversation. Ralph proudly showed photos from his wallet, and Ryan studied them appreciatively.

Finally, the man wished them goodbye and headed up the stairs.

Ryan, Francie, Alanna and Alex all exchanged a knowing look, but no one said anything in front of the Richardses.

After everyone had finished eating and started their separate ways, Francie asked, "Will Mr. Hanscom's thinking you're married be a problem after this?"

"I don't think so. I rarely see him. And only for business. I don't know why he'd mention it to anyone, and if he did, what difference would it make?"

"I didn't plan to mess up your life." She slowed down as they neared the door to the room.

"You haven't messed up anything." He slowed his pace to stay beside her.

"Dad, do you have change for the pop machine?" Alanna asked.

"You just ate."

"But now I'm thirsty."

Ryan dug into his pocket. Both kids stopped with him.

Francie went on ahead, finding her key and entering the room just as the phone rang. She grabbed it. "Hello?"

"I—I was calling for Ryan MacNair," the male voice said. "Do I have the wrong room?"

It sounded like the man they'd just seen by the pool. She hoped he wouldn't cause a problem for Ryan. "No, this is the right room. Hold on just a minute."

"Who's this?" the voice asked.

"This is his wife, hang on." She laid the receiver down and went to see if Ryan was coming.

He and the kids had almost reached the room.

"Someone's on the phone for you. Sounds like that guy we just saw by the pool."

He picked up the receiver. "Hello? Hello?" A few seconds later he hung it up. "No one there. That's odd."

She shrugged. "If it was important, they'll call back."

THE WEATHER COULDN'T have cooperated more. The sun shone brightly, yet it wouldn't be too hot to enjoy the day and the games. The picnic committee had gone whole hog just as every other committee had. There were games and contests planned for all ages, plenty of food and drinks on the way, and picnic tables and lawn chairs ready.

"There had better be real bathrooms," Alanna said as soon as they arrived at the park.

Ryan glanced at Francie. "I'm not sure," she said. "I haven't been here for years."

"If they're those awful stinky ones, you'll have to

drive me back to town to go.'' Alanna got out of the car and looked around.

The ride to the park had taken twenty-five minutes. Ryan's brows lowered into a thunderous frown.

"If they're outhouses, I'll drive you to that convenience shop we saw on the highway," Francie offered quickly, hooking the strap of her camera case around her neck. "That was only about ten miles back."

Alanna looked at Francie in surprise, but said nothing. She glanced from her to her father and nodded.

A van pulled into the gravel parking lot, and a couple of Alanna's new friends jumped out and ran to greet her. They carried a bulging bag and a CD case.

"I'll see you later." Alanna waved to her dad and walked toward a shade tree with the girls.

"S'pose that bag was full of makeup?" Ryan asked.

Francie grinned. "Seems likely."

"She wasn't always this difficult." He didn't know if he meant it as an excuse or as an apology. "I guess I'm to blame for much of her attitude."

The breeze tossed Francie's silky-looking hair. She threaded it away from her face with her fingers and replied, "Don't be too hard on yourself. You've done the best you knew how."

"Is it too late?" The question was directed more toward himself than to her. Could spending more time with Alanna make up for the past?

"It's not too late," she said, and surprised him by touching his arm. "She needed your attention, and

you're giving it to her. Give her a little time now.
She'll learn that you're there for her.''

They strolled across the grass. Alex took Ryan's
hand and then Francie's, forming a link between
them. He beamed his engaging smile at both. How
could Ryan have missed Alex's hunger for a woman's
attention? What could he have done if he had?

Holding the ever-present camera to her waist, Francie leaned down to say something to his son, and
when she straightened and smiled at Ryan, his heart
constricted. How had he not recognized his own need
for a woman's companionship? No, not just any
woman.

He returned her smile. *Francie.*

What kind of a chance did they have of continuing
their relationship once they returned to Chicago?
Would she want to see the kids? Would she care to
see him? She seemed to have changed her outlook on
the situation since their first meetings. She now appeared to regret inconveniencing them. He believed
the circumstances had changed for her as much as
they had for him. And the physical attraction was mutual. But would she wish to pursue this oddly entan-
gled association?

Perhaps she just needed a little persuading.

Francie's graduating class had been fertile. Children of all sizes and shapes lined up for the races and
games. Babies napped in playpens in the shade. Ryan
had never attended functions geared to families as this
was, and he regretted missing that.

Caterers carried in lunch, trays of chicken and tubs
of potato salad and slaws. Those who lived in Spring-

dale provided blankets and tablecloths for out-of-towners, and Francie spread a borrowed quilt in the shade for the MacNair family.

The kids ate quickly and raced off to play.

"Francie?" Ryan said.

Instinctively she prepared herself for what he was going to say and looked over at him.

"Is there a chance we could continue this...after we go back to Chicago?"

She took note of the seriousness in his dark eyes. "You don't mean keep pretending we're married."

"No."

As long as he'd said nothing she'd been able to pretend that there was nothing going on past a few impulsive kisses. "Trust me on this one, Mac, I'm not your type."

"What's my type?"

"You need somebody stable and dependable. Conservative and, well, you know, committed. Someone willing to dedicate herself to you and your kids."

"I didn't propose."

Heat climbed her neck and reached her cheeks. "So you just want to sleep with me when we get back home?"

"No. I mean...we don't have to make a commitment right away."

"But eventually. Sooner or later you'd want a commitment."

He shrugged.

"You would. It's the natural order of things, and it's who you are. It's what you should expect. But I'm not the one to expect it from."

He looked away, allowing her to study the sun dappling his perfect features through the leaves. That first day he'd come to her loft she'd never have imagined seeing through his impeccable demeanor to the vulnerable man inside.

"There are some things you just can't organize into a tidy little plan," she said.

"Then, could we just take it one day at a time?" he asked.

"We can," she agreed. "As long as you understand."

"That you would never want to marry me."

"That I couldn't."

"It's a lot to expect, asking a woman to take on a man with a ready-made family. But that's who I am, too."

"I know that." And that's why she would never set them up to let them down. He'd already had one unsuitable wife. He didn't need another. And knowing that, Francie couldn't let him think she might be any different.

The afternoon progressed, and more than once Francie heard her Nana's words. *"Don't be so afraid, Francesca... You can't love anybody too much... remember that."*

No, a person couldn't love too much. But they could love too little.

She and Alex stood along the sidelines in the sun while Ryan and Alanna took third place in a three-legged race. Ryan had had to convince his daughter to participate, but she'd quickly caught the competitive spirit and had accepted the plastic trophy with the same smile an Olympic athlete wore when she accepted her gold medal.

Alex asked Francie to be his partner for the boat-building match. She balked, knowing her skills were woefully inadequate, but Ryan's encouraging nod and Alex's pleading gray eyes won her over.

Lisa and Robert, the contest hosts, had laid out a variety of tools and supplies. No one could leave the area while building their boat. Only materials within the cordoned-off area could be used, and they had one hour.

Francie and Alex chose balsa wood and fast-drying glue for the base of their ship and dowels for the masts. Francie perused the selection of materials for sails and knew they hadn't created their boat heavy enough to hold the added weight.

"We need something heavy in the bottom to keep the whole thing from capsizing," she said, looking their project over thoughtfully.

"Rocks?" Alex asked.

"They are within the roped-off area, aren't they?" They grinned and Alex nonchalantly found a couple of smooth flat stones they could easily glue into the bottom.

"Now the sails," she said. "This stuff is all too heavy."

"Leaves?" he suggested, glancing around.

"Not sturdy enough. We need something practically weightless. Like cotton."

They glanced at each other's clothing.

Francie smiled immediately.

"What?" Alex asked.

She slipped her hand inside the neck of her shirt and pulled a shoulder pad loose from its Velcro mooring.

Alex giggled.

Francie ripped the cotton material away from the pad and discovered it was a suitable shape and size to make two sails.

With fifteen minutes left to spare, they picked glue from their fingers and kept their model hidden between them.

When the big moment arrived, the Richardses inspected and labeled the boats, and the launch was announced. Alex impatiently awaited their turn, watching as other crafts sank or capsized or traveled a few precarious yards in the swiftly moving creek.

At last their turn came. They traded hopeful looks. Francie nodded at Alex to do the honor. He removed his shoes and socks and waded out into the creek until the water reached his knees. Settling the little boat on the current, he released it.

Their masterpiece listed to one side and then righted itself to the collective groan of the onlookers. And then the current caught the vessel and carried it swiftly downstream. It hit a protruding stick once, spun in a circle and continued on its way.

The crowd cheered. Alex climbed the bank and ran alongside, following the boat until it reached a curve and neatly snagged in an outcropping of rocks.

Francie had never seen a bigger smile than the one on his face when he returned for his plastic trophy, carrying the water-darkened boat. She hugged him until he squealed.

Ryan enveloped Francie in an embrace that caught her by surprise and took her breath away. "Thank you."

She blinked back tears of happiness.

"I hope you don't mind," he said. "I took a few pictures."

She accepted her camera now, having forgotten it when she'd been elected to assist Alex. She never forgot her camera. She blinked. "You knew how to use it?"

"I've taken a few shots in my day. Did you mind?"

She shook her head. "Of course not. Alex, let's get a picture of you with the winning boat."

"Can we get a trophy case, Dad?" Alex asked, holding up the craft and grinning ear to ear.

Ryan smiled at his son's enthusiasm. "We'll see."

"They're just plastic," Alanna said. "They don't even have our names on them."

"I know that."

Francie snapped his photograph. "You can find someplace special to keep it, Alex."

"Will you help me find a place?" He stared up at her with wide questioning eyes.

Francie touched his cheek in a loving gesture. Here it was again. His desire to carry their bond past this week, past this game of pretend, and into the reality beyond. She caught Alanna's wistful expression before she masked it with practiced aloofness.

She met Ryan's eyes. He, too, had asked for an extension on their time together. He seemed to be waiting for her reply to his son to see if it was more satisfactory than her answer for him.

"Yes, Alex," she said finally. "I'll come help you find a special place for it."

Alex hugged her around the waist, and Ryan lifted his chin in acknowledgment. *I've only committed to this one thing,* she tried to tell him with her eyes. *I can't promise more than I know I have to give.*

She turned then to see Peyton studying them with an odd expression. Francie gave her a hesitant smile and the woman acknowledged it with a quick wave before turning away. What had that look been about? What had they said that Peyton might have overheard? Nothing incriminating, certainly.

Much later, another meal was laid out, this time barbecue sandwiches and chips and pickles. Watermelons were sliced and served, and near dark, several ice-cream makers were put into use, and Springdale's reunited class and their families ate their fill of homemade ice cream.

The grand finale of the evening came after full dark. A local expert put on a magnificent fireworks display.

Francie sat on the quilt with the MacNairs, full of ice cream, full of the most unexpected sense of completion she'd ever experienced. Alex's head lay in her lap, the boat still within his reach on the blanket. From time to time he touched it, ran a finger over the crude balsa wood structure as though it were an expensive treasure.

Alanna and her friends sat within sight and hearing on a blanket of their own. She seemed relaxed and sure of herself with the girls, and Francie loved seeing her that way.

Ryan moved until their hips met and stretched his much longer legs alongside hers. She moved the minuscule distance it took to incline her shoulder back against his, and leaned into his warmth and strength and his ever-present wonderful smell.

A myriad of starbursts exploded in the night sky above, and he wedged his nose behind her ear, along her neck. Delicious shivers raced down her arm and across her breasts. His breath gusted warm and soft at her ear. His lips opened against the column of her neck.

Pleasure washed through her in a wave of sensation. She wanted to turn and touch him, run her hand over his handsome face, his strong neck, his wide shoulders and hard chest. She wanted to open herself to his kisses, to forget time and place and the impossibility of their desire ever going anywhere. She wanted to toss caution in the creek like a stone and lose herself in the man. *Ryan.*

Instead she watched fireworks burst in the heavens while sensation throbbed in her body, and reminded herself what she wanted out of life, what she needed.

Francie Karr-Taylor had never cared about pleasing anyone but her grandmother. Since reaching adulthood she'd never had to depend on anyone to meet her needs. She wasn't accountable to anyone but herself. And she liked it that way. If she forgot a plan or blew an assignment, she let only herself down. If she wanted to change her life at any time, or in any way, she had the freedom to do so. There was no one to hurt. No one to let down or leave behind.

Against her back, Ryan's heart beat wild and strong, the heart of a man with wants and hopes and needs like those she'd denied for so long. And for the first time, she wished she had more to give.

9

RETURNING TO THE room late that night, the blinking light on the phone alerted them to a message. Alanna readied herself for bed and Ryan tucked Alex in.

Francie called the desk.

"Mr. MacNair is to phone his father in room 417 immediately," the woman on the other end of the line said.

"Room 417?" Francie asked, then said over her shoulder, "Ryan, do you know where to call your father?"

"If he's not at home, I have no idea," he replied.

"Where would that room be?" she asked the desk clerk. "Is there a phone number?"

"It's in the hotel," the voice replied. "You just dial eight and then the room number."

"In *this* hotel?" Her mind grappled with the thought for a moment. "All right. Thank you."

She hung up. "He's here. In this hotel."

"My father is where?" His brow wrinkled in puzzlement. "Here? What on earth would he be doing in Springdale?" He turned out the light over Alex's head and perched on Francie's bed to pick up the phone. After punching in the numbers, he waited.

Francie went about gathering her nightclothes, curious, but trying not to be nosy.

"Dad? Where are you? What are you doing here?" A lengthy pause. Ryan glanced at Francie. "That was you?" Another long pause. "I think we'd better talk. I'll be down in a few minutes."

He hung up the receiver.

Francie wadded the nightshirt she held and waited impatiently.

Finally he looked at her. "That was him you talked to on the phone this morning. The one who called asking for me."

"Is something wrong?"

"No. Yes. He called my office. My secretary told him I'd taken a vacation and gave him this number. I never take a vacation, so he found that unusual. Add to that the fact that you mentioned you were my wife when he called the room."

"Oh, boy."

"He didn't recognize your voice, didn't think I'd been seeing anyone seriously and so he wondered if we'd come here to meet..." His voice trailed off.

"What?" she asked. "Who?"

"Well, he was confused, and the thought that entered his mind was that the children's mother had somehow contacted us, and that we were meeting her. That idea upset him."

"I can see why," she thought aloud. She wanted to kick herself. She'd thought the voice on the phone had been Ryan's acquaintance they'd just seen near the pool. Now she'd gotten Ryan's father involved and left Ryan to do all the explaining.

"So he flew here today? Oh, my goodness. What will you say to him?"

"I'll just tell him," he replied simply.

"The truth?"

He stood and checked his pocket for the room key. "Why is the truth always the farthest thing from your mind?"

Chastised, she glanced over to see Alanna facing away from them on her pallet. Francie doubted she'd fallen asleep already, especially with this conversation going on. "Would you like me to do it?"

"Do what?"

"Explain to him? I'm the one who started this mess."

His dark-eyed gaze took in her face and hair. "You know, maybe he would understand better if he actually met you."

"I'll come with you then."

He nodded.

Francie freshened up before joining Ryan in the hall. They stood waiting for the elevator, watching the numbers, and she couldn't help remembering the kisses they'd shared within its confines. They entered the car and she knew he was reminded, too. He glanced at her once, then stared straight ahead, a muscle in his cheek jumping. The elevator took them down a floor, and they located the correct room.

Ryan knocked and the door opened immediately.

The tall gentleman, dressed in trousers and a belted wine red robe, did a double take at Francie's presence. Immediately he recovered his manners and invited them both into the suite.

"Dad, this is Francie Karr-Taylor. Francie, my father, Stuart MacNair."

"How do you do, Mr. MacNair?"

"Miss—is it Miss Karr-Taylor?"

"Call me Francie."

He accepted the hand she offered. "Please. Have a seat."

Thus Ryan's formality and gentility, she thought kindly, sitting in the chair he'd offered. Ryan's heritage. He and the still-handsome older man were strikingly similar in features and height, as well as mannerisms. Ryan waited until his father took the other chair, then seated himself on the sofa.

"Mr. MacNair, I asked Ryan to let me come along so I could explain this whole mess. I'm so sorry for any confusion or worry I may have caused you by what I said on the phone this morning. I feel so bad that you flew all this way after talking to me. I thought you were someone we'd just seen by the pool, an acquaintance of Ryan's from Chicago. He's a historian who collects Abraham Lincoln artifacts...do you know him?"

"I don't believe so." Stuart glanced at Ryan, then back at Francie.

"Well, we'd just seen this guy, and I thought he was calling Ryan about something. If I'd known it was you, I'd never have said I was Ryan's wife."

Amusement twitched at one side of Ryan's mouth, but he remained silent.

The silver-haired gentleman showed less tolerance for her explanation. "And it would have been...

normal for you to tell this historian person that you were my son's wife?''

''Yes. Well, Ryan had just introduced me that way. You see, we were with a group of my friends by the pool, and this fellow showed up, and Ryan didn't really have much choice.''

''No choice but to say you were his wife.''

''Right. Because my old classmates were there. They think we're married.''

Stuart MacNair looked decidedly confused. ''My son's private life is none of my business. If he registers into hotels with...*friends,* I don't need to know about it. I was only concerned when I didn't know whether or not you were someone who would try to hurt him or the children in some way.''

''We're not friends,'' she said before his words sank in, then stopped. He thought they had registered as married so as not to raise eyebrows at the hotel? He thought they were having an affair! ''Wait. It's not like that at all,'' she tried to explain. ''The children are in the room with us.''

The elderly gentleman's eyebrows climbed his forehead at that bit of information. ''My grandchildren are here?''

''Yes, but we're not...'' She raised a hand in a helpless gesture. ''We're not...''

''Sleeping together,'' Ryan finished for her.

She felt herself blush to the roots of her hair, and she dropped her hand to her lap. ''That's right. We just want people to *think* we're sleeping together.''

Stuart blinked as though he'd been abducted by

aliens and set down in a place he didn't recognize. He turned to his son. "You understand this?"

"Perfectly."

Francie realized she was sinking fast. "We're just pretending to be married for my grandmother's sake."

Ryan wore a composed expression and sat listening to her explanation. Francie glared at him suddenly. "Jump in here, anytime, Mac."

"You're doing just fine." He leaned back in smug repose and crossed one ankle over his bare knee.

At that action, Stuart seemed to take note of Ryan's grass-stained shirt and shorts. "Whatever have you been doing?"

"Oh. Fell during a three-legged race." He rubbed at a smudge on his knee. "Got third place, though."

"So you see," Francie continued, ignoring the interruption, "we really don't even know each other. But Nana's crazy about Jim and the kids, and pleased as punch with the whole situation. She thinks I'm settled down and happy."

She launched into an explanation about Nana's concerns for her marital status, the reunion invitation and how happy the children made Nana each time they visited.

"Alanna and Alex are well?" Stuart asked.

Ryan nodded. "Perfectly all right."

A niggle of exasperation tugged at Francie. Was this man even paying attention? She went on determinedly, at last mentioning the brooch.

"You have the brooch?" Stuart asked, as though

finally hearing something he understood. "My mother's brooch? Where is it?"

Ryan spoke up. "It's in the hotel safe now, Dad. Francie gave it to Alanna this morning. We voted to stay and finish the weekend anyway."

News of the piece of jewelry seemed to have softened the senior MacNair's opinion of her. Even his body language became less defensive, and he turned to her. "Thank you for giving my granddaughter the brooch, Miss Karr-Taylor. That piece means a lot to our family."

"I understand that," she replied. "I should have just given it to Ryan in the first place, but I was panicked over how I was going to pull off this week and still have Nana thinking I was happily married. I probably didn't use my best judgment."

"In selecting my son to carry out your deceitful plan, you mean?" He puffed out his chest.

"No, no, Ryan was perfect. He *is* perfect. I meant I didn't use good judgment in blackmailing him."

Ryan chuckled this time.

Stuart scowled.

"It wasn't blackmail," Ryan said, coming to her defense. "It was bartering. People do it all the time, remember?"

Had she actually used that argument to convince him to go along with her scheme? Once again, her impetuous nature had sprung her headlong into a predicament. Would she never learn? She caught herself twisting the wedding band and laced her fingers to keep them still.

"Francie is no threat to me or the children," Ryan

assured his father. "In fact she's been good for us. I'm sorry you had to come all this way to find that out. You could have waited to speak with me. Or I would have called you back."

"I probably wouldn't have believed you without seeing for myself. Without seeing *her* for myself."

Indignation brought a frown to Francie's brow. What was that supposed to mean?

"This is not like you," Stuart said, and she knew he meant *she* was not like the company Ryan normally kept.

Ryan rested his elbows on his knees and flattened his palms together. "It's not like I have been the past several years. I've been so absorbed in business that I haven't taken time to see how much Alanna and Alex needed me with them. That's all changed."

He took a long minute to look his father over, measuringly, and cast Francie a look she didn't quite understand.

An uncomfortable silence fell over the room.

Finally Francie stood. "I'll go. You two probably want some privacy."

"I'll be right up," Ryan said, and stood to hand her the key.

She nodded. "Good night, Mr. MacNair."

"Good night, Francie. If that *is* your name."

His sarcasm stung. She made her way to their room, knowing she'd embarrassed Ryan in front of his father, and knowing every bit of the damage done had been her fault. She could only hope that in trying to smooth it over she hadn't made it worse.

Alanna was sitting on the side of Francie's bed when she let herself in. "Was the old man mad?"

"He was worried."

"Did he ask about me and Alex?"

"Yes. He was pleased you had the brooch."

"Were you afraid of him?"

Francie studied the girl's features in the light that slipped through a crack in the drapes. Her skin was pink and flushed as though she'd recently scrubbed it hard. "No, Alanna. Why would I be? He's a perfect gentleman. Just like your father."

"Is he coming down here?"

Francie shook her head.

Alanna smoothed the hem of her nightshirt over her knees, visibly relaxing. "Did you tell him anything about me?"

Francie didn't understand. "What's to tell?"

"Nothing," Alanna said hastily. "I just wondered."

"You can see him tomorrow."

Alanna nodded and fell silent.

Francie located the nightshirt she'd taken out earlier.

"Thanks for being Alex's partner today," Alanna said. "That meant a lot to him."

Though the girl obviously didn't like to show it, she was sensitive to Alex's needs. She treated him like any big sister would, acting put out with him, but Francie had observed her protectiveness.

Her "thank you" came as a shock. Was Francie only imagining that a tiny window of communication was being opened here? "It meant a lot to me, too."

In the darkness, Alanna brushed her fingers over the bedspread.

"Thanks for being your dad's partner," Francie said. "That meant a lot to him."

The girl seemed to stiffen in the crack of light. "It's not your place to thank me. He's my dad."

That figurative window slammed and locked tightly. It had been fitting for Alanna to thank Francie, since Francie was an outsider. But not vice versa. The girl never missed an opportunity to point out that Francie was not really a part of their family.

"Thanks for pointing that out." Tiredly Francie padded into the bathroom and changed her clothes. By then Ryan tapped at the door, and she let him in. Alanna had gone back to her pallet and now lay silent, though she couldn't have been asleep.

Francie wanted to apologize to Ryan for his embarrassment. She wanted to know what Stuart had said after she'd left. Impetuously she took his hand, led him into the bathroom and closed the door. "What happened?"

"Thank you."

"For what?"

"I got a good hard look at where I was heading and I didn't like it," he replied, closing his hands over her upper arms.

Francie sensed a change in Ryan, a change that had something to do with the new light in his eyes and the spirited tone in his voice. "What are you talking about?"

"I'm talking about my father. I love him. But I

don't want to be him—buttoned up...reserved... indifferent. You saved me."

"*I* did?"

He nodded, stepping so close, she backed against the counter and reached to steady herself, knocking a comb to the floor. "Well, good. But, I meant what happened after I left?"

He threaded the fingers of one hand into the hair at her temple. "I assured him everything was fine. I told him we'd meet him for breakfast in the morning."

"You did?" Her heart fluttered at the touch of his fingertips against her scalp and hair.

He nodded.

This intense closeness and his electrifying touch caught her off guard. She'd pulled him into the bathroom in her impatience to know what had been said. She hadn't thought about the fact that she'd changed into her nightshirt, or what Ryan would think. Or how their confined closeness would feel. "What are you doing?"

"Getting ready to kiss you."

His words sent a thrill of anticipation along her nerve endings. "With no one watching, I might think you're doing it because you like it."

He brought his face closer to hers. "You might."

She read the purpose in his dark eyes. "Kissing me in here, like this, would be a reckless thing to do."

His lips came within a hairbreadth of hers. He raised his other hand and his fingers brushed her jaw. "Not well considered or advised, you mean."

Eager anticipation scattered her thoughts. "That's what I mean."

"I haven't done many reckless things…you'll have to let me know how I do." He touched his lips to hers, and if she'd had any resistance it fled in the wake of the sensation.

The ardent kiss awakened wants and longings she hadn't known she'd harbored. Self-reliant Francie needed Ryan MacNair. A feverish desire to have more, be more, feel more, flared to life, and she clung to his shoulders, raising herself fully into the experience, wondering all the while where her sense had flown to.

Through the fabric of his shirt, his skin was warm, the muscle beneath firm. Touching him like this, not by accident or for show, was heady in its own right. The fact that she'd closed them alone in the tiny space of the bathroom and that she was wearing nothing but her nightshirt and flimsy panties added a tantalizing electricity.

He plowed his fingers into her hair on either side of her head and held her still, availing her mouth to the onslaught of his lips. His head slanted, his urgency a living breathing force that made her senses reel and her skin tingle.

There was nothing cautious in the way he kissed her, none of his studious careful manner. Francie ran her palms down his strong back, grabbed fistfuls of his shirt and clung.

Ryan pressed closer, until she was sitting on the counter, her face raised above his, him standing in the V of her thighs. Behind her, bottles tipped and clanked and she dimly recognized the bristles of her hairbrush dimpling her backside. She leaned sideways and reached to dislodge it. Ryan moved with her, but their lips parted.

His breath ragged, he traced a path along her jaw with his lips, scattering goose bumps along her limbs. "How am I doing?"

She stopped the journey of his mouth by cupping his jaw and raising his face back to hers. "You get an *A* in reckless kissing, Mac."

She kissed him this time, spurred on by the flames of desire he'd ignited. Their breathing grew harsh and irregular, the sound magnified in the stillness of the enclosed space.

Ryan ran his hands down her sides and cupped her hips. She enjoyed that primal sensation until it wasn't enough. Grasping his wrists, she pulled his hands up to cover her breasts through her cotton nightshirt. He made a groaning noise in his throat.

"What are we doing?" she said against his mouth.

He kneaded her flesh gently. "We're doing what we've been thinking about doing for days."

"Did you think it would feel this good?"

"I didn't think anything felt this good."

"Oh, Ryan, I think we'd better stop."

"Okay."

"No, I mean really."

"Okay, you stop first."

His gentle tugs had her quivering. She closed her eyes and sought his lips once more.

His tongue drew hers this time, and she leaned into

the stirring pressure of his hands and the limitless allure of his sensual mouth.

The situation had grown way out of hand. "Okay," she said, drawing air. "We'll both stop at the same time."

"Okay," he said again, the word and his hands not in accord.

"Now," she said. "Stop."

She leaned away and caught her balance with one hand on the counter where she sat.

He raised both palms and took a step back.

They stared at each other.

Her lips were pink and swollen, her skin flushed.

His dark eyes held heavy-lidded desire.

Francie modestly tugged her nightshirt over her thighs and forced herself to look away from his face, willing her heart rate back to normal. "So, what did he say?"

"Who?"

"Your father."

"He, um. He just asked me if I'd lost my mind."

"And what did you say?"

"I said I didn't think so. But then that was before this."

"And then what?"

"And then I just reiterated what I'd said about wanting to change from the way I was before."

"And what did he say?"

"He said he liked me fine that way."

"And—"

"And I said I didn't. There. Geesh. You wanted to

give us privacy, now you want to know everything that was said."

She slid from the vanity counter, careful not to touch him. "I just thought he'd feel free to speak if I wasn't there. Or maybe you would. I don't know."

"I said everything I had to say while you were there."

"He thinks I'm a complete and total idiot."

"He thinks you're a little odd. We're all odd. Odd is relative."

She absorbed that one without comment, and edged around him to the door. "We'd better get some sleep."

"Somewhere," he said, stopping her with his palm against the door, "hidden inside that Francie who would've called an escort service to get a husband for a week..."

She didn't look up to meet his eyes.

"Would you have?"

She tilted her head. "Probably."

"...is a Francie who's very afraid to take chances."

She turned her back to him. "I'm not afraid."

"Yes you are."

"I'm not."

"Mmm-hmm. In there is a Francie in a stuffed shirt. Oh, it's probably red silk with matching pumps, but it's a stuffed shirt."

Finally she met his intent gaze in the mirror. "What are you talking about?"

"You're afraid to take a chance on me. On us."

He wasn't touching her anywhere now, but her

heart beat as fast as it had moments ago when he'd been kissing her senseless. "Relationships aren't about chances."

"It's *all* about taking chances," he insisted. "You have this hang-up because your parents left you. You're afraid you'll be like them and not be able to stick with a commitment."

"A child is a little more than a commitment, Ryan."

"Of course it is. But that fear keeps you from letting go."

"You really don't know me well enough to make that analysis. You don't know what my life has been like before I met you."

"Yes, I do."

She stared at him in the mirror, his eyes dark and more piercing than she was comfortable with. The heat from his body penetrated the back of her nightshirt.

"You live a free and easy life with nothing more entangling than a cat you can drop off at the cat sitter's—"

"Cat sitter's?"

"—because you're not willing to take the risk of really getting involved."

"You're a fine one to talk."

"I don't take chances with my kids or with business affairs. Yes, I was married once and it ended horribly. But I certainly don't think every woman is like Nikki. I don't think you're like her."

Ryan spoke that disclosure softly, his warm breath touching her neck and sending a shiver along her spine. She saw nothing but the blur of their combined reflection. The earnestness in his handsome expression tore away a little more of the restraint his words had eroded and that their sensual attraction had begun.

"Okay, you're right," she said, her voice not sounding at all like her own. "I'm afraid."

He said nothing.

"I've worked hard at making a name for myself and earning a reputation. I chose to go after what I wanted with my career, and I didn't let anything get in the way of that."

"And you think seeing me, maybe caring about me would get in the way of that?"

"I don't know." She passed a hand over her eyes and tried to put her feelings into words. "I'm not willing to give up my freedom."

"Freedom to do what?"

"Whatever I want."

"See other men?"

"No. It's not that."

"Francie, you can have a career, too. Lots of families make it work, find a balance. There's no reason why you can't have both. Trust yourself."

Hope swelled inside her, but she feared giving in to it. She wanted to turn around and fold herself against him, but she held back, and the self-denial left an ache in her chest.

"If being with me takes something away from you," he said softly, "then it's wrong. A relationship should add, not take away. You can have both. You can have it all. Your parents made a bad choice. That doesn't mean you have to.''

"Maybe it was the right choice for them."

"Maybe it was the right choice for you, too. You had Nana, didn't you? She loves you as much as any parent could.''

Yes, she'd had Nana. No one could ask for a more loving, more caring person to raise them. Francie lowered her gaze to the littered vanity and blinked back tears.

He moved away from the door, bent to pick up a comb and a can of mousse from the floor and returned them to the disarray on the counter. ''Think about it, Francie.''

She nodded, reaching for the doorknob. She would do little else but think about it. Would he press her? "We have a big day ahead of us."

"Will we be picking up Nana?"

She scrambled to collect her thoughts. "How about after breakfast?"

"All right. 'Night."

She fled from the confined space and scrambled into her bed, her whole body still tingling from the kisses and touches they'd shared, her mind numb from his suggestions. She had to be nuts for even thinking of continuing a relationship with Ryan. Why was it the whole family commitment thing she'd scoffed at for so long didn't seem quite so stifling any longer?

But even Ryan had allowed his career to overshadow his relationship with his children, and she knew how much he loved Alanna and Alex. If someone as steady and dependable as he couldn't juggle both acts, she didn't have a prayer.

That was an unfair assessment, she knew. Ryan had allowed his job to occupy his time to deaden the hurt of his wife's abandonment. And when he'd realized what his behavior was doing to his children, he'd chosen to correct that mistake immediately. But she knew only too well that his regret and change was not indicative of most career parents.

Hers had never come back for her. Never cared that she needed them.

Francie buried her head and refused to listen to Ryan climb into bed with his son. If she thought about him lying only four feet away from her she'd never rest.

Perhaps Stuart would discourage him from continuing to see her, anyway. Maybe in a week or so this whole infatuation would be blown over and behind them.

Maybe she'd better wait to make any decisions until she didn't have the feel of him on her skin and his taste on her lips.

Sure, and maybe it would rain pigs from the sky tomorrow.

The night was long.

10

SHE WAS AVOIDING him like a bad case of hives. All morning as they prepared to leave, she remained polite, but distant. Since checkout time came before the service would end, they packed so their bags could be loaded into the car.

They'd all dressed for the morning's event, planning to leave out casual attire for the plane ride. Ryan and Alex wore lightweight suits. Alanna had brought an ivory dress with a matching midriff jacket. Francie exited the bathroom in a short red dress that nearly stopped Ryan's heart.

The garment was cut straight and plain, not fancy at all, but the way it accentuated her curvy figure and bared her arms and legs kicked his hormones into overdrive.

She'd twisted her hair up into a gold clip in the back, with a few straight tendrils hanging against her neck and cheek, giving her an allover alluring appeal. She caught him staring, and he tried to smile appreciatively, rather than as lecherously as he felt. "Did that dress come with a warning label?"

It took her a second to figure out what he meant, and then she smiled. She handed Alanna a small silky-looking mauve bag, and they spoke with their heads together for a few moments. Alanna followed Francie into the bathroom and the door closed.

Ryan zipped his other suits into his garment bag, refusing to ponder the vagarious nature of women. Especially those two.

Alex sat beside his suitcase and the box that held his carefully packed prize-winning boat, and watched his father with forlorn gray eyes.

"Something wrong, son?"

"No."

Ryan made a neat stack of his luggage beside Alex's. "You sad about this being the last day of our vacation?"

"Kinda."

Ryan sat on the end of the bed he'd straightened and faced Alex. "I made a promise. We'll be taking more vacations together. I'm not going to forget that promise. The way we've done it in the past is not going to be the way it is from here on. We're making a fresh start."

An engaging grin showed off new teeth that still seemed too big for the gaps left by Alex's baby teeth and gave Ryan the bittersweet sensation he got whenever he thought of his children growing older. "Do you think we could go to Disney World?"

"Is that where you want to go?"

Alex nodded.

"If Alanna is agreeable, it sounds good to me."

"Alanna wants to go, too."

"Then I guess we go to Disney World."

Alex got up and stepped closer until he was resting against his dad's knee. "Thanks, Dad."

Ryan opened his thighs and pulled his son back into his lap, dismissing the fact that he wore one of his best suits and that it would probably wrinkle.

Alex reclined against his chest. "Dad?"

"What?"

"Can Francie come with us?"

He'd known the question was coming. Tightening his arm around Alex, he replied, "I'd be happy to have Francie come with us. But we have to remember she has her photography business and a life of her own. Her going would depend on whether or not the time we choose is good for her, and if she wants to come along."

"I bet she will. Francie likes to do fun stuff."

"We'll have to see."

The bathroom door opened and Francie and Alanna emerged, looking toward Ryan and Alex expectantly.

"You two ready?" Ryan asked.

With wide eyes, Francie stood a little behind Alanna. She bobbed her head to one side a couple of times. What on earth was wrong with the woman?

Now her mouth moved, too. She was trying to say something, but no sound was coming out. She kept her hand on Alanna's shoulder, only her face showing any movement.

"You look nice, Alanna," Alex remarked.

Alanna's expectant gaze locked on her father.

Ryan got worried.

Francie rolled her eyes. She'd been trying to tell

him something. He was supposed to do something. Say something. Notice something.

He looked hard at Alanna, trying to see what Alex had seen. She looked lovely, her skin a clean youthful pink. She was his beautiful Alanna.

What was he supposed to notice?

Perhaps she looked a little older, her eyes a little more defined, her lips shiny. Cosmetics? Yes, she was wearing makeup. But this time the effect was natural and becoming.

"You look nice, honey," he said. "Did you try some new makeup?"

His daughter's expectant face broke into a pleased smile. She nodded. "Francie bought it for me."

"It looks nice."

"You really think so?" she asked. "You aren't going to say I'm too young?"

"No. I'm not going to say that. Not as long as it looks this nice."

Alanna smiled.

Francie smiled.

Ryan released a sigh of relief.

Alex piped up, "We're gonna go to Disney World, and Francie, you can come, too!"

Francie's smile faltered.

Alanna's eyes darkened, her smile slipped.

Ryan patted Alex's shoulder. "It's not definite, though. We'll discuss our next vacation as a family, and if it's somewhere you want to go, Alanna, we'll decide together."

"And you said Francie could go," Alex persisted.

"I said if it works out for her and it's something she wants to do."

Alex stood up from his dad's lap and hurried over to Francie. "You want to, don't you?"

"That would be very nice, Alex, and thank you for asking me. We'll have to see how it works out."

Uncomfortably Ryan hoped Francie didn't think he'd placed the notion of pressuring her into Alex's head. And he didn't want Alanna to think they'd been making plans without her. He stood, brushed the creases from his trousers and picked up as many bags as he could carry. "I'll start loading the car."

"I'll help." Alex held the door open.

A half hour later, Stuart was waiting at a table when they arrived at the selected restaurant. He glanced pointedly at his watch.

"Hi, Grandfather," Alex said. "We're gonna go to Disney World."

Stuart's white eyebrows raised. "Oh?" His attention slid from Alex to Ryan to Francie, and his gaze took in the flattering red dress. He was old, but he wasn't dead, and Ryan stifled a laugh at the unnatural expression that crossed his father's face.

Stuart cleared his throat. "You and your sister come sit beside me."

Obediently Alex took a chair.

Alanna followed a little less eagerly.

Ryan held a chair for Francie before seating himself, and the waitress immediately brought menus and coffee.

"I have a few legal matters I want to go over with

you within the next week or two," Stuart said to his son. "We could do it over dinner one evening."

"Sounds good," Ryan replied. "I packed my planner, so I'll have to give you a call."

Stuart eyed him with obvious worry, then took a sip of his coffee.

In between ordering and the meal arriving, Alex chattered about the high school play and his boat-building trophy. Stuart listened and smiled stiffly.

"Dad and I got a trophy, too," Alanna said. "Didn't we, Dad?"

Ryan nodded with a smile.

Stuart eyed her as she spoke about the three-legged race. "Do you have on *makeup*, young lady?" he asked.

Alanna's expression flattened. "Yes."

Stuart looked at Ryan quizzically. "Isn't she too—"

"Doesn't she look lovely?" Francie interrupted before he could say the words. "Warm colors suit her perfectly. Because of her great hair, she can wear clothing in so many shades that not all of us can wear well. Like her ivory dress there...see how it complements her skin and eyes? I would completely wash out in that dress."

Ryan couldn't imagine Francie 'washing out' in anything, but Alanna sat a little straighter at the complimentary words.

"She has a light hand and a deft touch with a makeup brush," Francie continued. "She's every bit a proper young lady. Not like some of these girls nowadays who dye those awful red streaks in their hair and look like they put on their makeup with a spray gun.'' She made a face.

"And the clothes some of them wear!'' she went on. "Why, I don't know how their parents can let them out of the house. Alanna has exquisite taste, I'm sure you've noticed.''

"I don't see how your opinion on anything my granddaughter does makes any difference,'' Stuart said, laying his fork down.

"Dad,'' Ryan said gently, but there was a warning in the tone.

"She's—''

"Francie has been very helpful to Alanna this week, and Alanna *is* growing up,'' he said before Stuart could continue.

"However, she's not Alanna's mother, and what she thinks or doesn't think is not definitive.''

"No, she's not Alanna's mother, but I'm her father. This is my decision, Dad. My family. I'm happy. *We're* happy.''

Stuart stared at his son. "You *have* lost your mind.''

Ryan actually smiled at that. "Good. I hope it stays lost.''

Francie glanced back and forth from one man to the other, fearful Stuart would get up and leave. She didn't want to be the cause of a family quarrel. She knew it hadn't been her place to speak up, but she couldn't bear for Alanna to take any unwarranted criticism. At least this way the focus was drawn away from the girl and placed on Francie. She wasn't as fragile as Alanna.

Ryan defending both of them warmed Francie from the top of her head to the tips of her toes. Alanna had needed to hear that. And so, she guessed, had she.

"Perhaps you'll be replacing Mrs. Nelson, then?" Stuart said in a snide tone.

Ryan obviously had no intention of being goaded. "Mrs. Nelson is adequate as a housekeeper and cook. I see no reason to let her go. I plan to spend more time with the kids, but I don't plan to spend it cleaning and cooking."

Francie hid a grin behind her napkin.

"I meant replaced by *her*," Stuart said.

"If you mean Francie, she's *not* a housekeeper."

Stuart had been fishing as to whether or not this situation would be permanent, and Ryan hadn't answered. Francie wanted to kiss him for not feeling he needed to explain their personal relationship. Or lack of. She cast him an appreciative smile.

"Dad said Francie can go to Disney World with us," Alex announced. "It's not for sure, though," he clarified, glancing at his father as though proud he'd gotten it straight this time. "And we can share a room again. Dad said Francie's kind of messy, but it's okay. We don't mind."

Francie glanced at Ryan and found him staring at Alex with a combination of horror and confusion reddening his lean jaw and cheekbones. He'd said she was messy? Compared to his neurotic neatness, she guessed she was. She knew full well Alex had taken the statement out of context, but the laughable look on Ryan's face was worth a trip to Disney World. And definitely called for a little harassment.

"I'm messy?" she asked, deliberately raising one brow.

"I don't know why he brought that up. I never said it like that."

"How did you say it?"

"He said you take too much share in the bathroom," Alex said.

"He did, did he?"

Ryan looked as if he wanted to say something, but no words emerged.

"Yeah," Alex went on, "and I thought you guys were going to fix it up last night. You sure were in there together a *lo-ong* time."

It was Francie's turn to choke on her breakfast. She took a gulp of her orange juice and didn't look at Ryan or his father.

Lordy, what did *married* people do for privacy?

"Alex, why don't you tell your grandfather about Nana?" Ryan suggested, finally finding his voice.

Alex launched into an explanation of Nana and the wheelchair rides she gave him.

Good job, Mac. You should have thought to distract him earlier. Francie glanced at Alanna and found the girl's eyes truly twinkling with amusement. She was getting a kick out of their embarrassment! She actually grinned at Francie, and Francie couldn't help returning her smile with a wry shake of her head.

Once the subject had been changed, breakfast concluded in a lighter tone.

"Did you come in a cab?" Ryan asked as they left the restaurant.

His father nodded.

"Ride with us, then."

Francie got in back, with Alex between her and Alanna, and wondered how they'd pick up Nana and her wheelchair.

"We'll arrive at the school auditorium a little early," Ryan said, catching her eye in the rearview mirror. "You go in and get seats and I'll go back for Nana."

A guarded corner of her heart warmed toward him. That thoughtful suggestion hadn't come from only his methodic Type A mind; he was being considerate of her and her grandmother.

Of course, she realized, entering the building and seeing the first few inquisitive stares, his offer left *her* to introduce Stuart to her classmates. Had Ryan really been that generous?

Dressed in a flowing blue dress with a scarf that tied around her long neck and cascaded over her shoulder, Peyton sidled up. "Someone new," she crooned, smiling hungrily at Stuart as though she'd sniffed out his breeding and money.

"Peyton Armbruster, this is Stuart MacNair," Francie said reluctantly.

"MacNair! Oh!"

Francie held her breath.

"Francie's father-in-law," Peyton murmured and stepped closer. "What business are you in?"

Stuart didn't bat an eyelash. He didn't acknowledge the introduction, either. "Alex, come with me."

Alex took his hand, and they headed through the double doors into the auditorium, Stuart drawing questioning looks en route.

Immediately Peyton looked as if she'd bitten into a persimmon. The blue-tinged veins visible above the neck scarf stood out.

Francie flipped a hand nonchalantly. "He's senile," she said, and hurried after them, feigning an apologetic smile.

The auditorium had been spruced up with carnations dyed in Springdale High's school colors. A fringed banner numbered with the graduating year draped the podium.

They saved great seats near the stage, and Francie visited with those on either side. When Ryan wheeled Nana in, Francie sat on the aisle beside her chair and took her hand. The service began with an opening prayer by one of the local pastors. The class valedictorian gave a brief talk on continuing to follow their dreams, and the chorale group sang.

Though he had retired a few years ago and moved out of state, the past high school principal had returned to speak. The winners of all the games and contests were announced and cheered for.

And finally, the lights dimmed. A slide presentation, created from photographs from the class yearbook as well as the recent ones Francie had taken, all set to music, progressed. Francie had always been proud of her work, but never as proud as at this moment when Nana got tears in her eyes and patted her hand repeatedly.

Francie received an uncommon surprise when several shots of her were displayed in a row. Slightly off center, but capturing the concentration on both their faces, one photo showed her and Alex, heads bent together, gluing masts to their boat.

In the next one, Alex's freckled face tilted to hers, a look of adoration on his dear features, and at the vulnerability in that look, her heart caught.

For an amateur, Ryan had used light and angles to a visual advantage, pleasantly surprising her.

The next photo centered on Francie, sun glinting from her breeze-tossed hair, a smile of joy softening her features as she watched Alex receive their trophy. The look of love and pride could have belonged to…a mother.

A strange, undefinable feeling of warmth and joy blossomed in her chest. Her throat burned as if she had to cry, but she stifled the shaken-up sensation, because it was unfamiliar and it carved craters in her preconceived assumptions about her own nature.

She never saw pictures of herself. Her parents hadn't doted over her every growth process as did other mothers and fathers. They'd been taking pictures of news in the making, hell-bent on winning Pulitzers, not concerned with preserving memories of their only child growing up.

As soon as she'd been old enough, Francie had always been *behind* a camera lens.

So these photographs were special...but in more ways than one. Ryan had taken them.

And he'd taken them with as much sensitivity as an artist.

He'd taken them with love.

She had turned over the last few rolls of film to the baccalaureate committee last night, never imagining the shots he'd taken would be so moving, or that the committee would choose to use them.

Francie met his tender gaze over Alex's head in the semidarkness. The slides had affected him, too. Were her emotions as plainly visible as his?

He leaned in front of Alex. She bent to hear him whisper in her ear, "You are beautiful."

How did one reply to disturbing words like that? How had she lived so long without caring that a man had never said them to her, had never thought her beautiful? She sat back, hoping her expression didn't match the foolish fluttering in her chest.

The lights came up. Around them applause roared.

"That was you and me, huh, Francie!" Alex cried with pleasure.

She nodded and returned his hug, never taking her eyes from his father.

Finally Alanna said something to Ryan, and he turned to reply.

"I'm so proud of you, Francesca," Nana said from her other side.

Francie hugged her tearfully. "Thank you."

"Your parents would have been proud of you, too," she said, with a vigorous bob of her white-haired head.

"Maybe," Francie replied. "But you're the one who took care of me and loved me. All I really care about is what you think. And that you're happy."

"I'm happy, don't you give that a second thought. There isn't an old lady in all of Illinois who gets as good of care as I do. You've seen to that."

Francie pressed her cheek to her grandmother's, their warm tears of joy mingling.

The service had ended and people milled around them, raving over her photographs. Francie composed herself and swiped at her cheeks.

"Francie, I have all your slides," J.J. called over several heads. "Hang around."

She waved her understanding.

A light buffet lunch had been set up in the cafeteria so all the out-of-town attendees could eat before starting their trips home, as well as have a gathering place to say their final goodbyes.

The MacNairs, Alex pushing Nana, located a table, and Francie went through the food line for her grandmother and carried her plate back.

Nana had been a Springdale resident for nearly ninety years, and her presence attracted immediate attention. Friends, fellow church members, former neighbors, all stopped by to say hello.

Nana enjoyed the vigilance and the company more than the food. Every so often Francie reminded her to eat.

Distinctly out of place, Stuart ate a sandwich and nursed coffee from a foam cup. His scowl grew more fierce with each person who asked if he was Francie's father-in-law.

Finally the crowd thinned, but the core group stood nearby, spouting platitudes and promising to keep in touch better during the next ten years.

J.J. handed Francie an envelope. "Your slides."

Shari Donegan hurried to her side. "Francie, can I use those for the reunion book we're putting together? I'll send them to you as soon as it's finished. In fact, I was hoping you'd help me select the rest of the pictures."

"No problem," Francie replied.

Becka came closer, too. "Thank you for the wonderful pictures," she said with a sincere smile.

Don Armbruster walked over to Ryan's father. "I hope I get to see a Karr-Taylor exhibit soon. Have you seen all of her work?"

"I have no idea what you're talking about." Stuart's scowl turned on Francie. "Are you a professional photographer?"

Peyton caught that remark with her unerring ear. "How could you not know what she does for a living?"

"Never met her before yesterday."

Francie's heart plunged.

"You live in Chicago, don't you?" Peyton asked, her eyes narrowing.

"I do."

Peyton exchanged a haughty look with Shari, then

turned to Francie. "This whole thing with your little family has seemed fishy from the start. How come none of us met Ryan until now? If you'd caught yourself a man like this one, I'd think you'd have brought him to meet your grandmother before this. And that 'child,'" she said, indicating Alanna, "can't stand you, but you act like everything's all hunky dory. And not very good acting, by the way."

Peyton turned slightly. "Now this gentleman you say is your father-in-law says he's never met you before. You claimed to have been married six months as of Valentine's Day, though that's actually only five months, but your father-in-law, who lives in the same city, came all the way here to meet you for the first time? The whole story is more than shaky."

Francie couldn't run, as was her first inclination. She had Nana here to think of and to take home. In that moment, she realized that none of this really mattered, though. These people hadn't cared about her until she seemed to fit into their expectations. She never had to see them again if she chose not to.

And the MacNairs? They could all go home and forget this week had ever happened; they had their precious brooch…and each other.

But Nana. Nana did matter. And Nana cared whether or not Francie was married. In retrospect, would it have been better to let Nana worry over her marital state, rather than see her embarrassed and disappointed like this? The whole plan had been for her sake, to protect her from concern, but Nana wouldn't understand that.

She'd be disappointed in Francie. And rightly so. Francie had added an elaborate lie to her single status.

All that had ever mattered was Nana.

"If I'm the child you're talking about," Alanna said, coming to stand defensively beside Francie, "then you don't know kids very well. I guess I said some rotten things about Francie when I was mad that night I hid from my dad. But Francie's the best mom I ever had. I should have said I was sorry that night, but I didn't."

Alanna glanced from Francie to her dad, then looked back at Peyton. "Stepfamilies have a lot of adjusting to do," she continued, as though the woman needed a quick course in manners and family concerns. "I was mean to Francie because I was jealous of the love and attention my dad gives her. But I know my dad loves me, too. And I know Francie loves me. We're all just getting used to each other. We just need to keep communicating."

Francie didn't know whether that insight had come from Alanna's counseling sessions or an episode of "Montel," but it had sounded genuine enough and seemed to have had the desired quieting effect on Peyton.

"Francie loves me, too," Alex piped up. "And we're going to Disney World *next* time."

"My father's been out of the country," Ryan said, stepping around Alex and hugging Francie to him with one arm. "Otherwise he'd have met Francie by now. She's not exactly a wife I'd want to keep a secret now, is she?"

Ryan's quick cover up surprised Francie even more than the kids'. He'd been opposed to this from the start, and now here he was keeping her story afloat as though he was an accomplished fraud.

Stuart's expression conveyed his annoyance with the whole ridiculous scheme as well as a tinge of regret for not keeping his mouth shut and letting the others handle it.

Francie gave him a tentative smile so he'd know it had turned out okay.

From beside her, her grandmother spoke up. "You always were an uppity one, Peyton Baxter," Nana said, using Peyton's maiden name, the name that linked her to the town's furnace repairman, her father. "A body'd think you were jealous of Francie marrying a handsome rich man with such lovely children and still being able to have her photography career, while you kept Neiman Marcus in business."

"I'm not jealous," Peyton denied emphatically. "I just saw all the inconsistencies in her background stories all week. Nobody can say it wasn't odd."

"Odd is relative, you know," Francie said softly.

"Well, if there's one thing I love about Francie," Ryan said, ignoring her, "and there are many things I love about her, mind you, it's that she's full of inconsistencies. She's never boring, that's for sure." He kissed her cheek for emphasis.

Francie accepted the kiss, studied the warm assurance in his dark eyes and felt the loving support of this family to the tips of her toes. Each one of them had protected her story. Even Nana, bless her heart, who believed it to be true, and now wouldn't have to know Francie had lied to her.

Francie swallowed the lump in her throat. If only Ryan had meant those words of love.

With lowered lids, Peyton wished them goodbye, gathered her husband and son and left. The Donegans and the Richardses waved as Ryan wheeled Nana to the door and Francie, Stuart and the kids followed.

"I'll call a cab," Stuart suggested. "My flight leaves in forty-five minutes."

"I'll drop you off at the airport and come back for these guys," Ryan insisted. "We don't leave until later this afternoon."

Stuart accepted a peck on the cheek from his grandchildren, then turned to Francie. "Goodbye. It's been…unusual."

"Goodbye, Stuart." Francie waved him off.

11

WITHIN THE HOUR, they had returned Nana to the care center and settled her down to rest. "I want to speak with your nurses before I go," Francie told her.

Nana shooed her on her way. "Jim will sit with me until I fall asleep. Alanna, darling, why don't you go down and play something on the piano in the day-room? I can hear it from here."

"Okay. Come with me, Alex."

Ryan watched his children scamper off, hand in hand. "You and your granddaughter do have a good effect on those children of mine."

"They just need love. You can't love anybody too much."

"How right you are."

"You know, Ryan MacNair," she said, using his real name and narrowing her alert gaze on his face. "You have your work cut out for you in making Francesca see she's worthy of your love. It's not you she doesn't trust, it's herself. I don't know how she found you, or how you came to be here this week, but you're exactly what she needs."

Ryan stared at her in abashment.

"I think you need her, too."

He couldn't find his voice for a full minute, but finally he said, "I do."

"Then don't let her go."

She knew. She'd known all along. Her wise old eyes glistened with unshed tears.

He found his voice. "I've talked to her, Nana. But she's afraid to make a commitment."

"Because she thinks she'll let you down. But she won't. She's never let me down her whole life. Look what she did this week just to make me happy."

"You and I know that. Now I need to convince her."

Her eyes drifted shut. "You will," she said. "You will."

Ryan patted her hand and tucked the soft fringed throw around her. The lighthearted notes of a concerto drifted down the hallway. Alanna had probably drawn a crowd by now.

"She sleeping?"

He turned as Francie entered the room, and he nodded.

She gestured to the doorway, and led him out onto the shaded veranda where a few residents sat playing cards. "I spoke with her nurses about her care. Her doctors say she had a silent heart attack sometime over the past months. It's weakened her some, but she's doing as well as can be expected."

"I'd say she's doing very well." He glanced at his watch. "What do you want to do until flight time?"

She surveyed their pleasant surroundings. "Stay here?"

He agreed. "She'll probably wake up before we go, and we can say goodbye."

She nodded.

He pointed to a glider and they sat side by side. Ryan set it in gentle motion, and she watched his leg flex beneath his impeccably creased trousers.

A breeze caught her hair, and she tucked an errant strand behind her ear. They were so different, the two of them. How could anything come of this?

"You really are beautiful," he said.

Heat tinged her cheeks. She didn't look at him.

"I've learned a lot from you this week, Francie."

She looked over. "Like what?"

"Like life's too short to worry about what people think or to miss out on the things that are important."

"What kinds of things?"

"You know. Things like enjoying a day just because it's there and you'll never be able to get it back again. Things like appreciating the people who love you and seeing that spending time with them is far more important than simply providing for them."

"You already knew those things."

He nodded, a slow smile gracing his handsome features. "Maybe I knew them intellectually, but I didn't feel them. Those are two different things. I needed you to show me."

Was it possible that their differences were complementary? That they could actually be good for each other?

"I don't want our time together to end," he said. "I don't want to go back home and pretend I didn't feel anything."

"You don't have to pretend you don't feel anything." As soon as she'd said that, she followed it quickly with "What do you feel?"

"Like a different person. Like we're supposed to be a family."

He still looked the same, still wore an elegantly tailored suit and turned heads wherever he went. But he had changed. He wasn't the same buttoned-up man who had come seeking the brooch. And that amazing ability to change challenged her. Maybe he was right. Perhaps she was the one buttoned-up, the one too inflexible to alter her way of thinking. After all, hadn't she been contemplating the same things? Hadn't she been imagining herself with a family—with *this* family?

"Son, could you get an aide for me?" one of the gentleman on the veranda called.

With a rueful glance, Ryan stood and walked toward him. "What do you need, sir?"

"I'd like to go in and drain the radiator." The old fellow pointed to the doors.

"I think I can manage to push you in the right direction." Ryan steered the fellow's wheelchair into the building.

Francie got up and strolled across the lawn, rolling Ryan's words over in her mind. She questioned her motives in making the decision she'd made to remain emotionally unentangled.

She'd been living in fear. And she'd been untrusting of her own character. She'd been prepared to resent everything about family involvement. If someone had told her a month ago that bonding with a man and two children could be a rewarding and pleasurable experience, she'd have told them they were nuts.

In trying to make her grandmother happy, she'd found that the things she'd resisted with all her might really could make her happy, too: a man to love her—not that Ryan had ever said he loved her, but someone to be there for her when she needed emotional support, and children who looked up to her and defended her.

Those kids. They truly cared about her. And doggone it, she'd gone and fallen for them, too.

The irony struck her. Nana had been right all along. Oh, if she only knew the truth of it, she'd have a good laugh over the realization Francie was just now coming to.

Francie: self-reliant; risk taker; reckless. Afraid… *Alone.*

She found a spot of shade under a tree, but her skirt was too short to sit on the ground comfortably. She moved on to the fountain and perched on the concrete base.

Ryan, the man she'd called a stuffed shirt, was willing to give this alliance a shot. That took courage. And a belief in himself as well as her.

He crossed the lawn toward her now, his dark hair reflecting the sun. He'd removed his jacket, and it hung draped over his shoulder on one hooked finger. Here was the man she might just possibly love—*love?*

Her heartbeat snagged at the idea.

Had she ever said those words in her life? Had she told her parents before they left her? Surely she had. Had she ever told Nana? She hoped so.

Would saying them take anything away from her?

Just thinking them had given her something: a soul-deep gratification and joy. A new place of hope on the inside. He'd told Peyton he loved many things about her—but could he actually *love* her? Not just appreciate her, or desire her, but love her?

And in that moment, with the sun glinting from his hair, and her heart thudding as though she'd run all the way from Chicago, she knew without a doubt or a fear that she loved Ryan MacNair.

She raised her hand without thought, a half welcome, half warning. "I love you!"

Her voice carried across the lawn.

His step didn't falter. He didn't behave as though the earth had just turned on its axis and threatened to throw her off into space. He reached her within seconds and stopped, the afternoon sun at his back, shading her.

"I don't think I've ever said it before."

"I'm glad you did," he replied, "because now I can tell you I love you, too."

Her heart jumped giddily, and she grasped at words, afraid to hope. "I'm used to having my own way and doing what I please and not reporting to anyone."

"You've been considerate the entire week," he countered.

"I leave messes everywhere."

He shrugged. "I can't skate."

She smiled, daring to hope. "I don't cook."

"I have a housekeeper, but she can't kiss like you."

"You've kissed her?"

He smiled. "I plan my appointments weeks in advance and color code my calendar pertaining to the event."

"That *is* sick. What color is family time?"

"There hasn't been one until now."

"What color is romance?"

"What's *your* favorite color?"

She stood to face him, daring to believe. "You really love me?"

"I really do." He tossed his suit jacket on the cement bench and ran his hand down her arm to take her hand. "I make out all my checks at the beginning of the month and mail them five days before the due date."

"This is more serious than I thought."

"I did lay my jacket down without folding it."

"But you thought about it."

He chuckled, but then his face grew serious. "Does this mean you're giving us a chance?"

She nodded. "I'm giving myself a chance, too."

"We'll take it slow and easy," he said.

"Judging from the other night, I don't think you have a slow and easy switch."

"I just want to make you happy. And I want you to be comfortable with your decision."

"I am. On both counts. And Ryan, the very last thing I'd ever want to do is hurt Alanna and Alex. I know I'll only love them more and more as time passes, and as long as they want me for a friend or whatever they want me for, I'll be there for them."

"I know you will. Just be yourself, Francie. And

let us love you. That's all any of us wants or needs from you.''

She reached up to touch his face, her fingers skimming the strong curve of his jaw, his sensual lips, the tiny lines that fanned out beside his eye, her heart full with the wonder of this man's love. "How do people with children manage time alone?''

He brought a hand to her waist. "I think red would be an appropriate color.''

"For what?''

"For Alone Time on the calendar.''

He pulled her against him and she went willingly. "What if something more...spontaneous comes up?''

"There are locks.''

"Locks? I have my own apartment.''

His lips came within inches of hers. "I promise not to say anything about the mess.''

Their lips met then, a sensual fusion that sucked her breath away and started her heart leaping giddily.

She leaned into his embrace and lost herself to the magic of the sensations he created with his kisses and the joy of belonging.

"Dad! Francie!'' childish voices chorused.

Ryan ended the kiss, but kept her tucked snugly against his side as he turned. Alanna and Alex raced along the curving sidewalk that led to the fountain.

"Concert over?'' Ryan asked.

Alanna nodded. "They kept asking for more and more pieces. A lady even came and served cookies for everyone.''

"She was great, Dad.'' Alex took his dad's hand and leaned against him.

"I have some news," Ryan said.

His children looked up at him expectantly.

"I think Francie will be going to Disney World with us. That is if that's where you'd like to go, Alanna."

"Sure," she said easily. "That's cool." She eyed the two of them. "Does this mean you two are going to, like, go out?"

"Yes, we're going to 'go out,'" Francie replied. "But I'm not going to get in the way of your family time together. I think you should still have that time just for the three of you."

"What if we want you along during our family time?" Alanna asked.

"Yeah," Alex said.

Francie couldn't help her surprise or her tears of pleasure. "Well, then I'll be glad to join you."

They smiled at one another.

"I'd better go see if Nana's awake yet," Francie said finally. "I have to tell her I love her before we go."

Alanna moved beside her. "I'll go with you."

Ryan watched the two of them cross the lawn, his daughter in ivory, his...*Francie* in bright red. A lot had changed in the past week. Even more in the past day.

"Do you think you and Francie might get married, Dad?" Alex asked. "Could she be our mom?"

"If it's something she wants in the future, Alex. I'm going to pray it will be."

"I'll pray, too."

Later, after saying their goodbyes to Nana, and

promising to visit over Thanksgiving break, they stood in line waiting to board their plane.

"What are you going to do with those?" Francie asked, noting the laptop and briefcase at his feet.

"Store them overhead," he replied, convincing her of his remarkable transformation.

"Dad?"

He turned.

"Can I sit by Francie?"

After promising each of the kids they could have a turn sitting by Francie, he took her hand and kissed it.

She looked up with a smile, her heart full to bursting. "Thanks for being my husband this week," she said, caressing his fingers.

"Any time."

"Really?"

"Really."

"I mean *really* really?"

"Any kind of really you'd like."

"We could stop in Vegas on the way home."

He grinned. "This flight doesn't go to Vegas."

She glanced at the monitor over his shoulder. "No, but the next flight does."

His eyes widened, and he inspected his wild, impulsive Francie's expression. She was kidding. *Wasn't she?* "You would marry me, Francie?"

"Guess you won't know unless you ask."

His expression grew serious. His fingers found the gold band she hadn't removed since he'd given it to her. "What do you say to making this the real thing?

I love every crazy impulsive thing about you and I want you to be my wife. Will you marry me?''

She looked into his somber dark eyes. "On one condition."

"What's that?"

"That it's forever."

He pulled her hand to his lips and kissed her fingers. "I promise, Francie. I do promise."

She stood on her toes to accept a sweet soul-reaching kiss, then turned in his arms to find two sets of amused eyes watching them. "Change of plans, kids," she said with a husky voice. "We're taking the next flight to Las Vegas."

Their whoops echoed across the concourse.

NO RISK, NO OBLIGATION TO BUY...NOW OR EVER!

GUARANTEED

PLAY "ROLL A DOUBLE"
AND YOU GET FREE GIFTS!
HERE'S HOW TO PLAY:

1. Peel off label from front cover. Place it in space provided at right. With a coin, carefully scratch off the silver dice. Then check the claim chart to see what we have for you – TWO FREE BOOKS and a mystery gift – ALL YOURS! ALL FREE!

2. Send back this card and you'll receive brand-new Harlequin Duets™ novels. These books have a cover price of $5.99 each in the U.S. and $6.99 each in Canada, but they are yours to keep absolutely free.

3. There's no catch. You're under no obligation to buy anything. We charge nothing – ZERO – for your first shipment. And you don't have to make any minimum number of purchases – not even one!

4. The fact is, thousands of readers enjoy receiving books by mail from the Harlequin Reader Service®. They like the convenience of home delivery...they like getting the best new novels BEFORE they're available in stores...and they love our discount prices!

5. We hope that after receiving your free books you'll want to remain a subscriber. But the choice is yours – to continue or cancel any time at all! So why not take us up on our invitation, with no risk of any kind. You'll be glad you did!

THIS MYSTERY BONUS GIFT WILL BE YOURS _FREE_ WHEN YOU PLAY "ROLL A DOUBLE"

"ROLL A DOUBLE!"

Place label here

SCRATCH HERE

?

SEE CLAIM CHART BELOW

311 HDL CQV7

111 HDL CQVR
(H-D-07/99)

YES! I have placed my label from the front cover into the space provided above and scratched off the silver dice to reveal a double. Please send me all the gifts for which I qualify. I understand that I am under no obligation to purchase any books, as explained on the back and on the opposite page.

Name: _____
(PLEASE PRINT)

Address: _____ Apt.#: _____

City: _____ State/Prov.: _____ Postal Zip/Code: _____

CLAIM CHART

2 FREE BOOKS PLUS MYSTERY BONUS GIFT

2 FREE BOOKS

1 FREE BOOK

CLAIM NO.37-829

PRINTED IN U.S.A

The Harlequin Reader Service® — Here's how it works:

Accepting your 2 free books and mystery gift places you under no obligation to buy anything. You may keep the books and gift and return the shipping statement marked "cancel." If you do not cancel, about a month later we'll send you 2 additional novels and bill you just $5.14 each in the U.S., or $6.14 each in Canada, plus 50¢ delivery per book and applicable taxes if any.* That's the complete price and — compared to the cover price of $5.99 in the U.S. and $6.99 in Canada — it's quite a bargain! You may cancel at any time, but if you choose to continue, every month we'll send you 2 more books, which you may either purchase at the discount price or return to us and cancel your subscription.

*Terms and prices subject to change without notice. Sales tax applicable in N.Y. Canadian residents will be charged applicable provincial taxes and GST.

ALYSSA
DEAN

50 Clues He's
Mr. Right

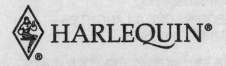

HARLEQUIN®

TORONTO • NEW YORK • LONDON
AMSTERDAM • PARIS • SYDNEY • HAMBURG
STOCKHOLM • ATHENS • TOKYO • MILAN • MADRID
PRAGUE • WARSAW • BUDAPEST • AUCKLAND

Dear Reader,

How can you tell he's Mr. Right? To find out, I conducted my own unofficial survey by asking every woman I know what she considered the qualities of a real man. "Taking out the garbage" was the number one answer, followed by "washes the dishes," and "has a great sense of humor." That might be true, but if a suave, debonair Cary Grant type came walking through the door, I doubt it would be garbage that we'd be thinking about!

Coming up with fifty qualities of a real man was a challenge, especially when I was trying to develop fifty qualities of a man in 1949! After quizzing my mother, I realized things hadn't changed that much. We're still looking for the suave, debonair guys with the great build and good jobs—although today we want them to cook, clean and take out the garbage!

Alyssa Dean

Books by Alyssa Dean
HARLEQUIN TEMPTATION
524—MAD ABOUT YOU
551—THE LAST HERO
636—RESCUING CHRISTINE
719—HER DESPERADO

HARLEQUIN LOVE & LAUGHTER
33—MISTLETOE MISCHIEF

Don't miss any of our special offers. Write to us at the following address for information on our newest releases.

Harlequin Reader Service
U.S.: 3010 Walden Ave., P.O. Box 1325, Buffalo, NY 14269
Canadian: P.O. Box 609, Fort Erie, Ont. L2A 5X3

For Winnie, Alison and Kathleen
three Real Women
and for Larry, Steve and Chris
my own Real Men

Real Men magazine—
the magazine aimed at
helping women find
romance with Mr. Right

Real men are hard to find. Haven't run across Mr. Right yet? Don't despair, ladies. Real men are worth the wait. You can recognize them by their suave and debonair appearance, their take-charge attitude and their confident approach to life. Trust me, darlings— there's a real man waiting around the corner just for you.

> —from "Forty-Nine Things You Need
> to Know about a Real Man,"
> *Real Men* magazine, April 1949

"I MUST BE HANGING AROUND the wrong corners," Tara muttered. She sat in Charlene's baby-blue carpeted office and studied the magazine spread open in front of her. It was the 1949 issue of *Real Men* magazine—the first issue, carefully preserved in plastic. The article Tara was reading was titled "FORTY-NINE THINGS YOU NEED TO KNOW ABOUT A REAL MAN." The title was in large block letters on the left-hand side of the page. On the right side was a black-and-white photograph of a young woman gazing up at an equally young-looking suit-and-tie-clad man. She had a wide-eyed dreamy expression on her face— which probably hadn't taken much acting, considering how strong and masculine and mouthwateringly gorgeous he was. "Either that or street corners like that got urban-renewed a long time ago."

Charlene Mortimer-Phelps, assistant features editor of

Real Men magazine, raised her blue eyes—exact shade of her carpet—to study Tara. "I beg your pardon?"

"That's what it says in this article. 'There's a real man waiting around the corner just for you.' That sure hasn't been my experience, Charlene. I've been in lots of cities and turned a number of corners and the only man waiting for me was a mugger!"

"I don't quite—"

"It certainly wasn't anyone like this. Just listen." Tara read from the magazine. "'Are you a woman who can't make up her mind? No need to worry. Decisiveness is one quality all real men share. Whether it's deciding what to eat, what to wear or where to go, your real man will have no problem making up his mind.'" She set down the magazine. "Now, I ask you, when was the last time you ran into a man like that?"

Charlene blinked. "I don't recall…"

"Me neither." Tara sat back. "The only man I've known who was like that was my father. Now there was a man for you! Charming. Polite. Distinguished-looking." She sighed. Her father had passed away years ago, but she had many fond memories of him. "I've never met anyone like that who was under eighty."

"Haven't you?" Charlene said vaguely. "Well, I'm sure you'll meet one someday. Now, as I was saying—"

"It certainly wasn't last Saturday," Tara complained. "You would not have believed my date. Dennis seemed so perfect when I met him, but he wasn't. He wasn't charming, he wasn't polite and he certainly wasn't decisive. Why, he dragged me from one restaurant to another, looking for one with a smaller menu. He said just reading all those entrées made him light-headed."

"How…fascinating."

Tara made a face as she recalled the episode. "It wasn't fascinating at all. Walking into a restaurant, demanding to see the menu, and then tossing it back to the maître d' and announcing 'It simply won't do' isn't my idea of a positive dating experience. Besides, I was hungry.''

Charlene's forehead creased into confusion. ''Hungry?''

''Starving,'' Tara confirmed with a decisive nod. ''And you know where we ended up eating? At a pizza place—because Dennis finally remembered he only likes one kind of pizza.'' She tapped a finger against the picture of the man in the magazine. ''Now this guy doesn't look like the type to take a woman to a pizza place on a first date. He'd do something more romantic…with candles, and wine…'' She sighed, because few of her dating experiences had involved either. ''Dennis even hinted that I should pick up half the tab. I bet the man in this picture wouldn't do that.''

Charlene's eyebrows rose. ''Of course he wouldn't, dear. He must be in his seventies now. If he planned for his retirement, he would be quite capable of paying for your meal.'' Her elegant forehead creased into another frown. ''Although I'm not sure he would ask you out at all, considering the difference in your ages.''

She looked so serious that Tara wondered if she was joking. Then she remembered who she was talking to, and decided she wasn't. Charlene might be the assistant features editor, a model of efficiency and not bad-looking for someone who seemed to be made entirely of plastic, but she'd been seriously shortchanged when it came to a sense of humor.

Tara set the magazine back on the glass-topped desk. ''I wasn't planning on dating this man, Charlene. I was just illustrating the fact that I haven't met any men who have the qualities mentioned in that article.''

Charlene gave her smooth auburn-haired head a shake that didn't disrupt a single strand. ''I'm not surprised. That article was written in 1949. Things have changed since then. Men have changed.''

Tara glanced back at the photograph of Mr. Suit and Tie. Not only was he good-looking, he also appeared to be suave and debonair and experienced. "They sure have," she murmured. Suave and debonair didn't describe any of the men she met. They were more likely to be clumsy, awkward and casually dressed.

"That's where you come in." Charlene's complexion was so smooth and so perfect that her staff sometimes speculated she'd had herself airbrushed. "As you've pointed out—I think—this list is badly out-of-date. We want you to fix that."

Tara had been freelancing for *Real Men* magazine for over three years now, but she still found Charlene difficult to follow. "I don't think I can change men, Charlene, at least I haven't been successful in changing any of the ones I've met. It's just something you have to learn to live with."

Charlene didn't even come close to cracking a smile. "Not the men, darling. The list. We want an updated version of this list."

Tara finally got it. "You want me to come up with forty-nine things you need to know about *today's* real man?"

"No, no. I want you to come up with *fifty* things." Charlene's eyes gleamed. "It was Sophia's idea, of course. One of the features to celebrate the fiftieth anniversary of the magazine."

"I should have guessed that." Sophia Watson, senior features editor of *Real Men* magazine, was going to make sure even first-time readers realized it was the magazine's fiftieth year. Every month was going to feature something about the number fifty, no matter how slight the connection. Numerous writers had been asked for ideas—Tara included—but she hadn't made much effort to join the fun. It wasn't that she had anything against the magazine. It was a smart, sexy, upbeat woman's magazine, it paid its contributing writers very well, and Tara had been delighted the first time they'd accepted one of her articles. However, she'd recently decided that it was time she wrote something with a little more substance than "Bedrooms That Say *Now*," "Clothes That Make You Feel Bold" or the one she was working on—"Food That Puts Him in the Mood."

A list of fifty things you needed to know about a real man just didn't qualify. "It does sound interesting," Tara assured Charlene. "But I'm not sure I'm the right person to do it. I mean, I haven't met that many real men so—"

"Oh, you don't have to worry about that. We've already lined them up for you."

Tara hadn't expected that. "You have?"

"Yes." Charlene opened a folder and passed over a few typewritten pages. "There are plenty of real men on this list."

Tara scanned the pages. "Enright Stefens. Harry Bakersfield. Tim McKewan." She looked up. "Who are these people?"

"Real men, of course." Charlene referred to her own copy. "Enright Stefens is an environmentalist, Harry Bakersfield teaches Latin at the university, Tim McKewan owns a nice little art gallery on the south side. And, of course, we've got the usual assortment of computer wizards, the owner of a men's boutique, a couple of entrepreneurs, a financial adviser—"

Tara made a face. "An environmentalist, a Latin professor and a bunch of computer gurus? These are examples of today's real men?" She shuddered. "They sound more like my date list, and believe me, Charlene, none of them were real men."

Charlene shrugged her elegant shoulders. "According to today's women they are." She set the list aside with a satisfied pat. "We asked our research department to come up with a list of today's real men—"

"And this is the best they could do?" Tara scowled at the list. "What about *real* real men? You know. Men like Gary Cooper and Cary Grant. Dashing, handsome, well-dressed."

Charlene dismissed this with a casual wave. "Passé, darling, passé. Women aren't interested in heroes who jump out of planes to rescue them anymore. Women today are quite capable of rescuing themselves."

Tara thought about the many dangers she'd encountered since moving to Chicago. The mugger on the street corner who had taken her purse. The weird guy on the subway who had followed her around. The footsteps behind her as she walked through the empty parking lot on the way home. "We might be capable of it, but that doesn't mean we wouldn't like a little help now and then."

"Today's women want men who are more—you know—up with the times. That's the sort of men you're going to be meeting. Isn't it thrilling?"

Tara had spent enough time with men like this. "It's delightful," she lied. "But, uh, why do I have to meet them? As a matter of fact, I don't understand why anyone has to meet them. Couldn't the research department just do a survey—"

Charlene's nod was crisp and approving. "I thought of that as well. But Sophia didn't care for the idea. She thought it would make a much more interesting article—and get more of a response from our readers—if you actually met them in person. Talked with them. Conducted your own little survey. Get your own insights into what they're like. And we can spice it up later with a few photographs of the real men you encounter."

Tara strongly doubted that photographs of computer gurus and environmentalists were going to spice up anything, including her career. Perhaps she should refuse. She'd resolved not to take on another fluff assignment, and that's certainly what this was.

There were other factors to consider, though. The stack of bills sitting on her kitchen table. The outrageous cost of her new apartment. The few serious assignments looming in her future. "I suppose, if that's what Sophia wants." She made another attempt to weasel out of it. "But, um, are you sure I'm the right person to do this? I mean, I'm flattered that you thought of me, but I am still working on 'Food That Puts Him in the Mood.' Besides, to be perfectly honest, I haven't done a lot of survey articles, so…"

Charlene looked shocked. "Sophia thinks you're the right person. And I agree with her. You've got all the right credentials."

Tara tried to think of one and came up empty. "If you mean my degree in journalism—"

"It's not that," Charlene said quickly. "Oh you're a fine writer, Tara, but that's not what I meant. I meant the fact that you're mature." She paused. "Mature and unattached."

Tara narrowed her eyes. "I'm only thirty-three."

"I know. Thirty-three and unencumbered. Unmarried. Footloose and fancy-free. You're just like the majority of our readers—desperately searching for that special someone to bring meaning to their lives."

Tara debated the wisdom of tossing one of Charlene's baby-blue ornaments at her. "I wouldn't call myself desperate."

"You know what I mean. You've got experience. You've dated a number of men. Why, every time I see you, you're dating another one."

"That doesn't make me an expert on men."

Charlene kept right on going. "And apart from that, there is the matter of your name."

"My name?"

"Yes. Tara is so today. So *modern*."

Tara scowled. "I was named after my great-aunt, and she was named after the house in *Gone With the Wind*."

"I'm sure she was a woman of her times as well." Charlene rose, a sure sign that the meeting was over. "It's all settled then. I do appreciate you taking this on, and I'm sure you'll write a tremendous article for us. Look at that wonderful piece you did on business clothes. It certainly perked up my wardrobe."

"It did?" Tara covertly studied Charlene's baby-blue suit, which looked pretty much the same as the baby-blue suit Charlene had worn the first time they'd met.

"Of course." Charlene rounded her desk and gave Tara's hand a brief, crisp shake. "I'll look forward to finding out what scintillating things you come up with this time."

"Scintillating." That was what she was going to come up with. A scintillating list of things you should know about a real man. No, *fifty* scintillating things women were dying to know about real men.

"Food That Puts Him in the Mood" was starting to sound better and better.

CHASE MONTGOMERY was thinking about food as well, but not about food that put him in the mood.

He was wondering who was in his kitchen.

He sat in the back room of his house—the room he used as an office—listening to the sounds of footsteps on linoleum with one part of his brain, while the other concentrated on what he was writing.

> There were a good dozen of Humphry Laromee's men on board that yacht—all heavily trained...and heavily armed. At the moment, a good portion of that armament was aimed directly at Hunter.

A cupboard door opened and closed in the kitchen. Chase paused for a moment to speculate on the identity of his uninvited guest. It could be one of his friends, he supposed. There were a number of them out there, all of whom he'd given keys to at one time or another, but most of them knew better than to drop in on him unexpectedly. Even his sister, Molly, called before she came over. Only his mother and his agent had the bad taste to show up without notice. His mother was on another of her scenic cruises, either checking out the fjords of Norway or, knowing her, organizing a mutiny. That reduced the list to his agent, Jerome, or a burglar.

Chase pondered the options. He liked Jerome well enough, but he didn't feel like having one of those "where is your next book and why aren't you finished yet" conversations.

A burglar, on the other hand, wouldn't want to talk. He'd just take things. That was okay. Apart from his large-screen television, which was too big to carry out, and his computer, which was in the room with him, there wasn't much around worth stealing. Any burglar worthy of the name would soon realize that and be gone.

If not, Chase could, like his fictional hero, run out there with guns blazing, easily overpower the intruder and call the police. However, since he didn't own a gun and had only ever fired one out on a range with paper targets, he rejected that idea and returned to his writing.

The cabin door opened, and Laromee waddled through, his short, squat stature emphasized by the tall willowiness of the silky blond woman by his side. He glared at Hunter through pale gray eyes filled with venom. "We meet again, Mr. McQuade."

"So it seems," said Hunter. He took another look around, judging his chances of escape. "Why don't you give it up, Laromee? You'll never get away with it."

Laromee grinned a vile, evil grin. "Who is going to stop me? I've captured the famous Hunter McQuade. If he can't stop me, who can?" He turned to the woman. "Bridgett, I don't believe you've met Mr. McQuade."

"I haven't," the blonde breathed. Her tone was cool but the expression in her violet eyes wasn't. Hunter watched her gaze travel over his features, then down his torso. There was a way out of this. All he had to do was convince Bridgett to give him a hand.

There was the sound of running water, the grunt of the coffeemaker, and finally, the smell of brew coffee wafting around him. Chase sighed and gave up. Unless burglars took coffee breaks, his mystery guest wasn't a thief.

"Don't worry, pal," he assured Hunter. "You'll get out of this. The lovely Bridgett has already fallen for you. She'll give you a helping hand, you'll save the world, and in between have a couple of pages of hot and heavy sex." It might be a trite plot, but along with a little danger and excitement, it should work. He clicked the save button on the computer, stopped by his bedroom to grab a T-shirt and trundled down the hall toward the kitchen.

The kitchen was a long narrow room, with the working area at one end and a wooden, picnic-style table at the other. Standing in the middle of the kitchen, in the process of pouring coffee out of the still-brewing pot, was a short, balding man wearing a dark business suit over a crisp, white shirt. His deductive skills were right on the mark, Chase decided. It was Jerome.

He rubbed his eyes and thought longingly of his burglar. Maybe a cat burglar all in black, an agent, sent to destroy the hero. He made a mental note to add a character like that in his next book. "Good morning, Jerome."

His agent gave him a disgusted look over the coffeepot. "It's almost noon. Don't tell me you're just getting up?"

"Not exactly." Chase shrugged the T-shirt over his boxer shorts, ambled across the kitchen and dropped onto the wooden bench beside the table. "I've been up since yesterday." He peered at the clock on the stove. "And it's not almost noon. It's only ten-thirty!"

Jerome brushed that aside. "In some parts of the country, it's well past noon." He poured out another coffee and plunked it down in front of Chase. "Here. You look like you could use this."

Chase scowled at the pitch-black liquid. "No, thanks. I only have that coffeemaker because you gave it to me. It's not something I use myself. I don't drink coffee at any time of the day. You shouldn't, either. All that caffeine—"

"Is exactly what you need to get you going."

It wasn't worth arguing about. Chase took a sip and shuddered. "That will certainly get you going, all right." He yawned, stretched and gave the back of his neck a rub. "Speaking of going, what brings you here? Shouldn't you be out hawking my books or something?"

Jerome raised an aristocratic eyebrow. "I'm your agent, Chase, not a street vendor. I don't hawk your books. I arrange for other people to hawk your books." He sat down. "Were you really up all night writing? Or were you doing something a little more interesting with Arla?" He peered down the hall. "She's not still here, is she?"

Chase was still recovering from the jolt of caffeine. "Who? Oh Arla? No, she's gone."

"Gone as in left, or gone as in...gone?"

"Gone as in gone," Chase admitted. "Finito. Finished. Done. I'm not seeing her anymore."

"You aren't?" Jerome blinked. "Why not? I thought you liked her."

"She was all right." He hadn't been crazy about her but he had liked her.

"Then what happened?"

"I don't know." He carried his mug over to the sink and dumped the contents down the drain. Any more caffeine and he'd be climbing the walls. "She just said she thought we'd be happier dating other people."

"Oh." Jerome watched him closely. "You don't seem too upset about it."

Chase considered it, then shook his head. "I'm not." Arla had been right. He knew he'd be happier dating other people, so he was sure she would be too.

"Well, you should be," said Jerome. "You crash and burn more times than the cars in your books."

"I do not!"

"You do so. You've been through more women than my ex-wives have through personal trainers." He settled back and creased his forehead, drawing his eyebrows into an upside-down vee. "This is not good for your image. You're supposed to be Mr. Macho Man, not the man every woman in Chicago has dumped." He tapped his fingers against the coffee cup. "You're a famous writer. You should be fighting women off. Instead, they're running away."

"They are *not* running away." Chase filled the kettle with water and plugged it in. Tea. That's what he needed. A nice soothing cup of tea and no more Jerome. "They're just…moving on with their lives…or something."

"They're certainly not staying around." Jerome looked around the room. "Not that I blame them."

Chase scowled at him. "What's that supposed to mean?"

Jerome took a long swallow of coffee. "Well, I don't want to hurt your feelings, but you aren't exactly Mr. Excitement. You spend half your life alone in the back room, writing."

This made sense? "I'm a writer! I have to spend some time writing. Otherwise, my publisher, my editor and you start getting on my case."

Jerome ignored that. "And when you aren't doing that, you're promoting your books, researching your books or playing with your nephews."

Chase leaned back against the cupboard and folded his arms. "I promote my books because you tell me to."

"No you don't. You love those book signings. You consider them a good opportunity to meet women."

Chase winced. "They are, but you still tell me I should do it. I research them because I need information—"

"And because you like librarians."

"Some of them are my biggest fans," he said, narrowing his eyes. "As for my nephews, there's nothing wrong with them."

"No, there isn't," Jerome agreed. "They're great kids if you like kids. They just don't belong on a date. Women want to be taken out places, to do things. Haven't you heard that three or more is a crowd?"

"I do things," Chase objected, stung.

"Not the right sort of things." Jerome took a contemplative sip from his mug. "For example, what did you do on your last date with Arla?"

"Broke up," Chase remembered. "It was a pretty short date. I picked her up, she gave her little 'you're a great guy but I think we'd be happier dating other people' speech, and that was pretty much that. I came home and polished off a couple of chapters."

Jerome sighed. "I didn't mean that date, Chase. I meant the date before that."

Chase put his head on a hand and thought about it. "We went for a drive. I wanted to scout out a place for Hunter to hide in the forest. Then we came here. We ordered pizza—the vegetarian low-fat one from that new place that just opened up. Helen's Healthy Takeout, I think it's called. You should try it, Jer. It's—"

"I'm not interested in the pizza," said Jerome. "I want to know what you did with Arla."

"Okay, okay. We ate pizza, then Molly's kids came over—"

"And you spent the rest of the evening choreographing a scene from your book?" Jerome guessed.

"Yes. But that couldn't be called boring. It's a thrilling scene, at least it would be if I could get it right. I'm going to have to get rid of one of the villains. Otherwise, the hero is never going to make it."

"Forget the scene and talk about Arla." Jerome eyed him suspiciously. "You didn't ask her to be one of your characters, did you?"

"Of course not," Chase said with mild disgust. "And I didn't ask her to be the helicopter, either. I only ask *you* to do that." He certainly wouldn't have asked Arla. The thought of her, with her perfect hair and perfect makeup, racing around the room, her arms outstretched, going *whopa-whopa-whopa* made him chuckle.

"That's not a date! You're supposed to take her out to dinner, go to a movie, or a play or concert. Women these days want sophistication, not to chomp hot dogs at a sports event, spend the rest of the evening watching you play cops and robbers, followed by a few hours in the bedroom."

Chase winced again. Apart from the fact that he never ate hot dogs, that did cover the way he spent most of his dates. But what did Jerome know about it anyway? He'd inherited a truckload of money, spent his life in elegant society, and, as far as Chase could tell, did the agent gig only because he wanted to, not because he had to. Jerome's idea of a good date was bound to be different than Chase's.

Then there were all his agent's ex-wives to consider. "What makes you an expert on women?" he demanded. "You've been divorced what…two times? Or is it three?"

"Three," said Jerome. "I'm not doing it again either. Vanna is definitely the one. Besides, at least I've made it to the altar. At the rate you're going, the only way you'll get there is if you pop the question on the first date."

Now that was a disquieting thought. Not that Chase was in a hurry to get married—the single life of a modestly rich, moderately famous bachelor had a lot of perks—but he didn't like the idea that he didn't even have the option of doing it. Perhaps he didn't. Jerome was right. He didn't have a good track record.

That wasn't his fault, though. He hadn't been looking for a wife, so naturally he didn't meet women who were wife material. Still, he had met—and dated—a number of women. Could all of them be wrong, or was it him?

He shoved that aside. Marriage was a long way off, a hazy something that would happen in the future. "If I don't get married this morning, my world won't come crashing to an end. And I'm sure you didn't come by here to discuss my failure rate with women."

"No, I didn't," said Jerome. "I wanted to talk to you about *Danger at Dawn*. When Hunter breaks into the electric plant, how does he know the villain has already armed the missile?"

Chase breathed a relieved sigh and settled back to discuss something he actually knew a little bit about.

STELLA BRISWORTH didn't share Tara's lack of enthusiasm for her latest assignment.

She stopped by that evening to give Tara a hand getting settled in her new apartment. While they sat on the shiny hardwood floor in Tara's living room, with boxes scattered around them, eating sandwiches, rearranging furniture and unpacking, Tara filled her in on the details of her assignment.

"It doesn't sound that bad," Stella consoled when Tara had finished. "At least you'll get to meet some interesting men. I never get to do that. The only men I meet want me to do their taxes."

"That's because you're an accountant." Tara started arranging the books in her wicker bookcase, then paused to survey the room. "Do you think this bookcase looks all right over here? Or do you think it would be better against the other wall?"

Stella shoved a hand through her short, fuzzy-blond hair, and pursed her lips consideringly. "Neither," she finally decided. "It will look awful in both places." She grabbed a handful of books and tossed them back into the box. "There's only one thing to do. Pack everything up and move back to your old apartment. The bookcase looked much better there."

"Stella!"

"Well, it did." Stella folded her blue-jeaned legs in front of her and clasped her hands around them. "I don't know why you moved. Your other place was closer to downtown, a little bigger and a lot cheaper." She gestured toward the ceiling. "Plus, the plaster there stayed on the ceiling where it belongs."

Tara smiled. "There's nothing wrong with the plaster, Stell."

"There's going to be," Stella warned. "My dad was in construction. I know these things. And I'm telling you that one day you're going to walk into this room to discover that your ceiling is now your floor. Besides, there isn't even an elevator."

"It's only two flights up. Exercise is good for you."

"Exercise is fine when you're supposed to be exercising. When you're carrying up groceries, it won't feel fine at all.'' Stella's hazel eyes darkened to mournful. ''But the best thing about your old apartment was that it was right across the hall from me. I'm really going to miss you, not to mention all that free baby-sitting.''

Tara listened to the sounds of Stella's six-year-old son playing in the bedroom and felt a pang of unease. ''I'm going to miss you, too.'' She thought about popping into Stella's for coffee, late-night gab sessions, playing cards with Matthew... Maybe moving hadn't been a good idea.

She took another look around the room, taking in the wide, old-fashioned wooden door frames, the interesting angles of the room and the high ceilings. No, moving had been the right thing to do. ''I had to move, Stella. This place is everything I pictured myself living in. It's taste-ful...elegant...old-fashioned.''

''It certainly is that,'' Stella agreed. ''Not to mention on the other side of town.''

''Don't worry.'' Tara reached over to pat Stella's knee. ''We'll still see each other, and I can take care of Matthew anytime you like.'' She mentally rearranged the room, decided the bookshelf was fine where it was and returned to filling it. ''I just hope I'm going to be able to afford this place.''

Stella handed over another stack of books. ''Why shouldn't you be able to afford it? You get lots of assignments.''

''I do all right, I suppose.'' She hadn't had much difficulty breaking into the freelance scene. Oh, there had been a tense time when she'd first started, but after she'd sold a few articles the work had been pretty steady. ''As long as all I want to write is fluff.''

''You don't just write fluff!''

Tara snorted. ''What do you call 'Clothes That Make You Feel Bold'...'Bedrooms That Say *Now*' and 'Food That Puts Him in the Mood'? Investigative journalism?''

"Well, no," said Stella. "I call it paying the rent. Besides, I liked 'Bedrooms That Say *Now*.' It gave me forewarning. Every time I see one, I run."

As far as Tara could tell, Stella ran no matter what the bedroom had to say. She was cute and perky and funny and she could have dated if she wanted to. Her ex-husband seemed to have turned her off men, because she seldom went out with anyone, and, apart from one salesman at work, showed little interest in doing so. "Scaring you off wasn't the point of the article."

"It sure helped me. And this one doesn't sound too bad. I mean, it's not like you have to think up fifty things you need to know about a real man. You just have to update the list."

"I suppose." Tara flopped back against the sofa. "I'm just not sure the list needs updating."

Stella gaped at her. "Excuse me?"

"I'm not," Tara confessed. "I've been thinking about this ever since I spoke with Charlene. She said I dated lots of men and she's right. I have. I've dated tons of today's men, and I wasn't impressed with any of them in an overall, real-man kind of way."

"Oh, come on." Stella drew her eyebrows together. "You've dated some great guys!"

Tara couldn't remember any. "Like who?"

"Like Derek for one. He was a real cutey. All that curly blond hair...great biceps—"

"He did have good biceps," Tara agreed. "But he should have, because he devoted his entire life to them. Sometimes he even talked to them... 'Don't worry, fellas. Tomorrow I'll take you both to the gym.'"

Stella giggled. "Come to think of it, he did introduce me to them."

"He introduced them to everyone. 'I'm Derek, and these

are my biceps.' It finally occurred to me that he was more involved with his muscles than he was with me."

"Maybe Derek wasn't a good example," Stella conceded. "Let's see. Who else was there?" She drummed her fingers on the floor. "How about Owen? He was darn good-looking, and he didn't spend his life in a gym."

"True enough." Tara pictured the dark-haired, well-dressed Owen. "He spent his time in therapy."

"There's nothing wrong with therapy. Lots of people—"

"Owen was obsessive about it," Tara remembered. "He was the only person I ever met who had more therapists than relatives. He didn't even know what problem he was trying to solve. He had a therapist to help him find a problem so he could go to another one to have it fixed. When he wasn't analyzing himself, he was busy analyzing me. He finally decided he was too insecure to make a commitment, which was fine with me. After three dates with him, I had more problems than he did!"

Stella nodded. "He was a little compulsive in that regard. It's too bad, though. He was such a cutey but not as dreamy as Angus. Now there was a hunk for you. All that white-blond hair and the unshaven look. He reminded me of Brad Pitt."

Angus had reminded Tara of Brad, too, which is why she'd gone out with him. "He was more like Brad would be if he didn't get a haircut and didn't have a job. He couldn't do any of those things, because he found them all too stressful."

"You had fun with Angus, though."

"Sure he was fun, but that's all he was. I couldn't see myself married to him. As a matter of fact, that was the problem with all of them. They were nice enough, but I couldn't see myself spending the rest of my life with any one of them." She stared pensively across her new living room. "That's because they were too…modern. Too…with it."

Stella crinkled her nose. "You want a man who's without it?"

Tara considered it, then nodded. "Yes. Let's face it, Stella. I've dated lots of men but I don't go out with them for good reasons. I go out with them for dumb reasons—they're good-looking, or have great biceps or just looking at them makes me tingle." They probably still could make her tingle, but she'd come to the conclusion that wasn't enough. "It wasn't because I thought they were good choices for a life partner."

Stella's blond curls bobbed with her nod. "I know what you mean there. I first went out with Bill because of his wide shoulders, and I think I married him for the same reason. As a matter of fact, the only reason our marriage lasted as long as it did was because I kept focusing on them. 'Sure he's a jerk,' I'd tell myself. 'But he's got such terrific shoulders.'" She shuddered delicately. "Take a hint from me. Shoulders are not good reason to marry anyone."

"That's exactly what I mean!" Tara exclaimed. "I go out with all these men because I'm attracted to them. That's not a good reason. From now on, I'm only going to go out with men who have husband potential." She slouched back against the couch, closed her eyes and imagined her Mr. Right. "I know just what I want too. I want one of the old-fashioned kind—strong, confident and well-dressed and polite…a man who'd give you his seat on the bus instead of making it into a footrace. Men like Cary Grant and Gregory Peck…or my father." She popped open her eyes to check Stella's reaction. "My father was perfect. Do you know that every morning he used to bring my mother a cup of tea in bed? I can't imagine any man I've met doing that."

"Neither can I," Stella said darkly. "I can't imagine any man I've met getting up before I do."

"My dad always did. He wanted to take care of my mother. Men today don't do that. They want you take care of them—and be grateful you have the opportunity to do it. And they spend all this time thinking about how they feel!"

"That's sort of our fault," Stella demurred. "We wanted men to get in touch with their feelings."

"They certainly did that. Now that they've got in touch with them, they keep having them! They're so concerned with how they feel, they don't bother worrying about how *you* feel. They want women to do everything, while they focus on the things they want—their career, their exercise program, their cholesterol count." She pushed a book into place on the crowded shelves. "They don't need a woman to have a relationship with because they're too busy having one with themselves."

"That's for sure," Stella muttered. "With men today, you're lucky if you get your child support payments on time."

Tara stopped thinking about her problems. "Not again?"

"Uh-huh. Bill quit his job." Stella looked more resigned than annoyed. "He decided that installing cable television wasn't fulfilling his needs. Here's a hint for you. Real men are not interested in finding themselves. Bill's been looking for himself for years. Unfortunately, he has yet to stumble across himself."

"Is that why you two split up?" Tara asked.

Stella nodded. "That and the fact that he kept looking for himself in the bedrooms of sexy blond women named Boopie." She snapped her fingers. "There's another one for you. Real men are monogamous. Hey, this isn't so hard!"

"It wouldn't be so hard if I was the one who got to think these up," Tara agreed. "I bet I could come up with a list in half an hour. Unfortunately, that's not the way Charlene wants it done. I've got to interview a bunch of men and figure them out.''

''That does make it harder.'' Stella finished emptying a box, pushed it aside and opened another one. ''You could always talk to Gerald. He looks a little like Cary.'' Her eyes narrowed. ''Unfortunately, he has a bad habit of bumping off people.''

''Gerald?'' Tara put a copy of *Romeo and Juliet* into the bookshelf. ''You don't mean that fellow who took over Wutherspoon Outerwear, do you?''

''Uh-huh.''

''I thought so.'' Stella had been fixated on poor Gerald ever since he'd inherited Wutherspoon Outerwear, where Stella worked as an accountant. ''Mr. Wutherspoon died because he had an allergic reaction, Stell.''

Stella drew her face into a too-familiar, suspicious expression. ''That's what they said, but I think it's pretty weird. I admit Franklin was allergic to fish, but he knew he was! He was very, very careful about what he ate.''

Tara stifled a sigh. They'd been over this a number of times since Franklin Wutherspoon's demise.

''And it happened right in the middle of our annual employee thank-you dinner!'' Stella had taken that as a personal affront. ''One minute he was just fine, and the next thing we knew, they were calling an ambulance. They said later that they thought he'd eaten shrimp in one of the appetizers, but I can't see him doing that.''

Tara had heard this before as well. ''Maybe he didn't know there was fish in it.''

''I suppose—although I wouldn't be one bit surprised if Gerald had something to do with it. After all he did inherit the company.'' She sighed a long, sad sigh, her gray eyes filled with regret. ''I wish Franklin had left it to someone else. Franklin was such a sweetheart. A real pleasure to work for. Now his nephew Gerald has taken over and he's making all these changes. We're even coming out with a line of leather underwear. Can you imagine? Mr. Wutherspoon must be rolling over in his grave.''

"Maybe they'll sell well," Tara offered, although she found it hard to imagine.

"Maybe." Stella sounded doubtful. "What do I know about it? I'm only the accountant. And I suppose Gerald isn't so bad. He's just not Mr. Wutherspoon." She looked pensive for a moment, then changed the subject. "You know who you really should talk to? Stanley Gruber. He's the salesman who started a few months ago. I think I've mentioned him a couple of times."

"It's more like a thousand times," Tara teased. That wasn't strictly true. Stella had mentioned Stanley a few times, but for Stella, that was a lot. The good news was, it sounded as if Stanley was just as interested.

Stella grabbed a pillow and smacked her with it. "It is not. Besides, Stanley is a great guy. He's charming and polite, and he's got a great sense of humor. He's not looking for himself, either. He knows exactly where he wants to go. He's just a salesman now, but in a few years, he'll be vice president of marketing. I can feel it in my bones."

"He certainly sounds a lot better than the men I have to interview," Tara grumbled. "A computer whiz, a gallery owner...the weatherman on Channel Three—"

Stella looked horrified. "You don't mean that guy who dresses up to do the weather?"

"I'm afraid so."

"You've got to be kidding. Last night he had on flannel jammies to illustrate that it would be a cold night. My idea of a real man is not one who wears flannel pajamas on television."

"He's the best of the bunch, Stell."

"I don't believe it," said Stella, shaking her head. "They can't all be that bad."

"I'll show you." Tara pushed herself up, dusted off her jeans and wandered into the kitchen to get her list of real men. She returned with two cans of soda, and handed one over to her friend, along with the list. "Take a look."

Stella took it from her and thumbed through it. "An engineer, a Greek philosopher and Howard Stern? You're right. These do sound pretty grim." She flipped another page. "There is a private detective in here. He might be interesting. Oh, and here's another good one. Hunter McQuade."

Tara paused in the midst of drinking her soft drink. "Don't tell me you actually *know* someone on that list?"

"I don't know him, but I know who he is. So do you."

Tara searched her memory banks and came up empty. "No, I don't."

Stella gave her a disgusted look. "You know who Hunter McQuade is! He's the hero in *Action at Sundown*. The book by Chase Montgomery. You must have read it. It was on the bestseller list for ages."

It was Tara's turn to look disgusted. "You have got to be kidding. Today's women think a real man is a guy a writer made up?"

Stella shrugged. "Maybe it's the closest they can get to one. Besides, I kind of agree with them. Hunter is magnificent. I'm sure you've read the book, Tara. As a matter of fact, I think I lent you my copy." She pawed through the books remaining in the box and pulled one out. "Here it is."

Tara peered at the plain black cover with Action at Sundown written in brilliant yellow and blood-red letters, and the author's name below. "Isn't that the one where the main character has to chase down one of those crazy 'take over the world' types, defeat an entire army of thugs and rescue a number of women from certain demise."

"That's the one," Stella confirmed.

Tara's contempt deepened. "The guy in that book was not my idea of a hero. All he did was race around blowing things up."

Stella wiggled her eyebrows. "That's not all he did."

"No, it isn't. Every time a woman came into the room, he took a time-out for a few obligatory sex scenes." Tara scowled. "That's not my idea of a real man."

"I don't know," Stella said thoughtfully. "After all, they were great sex scenes."

"They were imaginary sex scenes," Tara said, exasperated. "There's an entire army about to attack him so he jumps the nearest woman? What kind of a man is that?"

"Horny?" Stella turned the book over and gazed at the author's picture on the back with an expression approaching rapture. "Besides, if this guy was standing beside me when the world was about to end, I wouldn't mind if he jumped me. He's almost as good-looking as Stanley."

"Let me see that." Tara took the book from her and checked out the color photograph. Stella was right. Whatever faults Chase Montgomery had, one couldn't fault his looks. The man had short black hair cut in a sophisticated style, deep-set dark eyes that sparkled behind a pair of wire-rim glasses and a blunt-shaped nose reminiscent of Bruce Willis. His lips were curled into a knowing grin even more reminiscent of Bruce. "See what I mean," said Stella. "Isn't he a honey?"

"He does look interesting." Tara set down the book. "But he probably doesn't look anything like that in person. Even if he does, that doesn't mean either he or his heroes are real men."

"He still sounds a lot more interesting than a computer guru or a gallery owner," said Stella. "If I were you, I'd check him out."

2

Real men are punctual! Set your watches, girls. Your real man is a stickler for punctuality. When he says two o'clock, he means two o'clock—on the nose. Waiting for you can make him cranky. When he wants to see you, he wants to see you. This isn't a hardship though. You'll want to see a man like this too.

—from "Forty-Nine Things You Need
to Know about a Real Man,"
Real Men magazine, April 1949

EITHER CHASE MONTGOMERY didn't want to see her, or he wouldn't make the 1949 list of real men.

Tara checked the restaurant door for the tenth time, then settled back into her chair and frowned at her watch. The man was over half an hour late. Clearly, punctuality wasn't a quality of today's real men.

Not that she was expecting a whole lot from Chase Montgomery, but he was the most promising of the bunch. Besides, she'd spent the evening reading one of his books, and she had to admit that Stella was right. His heroes were pretty standard, but the sex scenes were outstanding. Besides, there was that photograph. Maybe he was a good example of today's real man.

She just wished he could tell time.

She swiveled to check the door again. An elderly couple entered, followed by a confused-looking man in his early thirties, casually and inappropriately dressed in a dark jacket, a purple T-shirt with a sports motif on it and blue jeans. Tara focused on the couple as the maître d' led them across the room, noting with a pang of envy the solicitous way the gentleman pulled out his companion's chair and ensured she was comfortable before taking his own seat. Now, *there* was a real man. Too bad he was in his seventies.

She turned again to check out Mr. Purple Shirt, who was now engaged in a conversation with the maître d'. He was a perfect example of what was wrong with men these days. He wasn't unattractive, if you liked the nerdy type, but those jeans could use a wash, and that shirt belonged in a garage sale, not a quality restaurant. She smiled as she watched the maître d' shaking his head. Apparently he agreed with her. He looked like a polite, well-dressed man. Maybe that's who she should be interviewing instead of this Chase Montgomery character.

Unfortunately, Charlene was unlikely to react positively to "Real Men Are Waiters."

She frowned as the maître d' turned and led the man into the room. So much for that theory. She had thought of another title though. "Real Men Don't Back Down." No, that was no good. If she wasn't careful, this article would turn into a men-bashing exercise, which wasn't what Charlene had in mind, either.

She turned back to her table, picked up her water glass, then set it down again. Mr. Purple Shirt had looked vaguely familiar. Surely he wasn't…

She checked. Sure enough, the maître d' was guiding him across the room, straight toward Tara's table, his lean, elegant face creased into a frown. They came to a full stop beside her table. "Ms. Butler?" he asked in a tone that could have frozen the equator.

Tara mentally cringed. "Yes?"

"The party you were waiting for has arrived." He gave said party a look of disdain and departed, his entire being emanating disapproval.

The man he'd left behind blinked after him, then slid into the seat across from her. "Hi," he said. "I'm Chase Montgomery."

No he wasn't. Where was the suit, the sophisticated haircut, the clean-shaven chin? He did have the same black hair, the same deep-set dark eyes, although the glasses were missing, the same blunt nose. "Tara Butler," said Tara. She extended her hand across the table.

His fingers closed around hers and her pulse gave an extra little beat. Tara pulled her hand away. Okay, he had a little charisma. That didn't make him man of the century. "I apologize for not recognizing you," she said, recovering. "You, uh, don't look much like your photograph."

"People are always telling me that." He reclined back in his seat. "I think it's the glasses. Either that or the fact that they spent hours getting me to look that way."

It was probably more like days and they'd had to buy him a new wardrobe. Tara tried not to stare at him as he refused the offer of a drink from the waiter. "Herbal tea if you have it," he said. "Otherwise, I'll just have water— bottled water."

Oh Lord, he was one of the "bottled water and herbal tea" types. Tara's heart sank another notch. Give him a chance, she encouraged herself. So he was a little weird about what he drank. That didn't make him a total write-off.

He focused on her now. "So what's this all about, Ms....uh...Butler?"

"Tara," Tara supplied. "And didn't your agent explain? I spoke with him a couple of days ago, and I believe the magazine—"

Chase waved that away with a gesture. "He didn't tell

me much more than that it's for *Real Men* magazine. What is that anyway? Something to do with hunting or fishing?''

"Well, no," said Tara. "It's a woman's magazine."

"Oh, one of those." Chase sprawled back, one arm spread across the top of the bench seat. "Let's see. Blue, salad with low-fat dressing and women just like you." Tara blinked and he chuckled. "That's what you wanted to ask me, isn't it? My favorite color, what I like to eat and what kinds of women I find attractive?"

Tara took one look at his complacent smile and shuddered. She knew his type. Smug. Arrogant. The kind who was never alone because he had his ego to keep him company. Talk about someone having a relationship with themselves. This guy was a master!

She cleared her throat. "Not exactly, no."

"No?" He grinned across the table at her. "That's great!" He lowered his voice. "To be perfectly honest, I don't have a favorite color. I just name whatever color comes into my head. So far I think I've said red, green, blue, navy and indigo. I don't even know what color indigo is."

His dark eyes sparkling mischief and the sincerity of his smile had Tara practically melting in her chair. Perhaps she'd been wrong about him. First impressions and all that. After all, he was good-looking even if he was poorly dressed, and she could understand not having a favorite color because she didn't have one herself and...

And what was she doing? Tara straightened her spine and forced herself to look away. She'd had reactions like this before. It meant chemistry, not manliness. From now on she was using her head, not her hormones. She wasn't going to fall for a guy with a great smile and a pair of bedroom eyes. She was going to hold out for Mr. Perfect, and there was little chance that Chase Montgomery was that.

She flipped open her bag and pulled out the "Real Man" folder. "Indigo is a shade of blue. But that has nothing to do with the reason I wanted to speak with you. You see, *Real Men* magazine is doing an article…"

"So I'm working on updating the list," Tara concluded.

"I see." Chase tore off a piece of the whole-wheat bun the waiter had brought him, and admired the woman sitting across the table. Interviews were a part of the writing business. According to Jerome, they "had a major impact on the marketplace," but Chase seldom enjoyed them. The interviewer was usually a tough no-nonsense type who asked the same questions: where he got his ideas, how he got started in the business, why he wrote what he wrote. This one was pleasantly different.

So was Tara. He settled back and watched her eat. He had been telling the truth when he'd told her that he was attracted to women like her. She didn't have the starving-waif look that was so popular with women these days. She had curves, and plenty of them, a healthy, girl-next-door face and sparkling green eyes that suggested a great sense of humor. Her dark red hair was swept back from her face and there were freckles on her nose. She looked like the type who *would* make a good helicopter. "So what you're doing is updating this list?"

"That's right." She nodded and her hair bobbed with the motion. "The magazine did a survey and came up with a list of men for me to talk to."

"I was on the list, was I?" Chase sat back and congratulated himself. So much for Jerome's theory that there was something wrong with him. Arla might have thought so, and Jerome might think so, but apparently other women didn't think so. Now he was really glad he'd agreed to do this interview. Ms. Butler wasn't wearing any rings. She had those great curves. His gaze wandered down her smooth throat, pausing at the patch of skin visible behind the top open button.

"Well, no," said Tara. "Hunter was on the list."

Chase's gaze snapped back to her face. "Who?"

"Hunter McQuade. The hero in *Action at Sundown.*"

Chase's elation faded. "You mean you're interviewing me because *Hunter* is on the list of real men?"

"That's right."

Chase set the bun onto the plate and leaned forward. "Hunter McQuade is hardly a good example of a real man. For one thing, he's not real! I made him up."

"I realize that," Tara said serenely. "The women in the survey were asked to identify a good example of a real man. It didn't say they couldn't be fictional."

"That's just great." His name wasn't on the list but the name of one of his fictional characters was. Chase didn't know if he should feel insulted or complimented.

Tara smiled brightly. "So I need to ask you a few questions about him."

"Yeah?" To hell with it. He felt insulted. "What do you want to know about him, Ms. Butler?"

"Tara, please. I just need to ask you a few questions about him. Nothing too difficult." She whipped a folder out of her bag and consulted the contents. Chase took a long swallow of water, struggling to compose himself. It wasn't that bad. At least his hero had made the list...and he was the one who'd invented him. In some ways he did identify with his character. Besides, although he'd done his share of publicity, women couldn't really feel they knew him the way they knew Hunter.

Tara tucked a few loose strands of red hair behind her ear and looked up. "Why don't we start with manners?"

"Manners?" Chase echoed.

"Uh-huh. How does Hunter feel about them? Would you say politeness is important to him?"

"Politeness?" Chase was lost. "What does politeness have to do with anything? My hero saves the world. He's too busy doing that to worry about being polite."

"I see." She pursed her lips. "So he doesn't consider manners important?"

"He doesn't consider them unimportant," Chase growled. "He just doesn't consider them."

"I see." She wrote busily into her notebook. "What about you? Is politeness something you care about?"

Was this a trick question? Chase started to sweat. "I don't like to be rude, if that's what you mean but, uh, I wouldn't call myself a master of etiquette."

"Ah." She ran a finger down a typed page in front of her. "How about fashion? Would you classify Hunter as well-dressed?"

"Not really, no." He saw her start to write that down. "But I wouldn't say he's poorly dressed. Most of the time he has to wear camouflage. Or black if it's after dark." He considered it. "I suppose I'd have to say that he's appropriately dressed."

"Hmm." She tapped the pen against the folder. "That's not exactly what I'm after. I need to know if fashion is a priority for him."

"It isn't," said Chase. "Saving the world is a priority for him. What he's wearing while he's doing it isn't a priority."

Ms. Butler appeared unimpressed by the serious nature of his creation's missions. "So if Hunter was in a situation requiring a suit and tie, he'd wear a suit and tie?"

Chase couldn't envisage his hero in a situation requiring formal attire. "I don't know. I suppose if he had to, he would."

"Oh," said Tara. She wrote down something while Chase tried to read her list upside down. He should have brought along his glasses. He didn't take them anywhere because he only used them for reading...and he hadn't expected to have to read during an interview.

"Let's move on to punctuality," Tara suggested. "What can you tell me about that?"

Great. He'd finally found something on this list Hunter was good at. "Punctuality is a big thing with him. He's always arriving just before the bomb goes off...although Hunter did cut it a little close one time, and I think—"

Tara's smile could only be classified as condescending. "That's not the kind of punctuality I had in mind. I'm more interested in date-type situations. Would he be on time for a date?"

A date? Did his hero ever have dates? Chase struggled to remember. "I'm sure he would be—unless there were mitigating circumstances."

"What sort of mitigating circumstances would that be?"

"You know." Chase gestured with a hand. "Being tied up, or locked up, or stranded in the desert. If any of those things happened, he could be late. Days late."

"Hmm." The disapproving look returned to her eyes in full force. "How would he feel about that? Would he be upset or concerned or—"

"He'd be more concerned about losing his life," Chase retorted, irritated. "Besides, my hero doesn't have a lot of dates, so it doesn't make much difference."

Tara blinked. "He doesn't consider establishing a meaningful relationship important?"

Chase was getting really tired of this interview. "Hunter has relationships!"

Her hair bounced around her shoulders as she shook her head. "Not in your books he doesn't. He starts a lot of relationships, but that's as far as he goes. He doesn't seem to be concerned about anything except his next adventure."

"Of course he doesn't!" Chase snarled. "They're action-adventure books, not romance novels. Although my hero is a good lover." He grinned across the table at her, oozing charm. "At least I try to write him that way."

Tara didn't look impressed. "Do you?" she said. "Well, he certainly does it enough. It seems every time a woman enters the room, your hero wants to jump her."

She made that sound like a bad thing. Chase scowled at her. "It's fiction, Ms. Butler."

"It certainly is," said Tara. "I mean, a man who doesn't care about punctuality, manners, relationships or proper attire would hardly make it in the real world, would he?" She returned to her list. "Let's move on to literature. Tell me, what sort of books does your hero like to read?"

Hunter took another look at the ocean. His plans hadn't included a burial at sea and he didn't have time for it right now—especially if the body being buried was his own.

Besides, the salt water wouldn't do one thing for the lacerations on his face.

He jerked his arms, trying, unsuccessfully, to free his wrists from the miles of duct tape Laromee's men had used. "Look, Bridgett, I have to stop him. I need your help to do it."

The blonde leaned closer, her tangy perfume touching his nostrils. "I might help you, Hunter," she breathed into his ear. "But first, I have to ask you something."

Hunter grinned. "Go ahead, honey."

"What sort of books do you like to read?"

CHASE SLAMMED his hands down onto the keyboard. "What sort of books do you like to read? What kind of question is that?"

He sat in his office later that day and pounded the computer keys to erase the question. That was not the way his stories went. The women took one look at the hero and did whatever he wanted. Besides, right now, the hero was in the middle of the ocean. He was surrounded by thugs and sharks. It was no time to worry about being polite, what he was wearing or what he was going to read.

On the other hand, if he was going to read, what *would* he read? Stephen King, maybe…or perhaps something along the lines of Tom Clancy. Chase didn't know. But he did know it would *not* be the next issue of *Real Men* magazine.

"Oh, hell," he muttered. He shoved back his chair and stomped into the kitchen to pour himself a glass of juice. That dumb interview had really gotten to him. He didn't know what bugged him more—the fact that he hadn't made the real man list, or the fact that he didn't think Hunter was going to, either.

He leaned against the fridge to drink his juice while he considered the question. He was probably more offended on his hero's behalf than his own, although he wasn't positive there was much of a difference. Hunter was based on his idea of a real man—and that idea was based on himself. Granted, he didn't run around saving the world—few people did stuff like that these days—but he did share a number of Hunter's qualities. He considered him a good example of what a man should be.

It was not an opinion Ms. Butler had shared. Chase frowned at the swirls in his orange juice. Tara sure hadn't been impressed with him, and that bothered him. He wasn't cocky enough to expect every woman in the world to fall at his feet, but when he felt a spark and she felt a spark…well, something usually happened. In this case it hadn't. If that look of disapproval in her green eyes was any indication, it wasn't going to happen, either. Nice eyes. And nice curves. He spent a few minutes mentally reviewing the way she'd looked, soft and warm and utterly feminine. The next woman he wrote about was going to look like her.

She was also going to rip off the hero's clothes the second she got a chance.

He was contemplating that image when someone rang the doorbell. Chase sighed and trudged down the hall to answer it, his mood not improved by the sight of Jerome on the other side, a sophisticated and urbane figure dressed in a dark suit and crisp white shirt. For some reason, his appearance annoyed Chase. "When I need to write about men's wardrobes, I'll have to use you," he grumbled as he opened the door.

"Go right ahead," Jerome said grandly. He followed Chase down the hall, into the kitchen. "But I can't imagine why your hero would go around in suits and ties. He probably doesn't even own one."

"He might," said Chase.

Jerome opened the fridge and pulled out a soft drink. "Is it my imagination, or are you in a bad mood?"

"Of course I'm in a bad mood," said Chase. "My hero is on a yacht in the middle of the ocean, surrounded by bad guys and sharks. The only way out is to get the girl to help him and she isn't going to if he doesn't read the right books!"

"*There's* an interesting plot twist." Jerome took a glass out of the cupboard. "What happens next?"

Chase threw up his hands. "It's obvious, Jer. He comes up with the wrong answer, gets thrown overboard, eaten by sharks, and the world, as we know it, comes crashing to an end."

Jerome poured his drink into the glass, apparently not too upset about the imminent end of both the hero and the world. "That's why you're in a bad mood?"

"Yes, that's why I'm in a bad mood," Chase said sarcastically. "You'd be in a bad mood too if your hero was just eaten by sharks. It makes for a very dull book.'' He led the way into the living room and threw himself into a chair. ''Then again, what do I know. Maybe *real* men like to get eaten by sharks.''

''I wouldn't think so,'' said Jerome. ''I know I never do.'' He sat down, drink in hand. ''How did the interview go with that magazine?''

''Not great.'' Chase rolled his hands around his glass of juice. ''As a matter of fact, I think I failed.''

''It was an interview, Chase, not a test.'' Jerome cleared his throat. ''What exactly do you mean by 'you failed'?''

''I didn't pass the 'real men' test.'' Chase frowned into the juice. ''But don't worry. I don't think Hunter did, either.''

''Who?''

''Hunter,'' Chase reminded him. ''You know. The hero in *Action at Sundown* and all seven other books.''

Jerome set his drink carefully on the table. ''This doesn't sound good. I think you'd better tell me all about it.''

''There isn't anything to tell,'' said Chase, but he did it anyway.

''Let me get this straight,'' Jerome said after Chase had finished. ''You didn't make the real man list but Hunter did?''

Chase nodded. ''And I think Hunter just got scratched. It was a dumb interview. Is Hunter polite? I don't know that!''

''Oh,'' said Jerome, looking worried.

''I don't even know if he *should* be polite. All he does is run around catching criminals and seducing women. He doesn't worry about being polite and punctual while he's doing that!''

''Maybe he should,'' Jerome said slowly.

Chase glowered at him. ''Excuse me?''

''I said, maybe he should. And maybe you should too.''

He got to his feet and paced across the room. "I enjoy your books, Chase, and they do sell well, but you have to admit your hero is a little one-dimensional."

"One-dimensional!" Chase echoed.

"He is, Chase. He doesn't seem to be real."

"He isn't real," Chase growled. "I made him up."

"I know you made him up, but your readers want to know about Hunter." He frowned in obvious concern. "This could be serious, you know. We don't want *Real Men* magazine announcing that neither you nor your hero is a real man."

Chase didn't want that, either. "It's just a woman's magazine, Jer."

"Who do you think buys your books? Women buy your books. You need that audience."

"I thought I had that audience."

Jerome's worried look increased. "This is a fickle business, pal. One day you can be hot, and the next day you're not. Women across North America chose your hero as a good example of a real man. The last thing your career needs is an article stating that he isn't, or that you aren't." He tapped his fingers together. "We're going to have to make some effort to repair the damage."

"Like what?"

"I don't know." Jerome considered it. "Maybe we can ask Ms. Butler to give you another chance. Tell her you were confused and upset because your girlfriend just dumped you."

Chase hated that idea. "That won't do a lot for my career either."

"You never know. Women might feel sorry for you."

Chase shuddered. "No thanks. Besides, even if I did talk to her again, it wouldn't do any good. You should have seen the list she had. There were dozens of things on it. I could make up a bunch of stuff about my hero, but I don't know the right answers. I could end up making up a guy women hated." He closed his eyes while he mulled over the problem. Real men. Apparently he didn't know as much about them as he thought he did. "Maybe we could get a copy of that list and you could give me the right answers."

Jerome coughed into his hand. "Who says I know?"

Chase stared at him. Just this morning, Jerome had been bragging about his talents in this area. Now he was wimping out? "You've been married four times, Jer. You must know something."

Jerome winced. "I've also been divorced three times." He turned his glass around and around between his palms and frowned down at it. "And it looks like I'm heading toward number four."

Chase took in his friend's slumped shoulders, the bend of his head and his general air of despondency. He did not look like a happy man. "I thought you said Vanna was 'the one.'"

"She is—for me." Jerome sighed heavily. "I'm not so sure I'm the one for her."

Chase studied him, concerned. He didn't know Jerome's fourth wife very well, but he'd seen them together on numerous occasions, and had even flown to Vegas for the wedding. As far as he could tell, the twenty-two-year-old model was a clone of Jerome's other three wives, but Jerome didn't think so. He'd gone on ad nauseam about the brunette's virtues, and she'd seemed just as enraptured with him as he was with her. "What are you talking about?"

Jerome gusted out another sigh. "Vanna has suggested we go for counseling."

That didn't sound good. "Counseling isn't so bad," he consoled. "It's not the same as moving out and taking all the furniture."

"It's virtually the same thing." Jerome grimaced. "I've

been through this, Chase. I know how it goes. First comes counseling. Then she moves out.''

Chase was at a loss for words. Jerome had seemed to take his divorces in stride, but the expression on his face suggested this one was going to be different. ''That's too bad, Jer.''

''Tell me about it.'' Jerome made an obvious effort to shake off his despondency. ''So I'd say that eliminates me as Mr. Authority on real men. You need to talk to someone else.'' He considered it. ''How about your brother-in-law?''

''Eddie?'' Chase's jaw dropped. ''Eddie sells furniture! Do you honestly think he knows anything about anything that isn't stuffed?''

''I suppose not. But I can't think of anyone else.''

''Neither can I.'' There were probably other men he could ask, but Chase didn't think wandering the streets of Chicago, asking men about politeness and clothing was going to do much for his reputation. Besides, he didn't know all the questions. ''I wish I did have that list of Tara's though. Then I could go look at some real men. Find out what women want.''

Jerome's eyes lit up. ''Now, *that*,'' he said, ''is a brilliant idea.''

IT WAS AFTER SIX when Tara arrived at her apartment. It was a warm day, and it had been a long one, and walking up two flights of stairs didn't help. By the time she unlocked the door, she was starting to wonder if she had made a mistake moving.

However, the gleaming hardwood floors, the elegant-looking living room with her things tastefully set around and the quiet hum of the ceiling fan made her feel better. There was nothing wrong with her apartment. The only problems she had were the assignments she'd taken on. She hadn't made much progress with either of them.

She put on leggings and a shirt, then paused when she caught sight of her reflection in the bedroom mirror. Leggings and a shirt might be comfortable, but they didn't go with this place. She should be wearing something more elegant, like one of those satin negligees she'd seen when she'd written "Luscious Loungewear for the Late-Night Lazies." What had she said in that article? "There's no need to schlep around the house in ripped blue jeans or your old comfy jammies. There's a whole line of lovely loungewear that's just as comfortable, and a lot more attractive. After all, you never know when he's going to come knocking at the door."

There wasn't any he in Tara's life right now, but, as she'd pointed out in the article, Mr. Gorgeous Perfect Stranger could show up at the door any time. It hadn't happened in her old apartment, but here, well, here anything was possible. There was a little boutique she'd visited for that article that had exactly the right thing. She'd stop by next time she was in the neighborhood.

She was in the kitchen, looking through cupboards for food, when Stella phoned. "I just felt like chatting," she said, sounding lonely and mournful. "My day was long and dull and I can't run across the hall to complain to you about it. How was yours?"

"Mine was pretty much the same," Tara reported. She held the cordless phone with one hand and tugged open the fridge door with the other. "I spent the entire afternoon talking to chefs for 'Food That Puts Him in the Mood,' and they all disagreed. So far, all I've found out is that practically anything puts him in the mood if you cooked it and he likes it." She pulled out a can of soda, a head of lettuce and other ingredients for a salad. "Oh, and I also found out that talking about food all afternoon makes me really, really hungry."

"I could have told you that," said Stella. "What about Chase Montgomery? Weren't you seeing him today?"

"Uh-huh." Tara opened the soda and took a sip. It was warm.

"Well?" Stella prompted. "Come on. Tell me. What's he like? Did you get lots of great stuff for your article?"

"No." Tara set down the soda and pulled out a carton of milk. It was warm too. She sniffed it and made a face. "He didn't give me anything for my article. He hardly knows anything about his hero, apart from the fact that he saves the world." She was still disappointed in Chase Montgomery. "He didn't even realize that he *should* know."

"Too bad. Although it's only to be expected, I suppose. The great-looking ones never seem to get the brains." She paused. "He was great-looking, wasn't he?"

Tara closed her eyes and thought about Chase. "I suppose. Sort of a nerdy-looking, herbal-tea-drinking Bruce Willis."

"Oh." Stella sounded as disappointed as Tara had felt. "He doesn't sound much like Hunter."

"He's not anything like Hunter." Tara returned to the fridge. The lettuce was wilted. "I guess I shouldn't have expected him to be, either. Hunter is a figment of his imagination. Chase made him up."

"What about those sex scenes? Do you think he made those up, as well?"

Tara thought about the tingle when they'd shaken hands. "No. I imagine those are real."

"Ah." Stella sounded intrigued. "Maybe you should find out."

"Excuse me?"

"Why not? It might spruce up your article."

Tara scowled at the phone. "I'm not going to sleep with

Chase Montgomery, or anyone else, to spruce up my article!''

''It was just an idea.'' Stella's tone changed to excitement. ''Speaking of sprucing things up, I had lunch with Stanley today. You know. Stanley Gruber.''

Tara chuckled. ''I know who you mean, Stell.''

''Do you? Good. Anyway, I mentioned your article to him and how you'd like to do something more investigative and he suggested you do a story about Wutherspoon Outerwear and all the changes that have taken place since Gerald took over. Isn't that a great idea?''

''It has possibilities.'' It did too. She had done a couple of pieces for a local business magazine and they'd said they'd be interested in seeing more of her work. It wasn't exactly what she wanted to get into, but it would be a start.

''And while you're at it, you could look into Franklin's death,'' Stella went on.

Tara froze in mid-thought. ''I could *what?*''

''Look into Franklin's death,'' Stella repeated. ''You know. Ask questions. Do your investigative reporter thing.''

''I don't have an investigative reporter thing,'' Tara objected. ''Besides, there's nothing to investigate.''

''There might be.'' Stella lowered her voice. ''You won't believe what I found out today. I was talking to Mrs. Kirpatrick from supplies, and she said that Marion Phillips told her that she had specifically mentioned to Franklin there was shrimp in that dish and he shouldn't eat it. What do you think of that?''

Tara dropped her head against the wall. ''Wasn't Franklin a little hard of hearing?''

''Yes he was but...''

''Well then maybe he didn't hear her.''

''Maybe,'' Stella conceded. ''Or maybe he didn't eat the shrimp at all!''

Her friend was definitely losing it. "He had to have. He died because of a fish allergy, remember?"

"Yes, I know he did, but he doesn't have to have eaten shrimp dip. Someone else could have ordered fish, and slipped it onto his plate. It would be easy to do. It was one of those weird French restaurants where everything has a sauce and it's all the same color. Someone could have mixed up something else with his meal. It could have happened, Tara. We were at that employee thank-you dinner. We were all milling about, talking to one another, moving from place to place. Franklin spent more time talking to people than he did sitting down. It's quite possible someone slipped something into his food without him, or anyone else, noticing."

"I suppose it's possible." It wasn't outside the realm of possibility, although it was darn close to the edge. "But I don't think…"

"We have to find out. Franklin was good to me. He gave me a job when I desperately needed one. If something sinister happened to him, I should *do* something about it."

Stella's dedication to her former boss was admirable, but rushing around accusing her co-workers, or her current boss, of murder sounded like a career-limiting move. "I know how you feel, but, um, I don't think you and I…"

"You and I are perfect. Motive, means and opportunity—that's what you need to commit murder. They're always saying that on television. You could use this article as an excuse to talk to people, to find out if anyone, besides Gerald, had a motive for getting rid of Franklin. I'll handle means and opportunity. I'll ask around…find out who was sitting where, and who was near Franklin's plate. We can make up a chart like they do in detective shows."

Tara pictured Stella drawing up a chart, with suspects down one side, and motive and opportunity across the top. "I don't know."

"Please, Tara," Stella coaxed. "Think of what a great article it would be if you identified a murderer."

It would be a major breakthrough, but Tara strongly doubted there was anything to find out. Still, an article in *Chicago Business* was better than anything she was working on. "I'll...think about it."

Stella took that as a yes. "Thank you thank you thank you! I'll get started on a list of people you should talk to right away. Gerald is first, but there are a number of others—"

By the time she hung up, Tara could have kicked herself. Stella clearly thought this was a done deal. If the business magazine wasn't interested, what was she going to do?

She'd barely replaced the receiver when the phone rang again. Tara picked it up, expecting to hear Stella with a few dozen more people for her to interview.

It wasn't Stella, though. It was Charlene, her usually bland tone brimming with excitement. "I'm so glad I caught you at home, Tara. I just wanted to tell you how thrilled we are here."

"You are?" Tara said blankly.

"Yes. You've outdone yourself on this one. Sophia was absolutely right. You are excellent."

"I am?" All she'd done so far was have a nonconversation with a nonreal man, and she hadn't told Charlene about that. "What exactly did I do?"

"What did you do? Darling, you know what you did. You had lunch with Chase Montgomery."

She made it sound as if Tara had rescued the *Titanic* single-handed. "Well, yes, I did, but, um, I wouldn't say it was an outstanding interview."

"That's not what Mr. Montgomery said."

Either she was remembering it wrong, or Chase's idea of a good interview was different than hers. "You've spoken with him?"

"Not him, no. I spoke with his agent. According to him, Chase was quite taken with the whole concept."

"He was?" Tara hadn't been sure Chase had understood the concept, much less been "taken" with it.

"Absolutely enthralled, I understand. He likes it so much he wants to be part of it."

Tara tapped the receiver. "He wants me to interview him again?"

"Not exactly, no. He wants to work with you on it."

She must be hearing things. "Chase Montgomery wants to work with me on coming up with a list of things you need to know about a real man?"

"That's right."

Tara collapsed back against the counter. "Are you sure that's a good idea, Charlene. I mean, it's an interesting angle and everything but—"

"It's exactly the angle we need."

"I suppose. But, um, it sounds expensive. I'm sure I could do a fine job without—"

"It's not expensive at all. Mr. Montgomery is volunteering his time. Isn't it wonderful? I'm just ecstatic, and I know Sophia is going to feel that way herself. It's splendid!"

"Splendid," Tara repeated. She slammed the fridge door. This was great. Her fridge wasn't working, there were no ice cubes, the lettuce was wilted and she was going to write an article with Chase Montgomery.

At least she had something else for her article. Real men, she decided, know when to mind their own business.

3

Real men don't eat oatmeal! Don't serve your man porridge for breakfast, ladies, and save that cold cereal for the children. Your real man needs a hearty breakfast. He should wake up to coffee brewing, bacon crackling in the pan, and you attractively dressed, hair coiffed, makeup in place, ready in the kitchen to cook those eggs the way he likes them.

> —from "Forty-Nine Things You Need
> to Know about a Real Man,"
> *Real Men* magazine, April 1949

"I'LL HAVE the oatmeal," said Chase.

He handed the menu to the waiter. "And herbal tea. You do have herbal tea, don't you?"

The waiter, a fresh-faced blond youth, looked properly shocked. "Of course we have herbal tea, sir. Which kind would you care for? The peppermint is particularly good in the morning, but we do have the lemon..."

Tara sat back in her chair, took a long swallow of her own strong, black coffee and watched in dismay as Chase and the waiter had a deep and meaningful conversation about the various kinds of herbal tea served at this restaurant, and the health benefits of each. It was a typical conversation between two of today's typical men. And what was it about? Tea!

Gregory Peck and Cary Grant had never once discussed tea.

She watched the waiter's earnest expression as he spoke. At least *he* had a good reason for being a herbal-tea expert. He had a customer. Chase didn't. Not that she cared what he drank—herbal probably was better for a person than her own caffeine-heavy coffee. She just wished he wouldn't make such a production out of it. Today's men always did that. They were preoccupied with what they put in their bodies. Her ideal Cary Grant-type man wouldn't do that. She couldn't imagine Cary even ordering the stuff, much less carrying on a five-minute conversation about it.

Of course, she couldn't imagine Cary Grant showing up at a fairly classy restaurant wearing a blue "Jogging Is My Life" T-shirt. Granted, Cary wouldn't look as good in it as Chase did. Chase had a hard-muscled chest. She couldn't recall ever seeing Cary's pectoral muscles, probably because they were usually covered by a well-tailored suit.

Her mind wandered on, first picturing Cary in Chase's garb, then vice versa. Neither image worked. Cary would look embarrassed dressed as Chase, and Chase wouldn't do a thing for a well-tailored suit. He was the type who'd misbutton the shirt, have the tail hanging out in ten seconds and spill ketchup on the tie—unless, of course, he had a girlfriend to keep after him about his appearance.

She drank more coffee while pondering that thought. Was there a woman in his life? She had a hazy recollection of a few articles linking him with this model or that lawyer…but nothing about anything serious. There must be someone though. True, he had a number of faults, but women today tended to overlook things like manners, punctuality and poise, focusing instead on fame, wealth, muscled chests and tanned arms. Her gaze went to Chase's tanned forearms, then returned to his chest. Maybe those women had a point.

The chest loomed closer. "Coffee seems to wake most

people up," Chase observed. "It looks like yours is putting you in a trance."

Tara set her cup down with a clatter. "Oh, um…sorry, I was just, uh…thinking about…" Your chest. Your muscles. The way you'd look in a suit. "My fridge."

"Your fridge?"

"It broke down last night." She made a face as she recalled the sour milk. "Actually, it turned out there was nothing wrong with the fridge. It's got something to do with the wiring in the building."

Chase frowned. "That doesn't sound safe. Today it's the fridge and tomorrow the whole place is going up in flames. If I were you, I'd give serious consideration to relocating."

"You mean move?" Tara shook her head. "No thanks. I just finished unpacking. Besides, I have to expect a few problems. After all, it's an old building. I think it was built in the forties."

"Where is it?" She told him and he made a face. "Why do you live there?"

Tara's spine stiffened in defense of her newfound haven. "It's an interesting neighborhood. It's got character… atmosphere."

Chase looked disgusted. "Atmosphere won't fix the cracks in the plaster or the faults in the wiring. If you ask me, they should tear them all down and build something that doesn't keep falling apart. Put in some decent housing people can afford, instead of turning places into condo units for the wealthy."

Tara shifted uncomfortably. She hated to admit it, but he did have a point. "And where do you live, Mr. Montgomery?"

She expected him to name an upscale part of town. Instead, he produced a smug grin and took another spoonful of oatmeal. "White Valley."

"White Valley?" Tara searched her memory. "You mean the suburb on the South Side?"

"That's the one."

"Oh." She set down her cup, intrigued. "What's a famous writer doing living in suburbia?"

Chase shrugged. "It's a great place. There are plenty of parks so I can go running, a number of excellent grocery stores that carry fresh vegetables, good schools—"

"Schools?" Tara digested that. "You have children?"

"Not that I know of," Chase said, grinning. "But my sister does. She lives a few blocks away. And my mother lives close by, as well."

Did that mean he was a family man or a mama's boy? More likely the latter. Mom probably even did his laundry, unless he had a staff to do it. That was it. He would have a few acres of land, a professionally decorated house and a cleaning staff to take care of it…maybe even a cook to ensure he got the right brand of tea. Tara opened her mouth to ask more questions, then changed her mind and curved her lips into her best professional smile. "That's interesting…but not what we're here to discuss. We need to talk about the article." Chase looked totally blank, so she explained. "The article for *Real Men* magazine."

"Sure," said Chase. "What do we need to discuss?"

"Lots of things. The concept. The approach. Why you're doing this…" She bit her lip on that one. She had been wondering, but she hadn't meant to blurt it out that way.

"Okay." Chase waited while the waiter placed a white china teapot in front of him. "The concept seems pretty obvious to me. You've got this article written in 1949, listing things women need to know about a real man. We're going to update it. Right?"

Tara nodded.

"The approach seems just as straightforward. You've got the list of men for us to talk to. We call them up and talk to them. I don't expect that it will take much more than a day or two.''

He was either putting her on or not too bright. "I'm afraid it's not going to be that simple," Tara explained carefully. "For one thing, we can't just call up these men and ask them how they feel about politeness and punctuality.''

"Why not? That's what you did to me.''

Tara squirmed. "The only reason I took that approach with you is that I was asking about one of your characters. I couldn't exactly spend a day with Hunter, now, could I?''

"I suppose not," said Chase. His eyes glinted mischief. "Although, I could write a scene where you do that.''

It would probably be one where Hunter was ripping off her clothes. "No thanks," said Tara, although the idea did hold some appeal. "I've got enough information about Hunter. But I don't have any information on the rest of these men.''

Chase scowled. "You're not suggesting we spend a day with each one, are you?''

"Not a day, perhaps...but a few hours—''

"Hours?" Chase blinked. "Just how many men are we talking about?''

"A couple of dozen.''

"Two dozen?" Now he looked horrified. "We can't spend hours with each one. That will take...hours.''

"More like days," Tara corrected. "Which is why I think it would be best if we split up the list." It was a plan she'd thought up after her conversation with Charlene last night, and it was a good one. "You can take the poet, the gallery owner, the guy who likes bungee jumping, and the others on this half of the list. I'll take the rest. We'll interview the ones on our lists, and come up with as many qualities as we can. Then we can merge the two. It will take a lot less time and we can both, uh, be creative.''

She sat back in triumph. Talk about a brilliant idea. Chase could do his thing, she could do hers. It would reduce the time she had to spend on this assignment, leaving her free to pursue other options. Not that she had a lot of "other options" right now, but the sooner she finished this, the sooner she could find some.

Chase took a spoonful of oatmeal, chewed thoughtfully—how could anyone chew oatmeal?—and swallowed. "I don't think so."

Tara gaped at him. "Excuse me?"

"I don't think that's a good idea." He reached across the table to pat her hand. "It does have some merit, I suppose, but it's just not the way I think we should do it."

Tara hadn't expected this. She lowered her lashes and glowered at him through the fringed curtain. "Oh? How do you think we should do it?"

"Together," Chase said promptly.

Tara closed her eyes and recited the first verse of "Mary Had a Little Lamb," which was her way of coping with frustration. *Mary had a little lamb. Its fleece was white as snow. And everywhere that Mary went, the lamb was sure to go.* "There's no reason for us to do the interviews together. This way it will take less time…"

Chase shrugged that off. "I'm not doing anything else. I can't write until I do this. My hero is in the middle of the ocean, surrounded by thugs and sharks, and there's no way out of it if he doesn't read the right kind of books."

"What?"

"It's a writer's thing," Chase explained. "I need inspiration, and meeting all these real men is bound to give me some."

Tara thought of the men they were going to meet. "I don't think gallery owners get eaten by sharks regularly."

Chase's grin was swift and disarming. "You never

know. I've heard a lot of interesting things about the art world.''

''Still, it would be better if we came up with our own lists…''

''We can still do that. I just think it would be better if we both talked to everyone at the same time.''

''I don't.'' If they did it his way, this assignment wouldn't just take the original month estimate—it would end up taking the rest of her life! She'd have her schedule to worry about, plus the interviewee's, plus Chase's. And the interviews themselves would probably take twice as long. Besides, if one of these men did turn out to be great and unattached and interested—long shots, perhaps, but still possible—she wouldn't have much chance with Chase around. ''I do think it would be best if we did it my way.''

''No, it wouldn't.'' Chase set down his spoon. ''The truth is, Tara, I'm not sure what I'm supposed to find out. Even if I did know, I doubt I'd have much success doing it. I write novels not magazine articles. I spend ninety percent of my time alone in my office. I don't interview people.''

He sat there looking charming and honest and helpless and irresistible. Tara tried to summon a little backbone. ''You must do some interviewing for your books.''

''Some, yes.'' He blinked wide and pathetic-looking eyes. ''I call up people and ask them technical questions about boats, planes…how a ballistic missile works…stuff like that. This sort of thing is a whole new area for me.''

''What about before you started writing?'' She had a hazy recollection of reading something about his life. What had he done? No, she couldn't remember, but it must have something to do with the journalistic world.

Chase didn't look as though he could remember, either. ''Let's see. I was a short-order cook when I was sixteen.'' He raised an eyebrow. ''Surprisingly enough, asking 'Do you want fries with that?' does not give you a lot of experience interviewing people. It does turn you off fried food, but interviewing people..." He shook his head. "Nope."

Tara could have shaken him. "How about between sixteen and now? Or were you making fries right up until you sold a couple of books?"

"No," said Chase. "There were a couple of years in there when I was working construction...driving a truck..."

Construction and a truck driver. That explained a lot.

"And then I taught physics for a while," Chase concluded.

Tara's jaw dropped. "You studied physics?"

Chase frowned, exasperated. "No, they let you teach it if you've got a few years of fry-making and nail-pounding behind you. Of course I studied physics. It's one of the requirements for teaching it, but I'm afraid it doesn't help me in this situation. I know why a helicopter can get off the ground and how to calculate the trajectory of a bullet, but they didn't have courses in interviewing people—unless that's what economics was all about. I never did understand that."

"If you didn't know anything about interviewing people, then why did you offer to do this?" Tara asked before she could stop herself.

Chase averted his eyes. "Didn't my agent explain that?"

"He did tell Charlene that you were fascinated by the concept, but—"

"That's it then!" Chase interrupted. "I'm fascinated by the concept." He narrowed his eyes in a pathetic attempt to look fascinated.

Tara wasn't convinced. "Honestly?"

"Honestly?" He winced. "Is honesty an important characteristic of a real man?"

"Uh-huh."

"Oh." He settled back with a sigh. "All right then. The truth is, I'm worried about my hero. I want to create a man that women like and admire. You seem to be working on the same thing. I can find out a lot about the type of men women like by working on this with you. But I am going to need your help." His smile was sweet and coaxing. "I need to watch you in action before I take off on my own." He took another spoonful of oatmeal. "Besides, how will I know what a real man is like without you to point it out to me?"

Tara couldn't think of a rebuttal for that one. She had already smoked his idea of a real man. And who knew what he'd come up with if she didn't lend a hand?

She collapsed back and watched him eat his oatmeal. There were no options here. She was going to have to do it his way. "I suppose we could do the first few interviews together. But you have to be on time for them."

"No problem."

She eyed his wardrobe. "And it would help if you would dress a little more formally. There will be a photographer accompanying us from time to time."

Chase looked surprised. "Sure."

"All right then." She rustled through her papers. "Who do you want to start with? The gallery owner, or one of the computer gurus?"

HALF AN HOUR LATER Tara pulled up in front of Wutherspoon Outerwear, still shaking her head after her encounter with Chase. She wasn't sure why he'd volunteered to do this, or why he'd made such a big deal about them doing the article together. However, one thing was clear. Now that he'd made up his mind to do it, he was going to do it. He approached the project with a single-minded determination that she hadn't expected. He'd spent a good hour quizzing her about the approach, exactly what she wanted to find out and how they were supposed to come up with the list of real-man qualities. She could hardly wait to see what he came up with. She just hoped he wasn't going to come up with inappropriate things like "can blow up a submarine without blinking an eye" or "can hop into bed with six women in as many pages."

She chuckled at the notion as she walked across the parking lot, and opened the door of the modified warehouse that served as both company headquarters and the main store.

The place was nothing like the way she remembered. Franklin Wutherspoon had been big on quality, but he'd placed no emphasis on ambience. The store had been nothing more than a huge room, with a concrete floor, harsh fluorescent lights, cracked walls and floor-to-ceiling coats, jackets and other outdoor paraphernalia.

All that was gone. A soft gray carpet covered the floor, the walls had been repainted, the ceiling lowered and the merchandise organized into departments. Tara wandered through the backpack section, paused to admire the jacket display and finally stopped in tents, where a stocky woman, wearing khaki pants and jacket, was struggling to dress a grouping of mannequins in jackets, hats and backpacks. They stood in half-naked splendor, looking pleased and outdoorsy as they admired a dark blue tent they'd apparently just finished assembling.

The clerk stopped what she was doing to give Tara a dour look. "You don't need help finding something, do you?"

"Oh no," Tara assured her. "I was just, uh, looking."

"Go ahead." The clerk, whose rectangular nametag firmly declared she was Wendy, gestured around. "Tents are here. Backpacks are over there. And if you're into climbing—" She eyed Tara up and down. "You aren't into climbing, are you?"

Tara shook her head.

"That's good because I don't know where they've put the climbing equipment." She sniffed. "You take a couple of weeks' vacation, and when you come back everything's changed."

"The place certainly does look different," Tara agreed.

"Tell me about it." Wendy clambered over a reclining mannequin to pick up a dark green jacket. "It's Mr. Charmichael. He's changing everything." She nodded her chin in the direction of the construction area. "We've been renovating ever since he took over."

"It's...very nice," Tara ventured.

"I suppose." Wendy's expression clearly said "I hate it." "Personally, I don't think it looks like the sort of place people would come to buy camping equipment. It looks more like—" she shuddered "—a boutique."

"Well, yes, I suppose it does."

"We're even carrying a line of leather underwear." Wendy scowled. "Mr. Wutherspoon must be spinning in his grave." After repeating Stella's words, she leaned forward and lowered her voice. "At this rate, I wouldn't be surprised if we're out of business in a year."

Tara tried a reassuring smile. "I wouldn't think so. I'm sure the store will do very well."

"I doubt it." Wendy sniffed again and stomped off to complain to some other customers, a young, outdoorsy-looking couple who were staring around the interior as if they'd been beamed in from another planet.

Tara watched her for a moment, then left the sales area, pushed through the glass doors at the rear and climbed the stairs to the second-floor offices. Mr. Charmichael had been at work up here, as well. The hall sported a new coat of paint, and the floor was covered by the same elegant gray carpet. Sarah Miles, who had been Mr. Wutherspoon's secretary, assistant and receptionist for years was gone, as well, replaced by a hipless young woman dressed in a green silk suit who was pounding on her computer keyboard with astonishing efficiency.

She stopped what she was doing when Tara entered and produced a smooth, polished smile. "Hello," she said. "Welcome to Wutherspoon Outerwear. How may I help you?"

"Well...uh...Angie," Tara responded, reading from the nameplate on the corner of the desk. "I wanted to talk to someone about doing an article—" She went on to explain that she was a freelance writer and thought there was an opportunity here. "I'd like to do an article about this place. You know, the changes that have happened since Mr. Charmichael took over and the effect that has had on the staff and the business in general."

"Really?" Angie smoothed her hands down her nonexistent hips. "Would there be photographs?"

"Of course," said Tara.

Angie beamed. "Well then, I can't think of a reason why we wouldn't do it." She patted her brown, red-streaked hair. "When would you be taking these photographs?"

"I'd have to check with my photographer," Tara improvised. She peered over Angie's shoulder at the closed office doors. "I suppose I should clear it with Mr. Charmichael first. How do you think he'll feel about the idea?"

"I wouldn't think he'd mind," said Angie. "He's very easygoing. A real gentleman, if you know what I mean. He does like things done just so, but he doesn't go around grabbing my butt or any of those things you get with men these days."

Angie didn't look as if she had much butt to grab, but Tara knew exactly what she meant. "I still think I should speak with him."

"You probably should, yes." Angie pressed buttons on the computer and examined the results. "He's not in right now, but he'll be in the office tomorrow. If you leave me your name and number, I'll have him give you a call.''

"Thank you." Tara fished one of her "freelance writer" business cards out of her purse and handed it over. "Oh, by the way, you wouldn't happen to know Stanley Gruber, would you? He's a salesman—"

"Stanley? Of course I know Stanley." She flushed. "Everyone knows Stanley." She assessed Tara from head-to-toe. "Are you his fiancée?"

Tara shook her head. "Oh no. No. Nothing like that. I—" She paused. "Stanley has a fiancée?"

"Does he ever!" Angie looked less than impressed. "She phones him at least half a dozen times every day."

"Does she?" Stella had never mentioned a fiancée.

Angie nodded confirmation. "She's probably just checking up on him. Not that I blame her. If I had a fiancée like Stanley, I'd want to check up on him too." She flushed again. "I'm sorry. I shouldn't have said that—you being a friend of his and all."

"I'm not a friend of his. I haven't even met him. I…uh…just heard his name from someone, that's all." She giggled. "She made him sound like the next Leonardo DiCaprio."

"He's a charmer all right." Angie got a dreamy expression on her face. "Too bad he's engaged."

"That's for sure," Tara muttered. She walked slowly down the stairs and out the door. Did Stella know about this fiancée? If not, how upset was she going to be to find out about her?

Stanley, she decided, was off her list of men to interview. A real man wouldn't lead a woman on unless he was available and interested.

On the good-news side, she was definitely going to do a piece on the changes at Wutherspoon Outerwear. It wasn't exactly investigative journalism, but it was a lot better than fifty fascinating things women needed to know about men.

Hunter pressed himself against the door, his gun clutched in his right hand while he tried to meld into the darkness. On the other side, he could hear Bridgett making small talk with Humphry. It almost sounded like she was interested in the guy. Hunter couldn't figure it. Apart from good manners and a number of expensive suits, Humphry had nothing going for him.

He glanced down at his black pants and black turtleneck. The second this was finished, he was going to shop for a new wardrobe.

"Shop for a new wardrobe?" Chase yelped. "Where did that come from?"

HE SLAMMED HIS HANDS on the keyboard and shoved himself away from the desk. "Do you think a new wardrobe is going to help you, Hunter? Here's a hint. It won't! Even if you dress well, figure out the right books and actually get around to reading them, that still leaves forty-seven other qualities you've got to worry about." No, he better make that forty-eight, since they had to come up with fifty qualities of today's real men. Fifty! Chase figured he only had three or four nailed down, and that was stretching it. As for Hunter, well, he was in big trouble.

He was still staring morosely at the screen when the phone rang. "Yeah?" he growled into it.

"It's me," announced Jerome. "I've just got a couple of questions. How did your meeting with Ms. Butler go, and is your hero out of the water yet?"

Chase swung his feet onto the desk and gazed morosely at the paragraphs on his computer screen. "Let's just say we're both sinking. As a matter of fact, right now I feel the same way Hunter does—sharks circling and little chance of survival.''

"Oh no! What happened this time?"

"With who?" Chase wondered. "Tara or the sharks?" He wasn't sure he knew the difference.

"Tara," Jerome explained. His tone turned anxious. "You didn't irritate her again, did you?"

"No." He hadn't irritated her, but he hadn't made a great impression, either. Hell, he'd had to use every trick in the book to get her to agree to do the interviews with him. Not that he was dying to spend more time with her. He wasn't even sure why he'd made such a big deal about it. He was quite capable of walking into a guy's office and finding out what qualities he had that made him a real man. Granted, he hadn't had a lot of practice at interviewing, but how hard could it be? Besides, doing it alone would be a lot better than doing it with a woman who clearly considered him something of a subspecies.

Damn but that irked him. Even when he wasn't a famous writer, women had been attracted to him. Okay, they hadn't stuck around, but they had been interested. Ms. Butler wasn't, which was fine with him because he wasn't interested in her, either.

"Chase?" asked Jerome.

Chase suddenly remembered he was in the middle of a conversation. "I didn't irritate her, Jer."

"So what happened? Did you get a copy of that list of hers?"

"Yup." Chase glowered at the paper on his desk. "She faxed over a copy."

"And…"

"And it isn't much help!" He swiped the offending list off his desk and scowled at it. "For one thing, it's a list of qualities men in 1949 were supposed to have. I don't know if men today are supposed to have them or not, but let me tell you, Jerome, if they are we're both in big trouble."

"How come?"

"You should see this! Real men are supposed to be punctual, polite, confident, well-organized, well-dressed, interested in decor—"

"Decor?" Jerome's tone brightened. "Hey, I like decor. As a matter of fact, I love decor."

Great. Jerome had a hit already. Maybe he... He took a look around his office. Shelves filled with reference books, misfiled magazines...a file cabinet. The rest of the house was like that. Furniture he bought because it was comfortable not because it matched anything. Nope, he couldn't say he was interested in decor. As for his hero...hell, he didn't give it a single thought. "Great. You've got one out of fifty."

"I'm also well-dressed," Jerome went on thoughtfully. "And I'm punctual, I'm polite...at least, I try to be—"

Chase felt worse than ever. Even Jerome had more of these qualities than he did. "Good for you. Now you've got three out of fifty. That's not even ten percent."

"Give me some more," Jerome urged. "I'm on a roll here."

"Okay. How about likes animals and is chivalrous?"

"Chivalrous?" Jerome sounded alarmed. "What does that mean? Do we have to take up jousting or something?"

"Who knows?" Chase tossed the list back onto his desk. "I'm telling you, Jer, this is impossible. How can anyone have all of these qualities? The only ones I have are liking sports and not liking housework!" Plus he ate oatmeal. What was he supposed to eat in the morning? Eggs? He shuddered.

"I don't like housework, either," Jerome mused. "I'm not big on sports, although I do enjoy the occasional round of golf. How important do you think that is?"

"I don't know. Maybe some qualities are more important than others. Besides, these are from '49. I don't know what still applies."

"Find out quick," Jerome advised. "Vanna's scheduled a counseling session for the end of the month. If I don't find out about this before then, she's going to dump me."

Chase hung up the phone. He wasn't sure he could help Jerome—or Hunter—or himself. As a matter of fact, if this list was any indication of what women wanted in a man, he was surprised they didn't dump everybody.

Real men can fix anything! Problem with the fridge or stove? Don't fret, dear. When your real man gets there, he'll have it fixed in a jiffy. Not only does he know how to do it, he likes doing it. You'll have plenty of time left to cook him that wonderful meal you've been working on all afternoon.

> —from "Forty-Nine Things You Need
> to Know about a Real Man,"
> *Real Men* magazine, April 1949

CHASE DIDN'T KNOW if Hubert Hendricks could fix a fridge or stove, but he could probably fix everything else—including a rainy day.

As far as Chase could tell, though, that was the only quality he had that would make him a real human being, much less Mr. Real Man.

Chase was in the high-tech office of Hendricks Computer Laboratories, becoming comatose as the intent-eyed Hubert began another discourse based entirely on three-letter acronyms. Tara had called yesterday with an alarming schedule of men they had to interview. Hubert was the first. "We're meeting him at his office," she'd told Chase. "Try to be on time." She'd sounded so doubtful about him managing this small request that Chase had volunteered to pick her up. "You can give me the rest of my instructions on the drive over," he'd told her.

She hadn't done much of that. "I'll ask the questions,"

she'd advised. "You can take notes and draw your own conclusions. Of course, if you have questions of your own—"

Chase hadn't, because he couldn't think of a subtle way of finding out if someone was a stickler for neatness, liked a well-run house or preferred demure women. Now he wished he had. They'd spent over an hour with Hubert, and so far he hadn't said three words that Chase understood. "It's the RAM," he explained now. "The way we utilize the RAM is what makes the project feasible."

Chase scanned the list he'd stapled to the inside of his notebook, searching for any quality that might explain why Hubert had made the real man list. They'd had to wait twenty minutes to see him, which eliminated punctuality. If his untidy office was any indication, he failed "well-organized," and his pale complexion suggested he wasn't interested in the great outdoors, which, according to the '49 article was a quality all real men shared. The only quality he seemed to have was intelligence. There was no doubt this was one clever dude. "My degree is from Cal Tech," he'd told them. "I received a full scholarship when I was sixteen."

There had to be more than intelligence though. Albert Einstein had been intelligent, and Chase wasn't positive he'd make the real-man cut.

His eyes stopped at number seven on the list. *Real men are fascinating. When one is talking, you'll find yourself hanging on every word.*

"The RAM is dual ported between the CPU and the real-time data-acquisition PLCs," Harold was explaining. "That solved the TLD variance problem as well as the closed-loop feedback performance."

"Really?" said Chase. So much for number seven. No one on the planet could possibly find this guy...

"How fascinating," said Tara.

Chase glared at her. She'd pinned her hair back from her face, so it fell across her shoulders in a profusion of gold, brown and auburn curls. He appreciated it for a moment, then let his gaze wander across her flushed cheeks, her wide, full lips, the curve of her throat. She was one attractive lady. He looked back at Hubert. Did women like her honestly find a man like him *fascinating?*

He checked out her expression while Hubert rambled on. She watched him with concentrated seriousness, as if she was hanging on every word. She hadn't looked like that when he'd been talking about Hunter. Surely she couldn't be more impressed with Hubert than she was with his hero—or with him?

Chase settled back into his chair. Maybe she could. After all, Hubert was on the real man list. Chase wasn't.

He took another look at Hubert and searched for adjectives to describe him. Short. Skinny. Okay, he did have a few muscles, acquired in the gym, no doubt, because his white skin suggested he hadn't been outside in the last decade, and his jerky manner indicated a diet laced with caffeine and preservatives. In a dark alley, he'd be useless. If he were thrown into the middle of an ocean, and surrounded by sharks, the only thing he could do was drown!

Unless he had a natural affinity with water. Chase pictured Hubert in a bathing suit and snickered.

To his surprise, Hubert stopped in midacronym. "Is something wrong, Mr. Montgomery."

You're boring, you don't look one bit like Hunter, and if Tara says "fascinating" one more time, I'm going to gag her. "I was just wondering if you know how to swim."

Hubert blinked his pale blue eyes three times. "Excuse me?"

"Swim." Chase moved his arms in an imitation of the front crawl. "You know. In the water."

"Oh," said Hubert. "No, I'm afraid I don't."

"I didn't think so." Of course this guy couldn't swim. There was a strong possibility that he couldn't do much of anything that didn't involve integrated circuits, RAM—whatever that was—and hard drives.

Hubert went back into his monologue. Chase tried to focus on what the man was saying, hoping for a clue.

"As you can see, this revolutionary CPU design—"

Chase gave up. "I don't see it," he interrupted. "It looks like every other computer I've ever seen." He peered at the machine, looking for the on/off button. "How about turning this thing on and giving us a demo?"

Hubert looked flustered. "I can't do that, I'm afraid. This isn't a working model. It's a prototype."

"Shouldn't it prototype a model that *does* work?"

Hubert gave him a patient, patronizing look. "You don't work in this industry, do you?"

"No, I don't. However, my hero knows a lot about it."

"Your...hero?" Hubert echoed very slowly and very blankly.

Chase ground his teeth. Apparently, Hubert didn't brighten his otherwise dull existence by reading Chase Montgomery books.

"Chase is a writer," Tara explained. "Action-adventure novels like...um...*Sunset to Disaster* or...?"

Hubert shook his head. "Never heard of them."

Tara gave Chase a wry look. "Perhaps they're just not the sort of books you read."

"What sort of books *do* you read?" Chase interjected. "You do read books, don't you? Or do you have a working model of this thing that reads them to you?"

Tara's green eyes flashed a rebuke. "I'm sure Hubert is a very well-read man." She looked expectantly at Hubert, who stared at her for a moment before answering.

"Of course I am, Tara. Why, I have over two hundred

books on electronic circuitry alone, and I've read them from cover to cover.''

Tara blinked, but didn't give her ''that's not what I meant'' lecture. ''How fascinating,'' she said instead.

Hubert gave her a calflike look of adoration before launching into another technical discussion. Chase scowled at both of them. It wasn't fascinating at all. *Hunter spent the evening reading a circuitry manual.* That would make one dull sentence. Make a chapter about it and he'd be back on a construction site, hucking around heavy boards for a living, or trying to teach the concept of velocity to uninterested teenagers.

Worse, it could be the death of his hero:

''What's that you're reading?'' asked Bridgett.

Hunter turned a page. ''A circuitry manual. I've got literally hundreds of them and I've read them from cover to cover.''

''Oh,'' said Bridgett. ''That's really boring.'' She gave him a shove. Hunter overbalanced, toppled over the railing and into the ocean. ''Sorry,'' she called down after him. ''I never help boring men save the world.''

IT WAS AFTER FOUR when Tara decided she had as much information about Hubert as she was going to get.

It wasn't as much as she'd hoped for. She had no idea how he felt about housework, if he was interested in decor, or what he liked to eat. However, she didn't think there was any way of finding out, because every time she asked a question, Hubert started talking about his work. She might not have learned a lot about real men, she thought philosophically as they left the building, but she had picked up a great deal of information about computers.

''I give up,'' Chase announced from behind her.

Tara looked over her shoulder at him. He was strolling along, his hands shoved deep in his pockets, his creased forehead indicating his thoughts were equally as deep. "You're giving up on doing this?"

"No." He came up beside her. "I'm giving up on Hubert."

"Hubert?" Tara squinted at him in the bright sunshine. He'd exchanged his T-shirt-and-jeans outfit for a green golf shirt and khakis, making him look rakishly handsome, but certainly not suave and debonair. However, he was head and shoulders above Hubert.

He rocked back on his heels. "That's right. I've given this careful consideration, and I've got to tell you, I can't figure out one thing that would make that character a real man."

Neither could she, especially compared with him. Hubert had been intelligent, but he didn't have one ounce of the masculine appeal Chase exuded.

Chase unlocked the passenger door of his car and opened it for her. "The only thing I can come up with is that real men are incredibly, astoundingly, amazingly dull."

Tara climbed in, astonished by his small gesture of good manners. "He was a little obsessive, I suppose, but—"

Chase snorted. "A little obsessive? The only thing he could talk about was his computers." He closed the door with a disgusted slam and wandered around to slide in behind the wheel, still complaining. "He wasn't well-dressed, unless you consider the no-tie, no-socks look high fashion. He wasn't particularly polite, I wouldn't call him good-looking and he can't swim." He switched on the engine. "I know we're supposed to come up with our own lists, but you're going to have to give me a little help here because I'm drawing a blank."

So was Tara. She rolled down the window a few inches

and rested her head back. "Don't feel too bad. It wasn't obvious to me, either."

"It wasn't?" She could hear the surprise in his voice. "It must have been. You're the one who kept saying he was fascinating."

"I was also the one who was trying to change the subject." She had found it difficult to concentrate with Chase in the room. Chase practically oozed masculinity. Hubert, poor fellow, didn't. If she put Chase and Hubert in a lineup and asked a dozen women which one was a real man, they'd all pick Chase. So would she. "But I think I know why women consider men like Hubert real men."

"You do?"

"Uh-huh. I suspect it's because they're so...how do I put this...uh...technologically aware."

"Technologically aware?" Chase braked to a jolting stop at a red light. "Women actually *like* men who are boring?"

He sounded so incredulous Tara had to smile. "Boring—no. But up-to-date on technology—yes. It's a big thing these days, Chase. Women know about computers. They want a man who is just as knowledgeable as they are. They find it attractive."

Chase stared at her, then turned his attention back to the road. "I never would have guessed that."

"It's kind of subtle."

"No kidding." He was silent for a while, apparently mulling that over while Tara tried not to notice the flutter of his hair in the breeze, the lazy ease with which he drove the car, the scent of his aftershave. That was another thing she'd put on her list. Real men smelled good.

Chase finally broke the silence. "Tell me something. How would a woman know a man was technologically aware? Would she ask him when she met him?"

"No." Tara closed her eyes to stop herself from staring at him. "Men like that bring it up."

"How? It doesn't fit naturally into a conversation. Or do they do it when they introduce themselves? 'How do you do. My name is Ben. I'm technologically aware. Let's go to my place so I can jump you.'"

Tara laughed. "It's not that simple. It usually happens somewhere between the first and second date. He comes by to pick you up, catches sight of your computer, and the next thing you know, you're spending the evening watching him fix a whole bunch of stupid little problems you didn't even know you had, instead of going out to dinner."

"Sounds like you've had a lot of experience in that area."

Tara made a face. "I have."

Chase was quiet for minute. Then, "Are you still seeing him?"

"Seeing who?" She opened her eyes to look at him, then closed them again. "Oh, you mean Mr. Technologically Aware? I'm not seeing him socially, no, although I do call him up when my computer breaks down."

"Why not?" Chase wondered.

"What?"

"Why aren't you still seeing him. I mean, if women are so attracted to these types, and you had one, why did you—"

"I'm not typical of today's women," Tara admitted. "Besides, I don't want a man who is more interested in my computer than he is in me."

"Fair enough." He paused. "So what kind of man do you want?"

"The old-fashioned type," Tara said promptly. "Someone like Cary Grant or Gregory Peck."

Chase chuckled. "I don't think Cary could be classified as technologically aware."

"A modern Cary Grant would be." She built a mental image of Mr. Perfect, complete with suit and tie, and, unlike Hubert, socks. "He'd know the theory behind it all, and when my printer didn't work he'd know how to fix it, but he wouldn't be so hung up on it that taking one apart was his entire reason for existing."

"I see," said Chase. He parked in front of her apartment building and switched off the engine. "Are you inviting me in for coffee?"

"I didn't think you drank coffee."

"I don't." He got out. "But I'll come in anyway."

He followed her up the stairs to her second-floor apartment. "I suppose this is one way to fit in your exercise regime," he commented as she unlocked the door. "But frankly, I'd rather be jogging."

Tara wasn't sure what to do with him when they got inside. "Do you really want coffee or...?"

"Just water, thanks." Chase followed her into the kitchen, then stopped beside her at the door and stared at the floor. "Now, that's an interesting place to keep your water. Most people keep it in the tap...or in the fridge if it's bottled, which it should be in this day and age. But you seem to keep yours on the floor."

"Oh no." Tara stared in horrified disbelief at the smooth hardwood. There wasn't just a puddle in the kitchen. There was a lake in the kitchen—a lake that was getting deeper by the second, fed by a fountain that appeared to originate from under the sink. "There must be a problem with the plumbing," she muttered as she watched a bottle of glass cleaner float by.

"Good guess," said Chase. "Either that, or you've invented a new way to wash your floors. If that's the case, I'd say it's a nonworking prototype."

The sparkle in his eyes reflected his amusement. Tara could have strangled him. "I suppose I should call the building manager."

"That might be a good idea."

She hurried to the phone in the hall and dialed. Chase shoved his hands in his pockets and watched as she listened to ring after ring. She finally slammed the phone back into the cradle. "There's no answer." She turned to Chase. "I don't suppose you know anything about—"

Chase shook his head. "Nope. Broken plumbing isn't a plot twist I've ever used, although it does have possibilities."

"Figures." Where was Cary when she needed him? Cary would know what to do. Even Hubert would know what to do. Unfortunately, the only man here was Chase, and he didn't seem to know anything. It was up to her to do something.

Water. Plumbing. That's what she should do. She should call…

"Maybe you should try a plumber," Chase suggested from the doorway.

Great revelation, Sherlock! Tara gave him a fulminating look. "I already thought of that." She pulled out the Yellow Pages and started thumbing through them. Let's see. Plumbing Supplies. No. Plumbing Wholesale…"

"Try Gus's Plumbing on Thirty-third."

"What?"

"Gus's—" He took the phone away from her. "You better let me do this, Tara. Otherwise we'll drown." He dialed a number. A few seconds later he was speaking into the receiver. "Hey, Gus, it's me, Chase… No, no, I didn't break anything this time. It's for a friend of mine… Yeah, it's an emergency. There's water all over the floor and it's getting deeper by the second. I need someone here right now. Immediately. No later than the next second. In the meantime, what in hell do we turn off to stop the fountain of youth here?"

"THEN WHAT HAPPENED?" asked Stella.

She handed Tara a can of cola and settled onto one of

the green chairs in her living room.

"Nothing much," Tara reported. She tipped the can and took a long gulp. "Chase helped me mop up the mess. Gus arrived with a whole parcel of tools and fixed whatever needed to be fixed. Then he and Chase went out to do a male-bonding thing over a beer—or in Chase's case, a bottle of water. I interviewed two more chefs for the foods article, made appointments to see more 'real men' and called it a day."

"Sounds like a pretty exciting day to me."

"It wasn't." Tara plopped down on Stella's old plaid sofa. "I must have gained five pounds sampling food, and none of them put me in the mood for anything." She took a handful of chips from the bag and swung her legs up onto the coffee table. "To top it off, Hubert turned out to be a dud."

Stella sat beside her and stacked her feet on the coffee table as well. "It sounds as if Chase came through with flying colors though."

"I suppose." Tara didn't feel like talking about Chase. She was still stunned by the way he'd handled the plumbing issue. It hadn't been in the usual "I'll fix it" way, but he had gotten the job done. "What about you? Is anything exciting happening at Wutherspoon Outerwear these days?"

"Not unless you count the leather-underwear display. Oh, and I had lunch with Stanley again today."

"Stanley?" Tara winced. She'd forgotten about Stanley. "Listen, Stella, I stopped by Wutherspoon's yesterday. To look into doing an article."

"About Mr. Wutherspoon's death?" Stella asked eagerly.

"No. About the changes in the company. But it will give me a good opportunity to talk to everyone."

Stella practically glowed. "That's terrific, Tar! Terrific. Maybe now we'll find out what's going on. Did you talk to Gerald?"

"No." Tara cleared her throat. "While I was there, I had a chat with the receptionist."

"Angie?" Stella shook her head. "I don't think she'll be a good source of information. She started after Gerald took over."

"She mentioned that." Tara cleared her throat again and tried to find a way to approach the subject delicately. "She also mentioned that Stanley has a fiancée."

"She did?" Stella blinked. "How did that come up?"

"It just did," Tara said vaguely. Stella hadn't looked too surprised when she mentioned a fiancée. "You knew Stanley was engaged?"

"Everyone knows, Tara. It's hard not to know. Lorraine calls him every chance she gets. She must phone him ten times a day." She leaned forward. "I think she does it because she wants to check up on him. She shouldn't do that, you know. Stanley is extremely trustworthy."

Was he? If so, Stella must know a different definition for the word *trust*. "I thought he took you to lunch."

"He did," said Stella. "But that has nothing to do with anything. We're just two friends having lunch. We didn't even get to finish it, either. I had just started to tell him about my suspicions regarding Franklin, and guess who calls him on his cell?"

"Lorraine?"

"Right. There was something wrong with her car, so Stanley had to drop everything and rush over there to fix it."

Tara blinked. "Stanley knows how to fix a car?"

"Sure. I told you. He's a real man. Why don't you come around. I'll introduce you to him."

"Maybe." Tara sat back. She doubted Chase knew how to fix a car any more than he knew how to fix plumbing.

On the other hand, maybe a real man didn't have to know how to fix something if he was smart enough to know how to get it fixed.

"YOU'VE GOT TO BE technologically aware," Chase reported over the phone to Jerome that evening. "Apparently it's a big thing with women these days." He pulled a bottle of orange juice out of the fridge and carried it and the phone to the back office.

"Technologically aware of what?" Jerome wondered.

"Computers." Chase sat down in front of his and twisted the cap off the juice. He'd spent the past hour reading a *Computers for Dummies* book, and so far all he'd figured out was how to switch the damn thing off and on—and he'd already known that.

"Computers?" Jerome sounded puzzled. "I know all about computers. I use one at work, and I send E-mail by the truckload. Hell, I even know how to surf the Net, but I don't think that's going to impress Vanna."

"It's not going to impress anybody. Everyone knows that stuff. But what do you know about your RAM and your hard drive?"

Jerome hesitated. "Not much," he finally admitted. "But I don't think Vanna cares if I do or not."

"Have you ever asked her?"

"No, but…but Vanna doesn't care about computers, Chase. She doesn't have one, she doesn't use one, and I can't see that taking one apart in front of her is going to save my marriage."

It did sound like a long shot, but… "According to Tara, it's a big thing with women these days. And I think she might be right. Do you know, today I got cash from an automatic teller machine, paid for my groceries with a debit card and wrote a chapter on my computer, and I don't have a clue how I did any of it except for the typing part. I don't know how any of this stuff works. I think I should—and so should you.''

"Maybe." Jerome sounded dubious. "I suppose I could learn a little more about it."

"It might help," said Chase. "It's certainly doing something for Hunter."

Jerome's voice sharpened. "You're not making your hero into a nerd, are you?"

"Not exactly." Chase hung up the phone and turned back to Hunter.

"Now here's the plan," said Hunter. "We're going to sneak onto that yacht. I'm going to find the missile-launching system in the cabin, and I'm going to disarm it."

"You know how to do that?" Bridgett looked impressed.

"Yup." Hunter patted her shoulder. "It isn't that difficult, Bridgett—just a simple matter of changing the RAM. It's not being properly utilized anyway, so a little zap to the hard drive should easily destroy it."

Chase sat back and reread the scene. It was pretty good all right. It made Hunter sound less like a thug and more like an intelligent human being.

Which would impress Bridgett no end.

He sat down and started rewriting the scene. It did work. And it did give his hero more depth. It sounded as if it did something for Bridgett as well. As soon as they got the chance, she was going to start ripping off Hunter's clothes with her teeth.

5

Real men *know* they are real men! Is self-confidence a problem for you? Don't worry about it. Your real man has enough for both of you. No matter what the situation, your real man is cool, confident and self-assured.

> —from "Forty-Nine Things You Need
> to Know about a Real Man,"
> *Real Men* magazine, April 1949

COOL, confident and self-assured described Gerald Charmichael to a tee.

He was in his office at Wutherspoon Outerwear when Tara arrived to keep their appointment—a dapper-looking man in his late fifties, with graying hair, a tailored suit and a courtly manner. He rose from the chair behind his desk when she entered the room, and shook her hand with just the right degree of pressure. "I'm delighted to meet you," he said as he ushered her into a seat at a small table in the corner of his office. "It's so kind of you to take an interest in our little operation."

"Not at all," said Tara. Gerald didn't look like the type of person who would bump off his uncle—not that she knew what a bumping-off-your-uncle type looked like, but she suspected there would be something sinister about them. There wasn't one thing sinister about Gerald. As a matter of fact, he reminded her of a shorter, elderly Cary

Grant. A tall, fit Cary had never looked sinister, so the smaller, older version certainly didn't.

He sat down next to her and folded his hands together on the table. "What made you decided to write about us?"

My friend thinks you bumped off your uncle. Tara crossed her legs, smoothed down her skirt and launched into an explanation about Stella, her own freelance activities and her ideas for the article. "I do a little freelance work for the local paper and it occurred to me that an article about the changes you've made to your business would be interesting to their readers. If you wouldn't mind, of course."

Gerald shook his head. "Well, Tara... Do you mind if I call you Tara? Or would you prefer Ms. Butler?"

"Tara is fine."

"Thank you. As I was saying, Tara, we never turn our back on publicity." His smile was warm and genuine. "What sort of information are you after?"

"The renovations you're making. The direction your business is taking. The reasons you chose that direction." *If you had anything to do with Franklin's death.*

"All right," said Gerald. "Why don't we start with a tour? I can explain on the way what renovations I've got in mind."

He took her through the whole building, politely opening doors for her, gesturing for her to proceed him, walking beside her with his head bent in her direction while he explained his ideas.

They finished up in front of the mannequin display. While the mannequins beamed at their recently set-up tent, Tara tried to find a way to lead into the subject of Franklin Wutherspoon, and the change of ownership. "It certainly does look different around here," she said.

"I know." Gerald sighed. "Things had to change, Tara...although my uncle couldn't see it."

"You mean Franklin Wutherspoon?"

"Yes." Gerald coughed discreetly into his hand. "I was very fond of Uncle Frank. He was a good, decent person. All the employees were attached to him and so was I." He gestured around. "Sometimes when I walk around here, I can see him."

He touched a finger to the corner of an eye and a lump rose in Tara's throat. She was an idiot. She should never have listened to Stella. How could anyone suspect this charming man of having anything to do with Franklin's death? "I'm so sorry, Gerald."

"So am I." He sighed again. "I suppose you heard what happened to him."

"I, uh, did hear something about it. A food allergy, I believe?"

"That's right," Gerald told her the same story Stella had. "I just wish I'd seen him take that shrimp dip. I would have stopped him. Of course, I didn't eat any."

"You didn't?"

"No. I'm allergic to fish, as well. It's so sad, isn't it? Such a tragedy." He was silent for a moment while he composed himself. "Unfortunately, Uncle Frank was a little behind the times. I tried to talk to him about it, but he didn't agree with me. He didn't want things to change. They have to change. More and more people are getting into outdoor activities. They don't want to shop at a warehouse. They want to shop in a place that looks and feels more upscale."

Tara wasn't sure she agreed with his assessment. The outdoorsy types she met seemed more interested in getting a good deal than in what the place looked like. And it sounded as if he and his uncle hadn't gotten along all that well.

"I guess he did agree with me in the end though," Gerald said thoughtfully. "After all, he did leave me the company. I was totally taken by surprise when I found that out.''

''You weren't aware that he'd left it to you?''

''No, I wasn't.'' He sighed a third time. ''I'm grateful he did. It made me feel a lot better about those disagreements we had.''

That was a good point. Why would Franklin leave Gerald his company if they hadn't gotten along?

Gerald put a hand on her back and gestured toward the next display. ''Come over here. I'd like to show you our new line of leather underwear.''

TARA SPENT so long at Wutherspoon's that she was fifteen minutes late for the three-thirty interview she'd scheduled with the entrepreneur Anthony Stevens.

She found a parking spot and plugged quarters into the parking meter outside the Holiday Inn, where Anthony had arranged to meet her and Chase. ''I'm in the process of setting up a new company,'' he had explained. ''I don't have a formal office at the present time.''

She hurried inside, her mind still occupied with thoughts of Gerald. Stella was right about the changes he was making. She wasn't sure about them, either. However, she doubted he'd had anything to do with his uncle's death.

Chase, thank goodness, was already in the lounge when she arrived. He was sitting on a sofa in the back of the room, heavily involved in a discussion with a wide-shouldered, fair-haired man she assumed was Anthony. Anthony was wearing a suit and a tie. So was Chase.

Tara walked slowly toward them. Anthony was the fourth man they'd interviewed. After Hubert had come the gallery owner, who she thought had good taste and Chase thought had none, then the Latin professor whose only quality seemed to be ''well-educated.'' They'd all been pleasant enough men in their own way, but none of them were men of her dreams. She hoped Anthony would be different.

Chase performed the introductions. Anthony shook her hand with enthusiasm, assured her that he was delighted to meet her, then excused himself to make a call on his cellular phone. Tara took a seat and tried not to stare at Chase. His suit wasn't the dark blue pinstripes of Anthony's. Instead, he'd chosen a pair of black khakis, with a gray shirt underneath a darker gray blazer. He had completed the outfit with a deep purple tie. It wasn't the serious, respectable look of her movie-star heroes, but it was an improvement on his usual attire. "Nice tie," Tara commented. "I didn't know you owned one."

"I own tons of them," Chase retorted. "As a matter of fact, my closet is brimming with suits and ties." He leaned forward and lowered his voice. "Where were you?"

He might look unnatural in a suit and a purple tie but he still looked great. He looked as if he tasted great too. "Tara?" he asked.

Where had she been? Oh yes, Wutherspoon Outerwear. "Looking at leather underwear," she murmured. She pictured him in leather Jockey shorts—the black ones. They'd looked interesting on the mannequin, but since it didn't have all the right equipment, it had been difficult to get the proper mental image. On a man like Chase, they'd look terrific.

"Pardon me?"

She'd tried to picture the underwear on Gerald, but the image hadn't worked. Gerald wasn't the type of man to wear leather underwear, and a younger version of Gerald didn't work, either. That wasn't a character flaw, though. Cary Grant probably didn't wear leather underwear, either. "I was working on another assignment," said Tara. Focus, Tara, focus.

Chase frowned. "I'd appreciate it if you could be on

time. I thought I was going to have to do this by myself and I'm not very good at it!''

"Really?'' If those sex scenes he wrote were any indication, he was great at it. She sat back, away from him, struggling for composure. "You and Anthony seem to have established a rapport.''

Chase made a face. "We haven't talked about anything except my books—and all he did was critique them. Apparently, he knows more about writing than I do.''

"Does he?'' Tara watched Anthony stride through the lounge toward them. He looked like the strong, mature, decisive type, he dressed well, and although he wasn't handsome, he wasn't dog meat either. Did he know anything about writing sex scenes? If so, Tara really wanted to get to know him.

Unfortunately, Anthony didn't appear to be the type who knew much about writing smut, although he did seem to consider himself an expert on everything else, from how Tara should tackle this assignment—"You have taken an interesting approach, but I would have thought something a little more scientific would give you better results''—to the hotel decor, as well as a number of business issues. Over a drink he'd ordered for Tara without consulting her, he held forth about manliness, while Tara took notes and tried not to think about leather underwear. Chase looked more and more disgusted with each passing second.

"Today's man,'' Anthony ruminated. "I'd have to say that I think a man today has to know where's he going and have the confidence and intelligence to know he can get there. He has to have balls.'' He swung his head to look at Chase. "Don't you agree, Mr. Montgomery?''

"Chase,'' said Chase. "And I certainly agree that men have to have balls. As a matter of fact, I believe they're pretty standard pieces of equipment.''

"Exactly.'' Anthony settled back, exuding confidence

and intelligence. "Take me, for example. I've established three companies within the last five years, and I'm in the process of setting up my fourth. It's an innovative business venture—"

Chase shifted in his chair. "What happened to the other three?"

Anthony frowned. "Excuse me?"

"The other three companies you started. What happened to them? Were they successful?"

Anthony smiled a small, patronizing smile. "Success is a matter of opinion. They were certainly viable opportunities at the time."

"I'm sure they were," Chase said equitably. "But are they still in operation today?"

Anthony looked edgy. "Some are. Some aren't. I haven't really kept up with them. That's not what I do. I get things operational...line up investors...then I sell off my interest and move on." He focused on Tara. "That's something else you should put in your article. Men today like a challenge."

Tara nodded. "Maybe that point should be on the list." She started writing it down.

Chase surprised her by arguing. "I don't think it should be."

Tara turned her head to frown at him, but got caught up in her leather-underwear fantasy again. It didn't make sense. She'd been wishing he'd turn up in a suit, and when he did, she wanted him to take it off. "Why not?" she murmured.

"It's too general. Everyone likes a challenge. It's part of human nature. Besides, wouldn't it be just as challenging, if not more, to work on making a company successful, not just starting it up? I mean, if all my hero did was start things, the world would end on page three."

Anthony set his jaw. "That's how some people work, I suppose, but that's not—"

"I believe follow-through is the important thing," said Chase. "What do you think, Tara?"

Tara squirmed. "Well, um, both parts do have validity, I suppose, but…"

"And that does lead to the question of if your idea of a challenge spills over into your personal life," Chase went on, beginning to enjoy himself. "Are you the type who just starts relationships or do you work on establishing something meaningful?"

Anthony's classic-shaped jaw bunched. "That's a little personal, Mr. Montgomery."

"We're doing an article about real men, Mr. Stevens," Chase retorted. "Didn't you expect that at some point it would get personal?"

Tara set down her cup. The two men were staring at each other, Anthony with blue eyes blazing, Chase's dark ones bland and innocent. If this got any more personal, they were going to be wiping the floor with each other. "I don't think we have to—"

Anthony laughed lightly. "I don't know what you're after, but I play the field, if that's what you want to know."

"That's what I wanted to know," said Chase.

"That's, um, fascinating," Tara said brightly. She glowered at Chase and then smiled at Anthony. "Why don't we talk about…about—"

"Emotions," Chase put in. He settled back in his chair and grinned. "Tell me, Anthony, do you often lose your temper?"

"DO YOU OFTEN LOSE your temper?" Tara seethed.

She marched out of the Holiday Inn in front of Chase, her head held high. "What kind of a question is that?"

"A good one?" Chase guessed. He gave himself a mental pat on the back. He'd handled that situation pretty well, if he did say so himself. Tall, well-dressed, good-looking Anthony hadn't come out of that one in good shape. "It's on our list. Real men are even-tempered. I wanted to know—"

"You didn't have to ask him!" Tara stopped beside a blue Pontiac parked on the street and rounded on him. "All you had to do was look at him! I thought he was going to punch you."

"So did I." Chase shrugged off his uncomfortable suit jacket and tossed it on top of what he assumed was her car. His tie followed. "You didn't need to worry, though. I could take Anthony. I know at least five great karate moves."

"Really?" Her eyes followed him as he rolled up the sleeves on his shirt. "I...uh...didn't know you knew karate."

"I don't. I know five karate moves. But I'm willing to bet that's five more than Anthony knows."

"Right." Tara gazed at his forearms and licked her lips. Then she shook her head and looked up at him. "That doesn't matter. I wasn't worried about him beating you up. I was worried about the effect a brawl would have on the article."

"Thanks a lot," Chase muttered. His heroines didn't act this way. After any sort of altercation, they would be clinging to the hero, cooing, "Oh, Chase. I was so frightened that you might get hurt."

Tara dragged him back from that pleasant scene. "You were baiting him!"

Chase looked back at her. Her hair glowed, her green eyes glittered. Her cheeks were flushed and her lips were moist, and if he bent his head, he could lick the moisture off with a swipe of his tongue.

Right. Then she'd knee him in the groin and beat him to

death with her purse. "Anthony bugged me," he defended. "He ordered me a martini as soon as I got there. He didn't even ask me. He just ordered it, and when I told him I didn't drink martinis, he told me that I should start!" He scowled. "I haven't got a clue how he made anyone's list...unless real men are pompous asses."

Tara turned away and started rummaging through her purse for her keys. "He wasn't pompous. He was...self-assured. Confident. In-charge."

"Obnoxious," Chase said under his breath.

Tara giggled. "Okay, maybe he had a little too much confidence, but women today like that. They appreciate a man who knows who he is and where he's going."

Chase snorted derision. "That guy didn't know where he was going. All he knows is how to start something. He doesn't know how to keep it running. And he's got far too much confidence. He's absolutely positive that his latest venture is going to be a huge success."

Tara sighed. "He should be confident. He's started a number of businesses."

"Businesses that have all failed." Chase stretched out an arm and rested it against her car door. "Or if they haven't failed, they haven't been roaring successes. The guy who took over his stationery-supply business told me that he'd had a hard time just keeping it afloat."

Tara blinked. "You know the guy who took over one of Anthony's businesses?"

"No," said Chase. "I found out about it and gave him a call." She looked so surprised that he added, "I might not have much experience at interviews, but I'm great at research."

"Oh." She found her keys in her purse. "That's good, but you don't really need to go into that much depth here. We're not writing an exposé or a character assassination. These men just represent what women think today's men should be like. And after talking with Anthony, I'd say that women like men who are confident.''

''I see.'' Chase wasn't ready to end this conversation. He picked up his clothes from the top of her car, took her arm and started walking down the sidewalk. ''Well, if that's the case, we writers are in big trouble, aren't we?''

''Why?'' asked Tara, sounding confused.

''Because of what we do. Writers are filled with self-doubt.'' He glanced down at her. ''Don't you agree? I mean, just because your last book sold well doesn't mean your next book will sell. You're always worried about it.''

Tara stopped walking and faced him. ''That's how you feel?''

''Yes, that's how I feel,'' Chase admitted. ''I know it's not the confidence a real man is supposed to project, but it's the truth.'' Maybe that was why he hadn't made the real man list and Hunter had. Hunter had tons of confidence.

''I think it's better,'' Tara said slowly. ''Women like men who have a few vulnerabilities...as long as they aren't obsessive about them.''

Chase peered into her face. ''Honestly?''

Tara nodded solemnly. ''Honestly.''

''That's great.'' He continued to gaze into her pretty, upturned face. He'd like nothing more than to pull her back against the nearest building, tuck her tight round bottom against him and show her just how vulnerable he was to her.

Another bad idea. Chase took her arm and resumed walking. ''Let's go.''

Tara hurried to keep up with him. ''Where are we going?''

''There's a place up here that serves the best tea in the city.'' He grinned at her. ''After that little chat with Anthony...along with two swallows of a martini...I need a cup of tea."

"I think I do, too," said Tara.

TARA STOPPED at Lovely Lounging on her way home, had a nice chat with the owner and spent far too much money on a brilliant green and aqua silk negligee set. She changed into it as soon as she got home and checked it out in the bedroom mirror. It was perfect. She looked elegant and sophisticated and a little old-fashioned, just like her apartment. Granted, this wasn't the outfit for washing floors and cleaning toilets, but she didn't plan on cleaning any toilets right now.

She poured herself a glass of wine and settled at the kitchen table with her papers spread around her. This was how she wanted to live...elegant, sophisticated...with a charming, old-fashioned man as a companion and lover. A charming, well-dressed, old-fashioned man who had nothing, nothing to do with leather underwear!

But if he did have something to do with leather underwear, he'd look great in it.

She pushed that fantasy aside and started transcribing her notes. She'd just finished writing up her findings from Wutherspoon when Stella dropped by. "Matthew's with a friend," she explained. "I have a little time before I have to pick him up, so I thought I'd pop over and see if you had any news."

"Sure," said Tara. "I've got tons of news. Anthony is pompous and Chase looks uncomfortable in a suit and owns a purple tie. Oh, and if you feed a man a steak, it doesn't turn him on. Apparently, it makes him too full and too dopey to do much."

Stella waved that away. "That's not the sort of news I meant. I want to know about your progress in the Wuth-

50 Clues He's Mr. Right

erspoon case. You were going to meet with Gerald today, weren't you?"

"Oh yes. Gerald." Tara had almost forgotten about him. "Yes, I met with him."

Stella's eyes lit up. "What happened? Did he say anything about his uncle?"

"He didn't admit to bumping him off, if that's what you mean. He showed me around the store, and told me about all the things he was going to change in the place. Oh, and I did see the new line of leather underwear. You're right. I will be surprised if it sells well...although Gerald said there's a big market for it."

"He's wrong, but I'm not worried about that right now. Go on. What else did you find out? Did he mention Franklin at all?"

Tara set down her wineglass. "Yes, he did. He said he was very fond of him."

"I bet," Stella muttered.

"And that he was shocked when he discovered Franklin had left the business to him."

"Really?" asked Stella. "Who did he expect Franklin to leave it to? Gerald was pretty much the only relative he had, unless you count his canary."

Tara hesitated. "He didn't mention that. But he did mention that he didn't eat any of the shrimp dip so he couldn't have fed it to his uncle."

"You never know," said Stella. "Go on, what else did you find out?"

"Not much." Stella looked so disappointed that Tara added, "But I'll have more after next week. I'm going to talk with everyone who works at Wutherspoon. And I'm having dinner with Gerald on Saturday night."

Stella's lip curled in disgust. "Terrific strategy, Tar. Date a murderer. I'm sure that will add something to your real men article." She got to her feet. "Can I use your bathroom before I spend another forty minutes in the car?"

"Sure." Tara watched her disappear down the hall. "I don't think he's a murderer and I'm not dating him," she called after her. "He's just going to update me on the changes he's made, and what he's trying to accomplish." *Do you mind if we discuss it over dinner?* Gerald had asked. *Call me old-fashioned, but I just find it difficult to have a discussion with an attractive woman in a warehouse.* "You never know what I'll find out."

"I'm expecting to find out something," Stella called back. "I'm having a drink with Stanley tomorrow night."

Tara scowled at that. "You don't mean Stanley Gruber?"

"Uh-huh. Can you watch Matthew for me?"

Tara narrowed her eyes. "Sure, but..." But what about Lorraine? "I thought Stanley was engaged."

"He is." Stella came out of the bathroom and caught Tara's frown. "Get your mind out of the gutter. Stanley is just having a drink with me to discuss the Franklin Files."

Tara blinked. "What are the Franklin Files?"

"That's the code name I've given this case." Stella beamed. "How do you like it? It sounds like a book...or maybe a good title for your article."

Terrific. Stella was still playing undercover detective. "I don't know about this."

"What? The Franklin Files? I wasn't sure, either. I did come up with the Fishy Franklin Files—"

Tara shook her head. "Not that. This...investigation. I don't know that there's any point. I'm not convinced it wasn't just an accident, and I'm positive Gerald had nothing to do with it if it wasn't."

Stella rubbed a palm around her chin in a thoughtful, detective-type pose. "I'm not so sure. But even if you're right, and he didn't do it, then maybe someone else did.

I'm not alone in my suspicions, either. Stanley agrees with me.''

"He does?"

"Yes, he does.'' Stella nodded. "That's why we're meeting tomorrow night. Stanley wants to compare notes. He wants to tell me what he knows.''

"Assuming Stanley knows something—which I strongly doubt—why would he want to tell you about it?"

"Because I'm an accountant, of course.'' Stella raised her chin. "People tell accountants all kinds of things. We're sort of like priests in that regard.''

"Uh-huh.''

"Oh, come on, Tara. Why else would he ask me out for a drink?''

"You never know,'' said Tara. "Maybe it's because he's heterosexual.''

"He is not!'' said Stella. "He's a Capricorn. He told me so at lunch.'' She picked up her purse. "Oh, by the way, do you remember the name of that plumber you called the other day?''

"Gus,'' said Tara.

"Do you know his phone number?''

"I think so. Why?''

Stella winced. "You might want to give him a call. Your toilet is backed up.'' She slipped on her jacket. "I'd stay and help but I've got to pick up Matthew.''

"No problem.'' Tara growled. "I've got the routine down now.'' She walked Stella to the door, closed it behind her, then stomped over to the phone. This apartment might be lovely and elegant, but it sure needed fixing up!

WHILE TARA WAS QUIZZING Gerald, and Stella was quizzing Stanley, Chase decided to quiz his sister.

He dropped by late that evening to pick up the boys. He still wasn't happy with his helicopter scene, and needed a couple of willing actors to help him choreograph it. While he waited for them to gather up their toy guns and other paraphernalia they considered necessary for this activity, Chase leaned against the counter and told Molly about the assignment.

Molly had not only heard of *Real Men* magazine, she was also an avid reader, and more impressed with Chase's association with it than Chase felt the situation warranted. "You're writing an article for *Real Men* magazine," she exclaimed, wide-eyed. "Wow, Chase! That's incredible!"

For some reason, her amazement seemed insulting. "I've written half a dozen bestsellers and been in lots of magazines, Molly. This is just a small article."

"Yes, but it's for *Real Men!* I mean, I was impressed when your books started turning up in the supermarket, and I'm always astonished when I see you featured in some magazine. Although I've never understood why your favorite color keeps changing."

"It depends on my mood," Chase said vaguely. "I didn't know you read *Real Men* magazine."

"Every woman reads it. All the best men turn up there. They even did an article on Leonardo DiCaprio. And now you're doing an article for them!" She eyed him. "You're not posing in the nude or anything, are you?"

Chase shuddered at the thought. "Good God, no. And I'm not really doing an article for them, either. I'm working with Tara on the article she's doing for them."

"Tara?" Molly's eyes widened. "You don't mean Tara Butler?" Chase nodded and she put a hand over her mouth. "OhmyGod. You know Tara Butler! I can't believe this!"

Chase had met a number of famous people, including politicians, movie stars and models, and Molly hadn't reacted like this. "She's just a freelance writer, Molly."

"I know, but she's good! 'Sex and the Single Scene' was a classic!"

"Sex and the Single Scene"? Tara had written about sex and the single scene? How had she researched *that?*

"And the article she did on clothes that make you feel bold was fascinating," Molly burbled on. "I ran out and bought a new pair of sneakers right after I read it."

"Sneakers? What do sneakers have to do with—"

"It's a woman's thing." She studied him with outright curiosity. "What kind of article are you working on with her?"

"It has nothing to do with sneakers. It's about men. Real men." He cleared his throat. "As a matter of fact, I wanted to ask you about that." He leaned against the counter. "What would you say were the qualities of a real man?"

Molly wrinkled her nose while she considered the question. "Let's see. Good looks. A great sense of humor…intelligent…" She chewed on her bottom lip. "I guess I'd have to say someone just like Eddie."

"Eddie?" Chase tried to reconcile his brother-in-law with the adjectives Molly had used but couldn't. "You mean, your husband, Eddie?"

Molly frowned disgust. "No, I meant Frasier's dog, Eddie! Of course I meant my husband, dummy."

"Oh." Chase couldn't think of a response to that. Eddie owned a furniture store. He was a decent enough guy, but his entire conversation seemed to revolve around sofas. Chase had a hard time fitting that into the image of a real man. "What about me? Would you consider me a real man?"

Molly put her head on one side. "You're my brother, Chase. I don't think of you as a man at all."

"Gee, thanks."

"But if I did, I suppose I'd think you were a real man. You've sure been a good brother to me. Look how you've helped Eddie get his furniture store set up, not to mention the money you put up for my education, the things you've gotten for Mother. You've been wonderful."

Chase shrugged that off as unimportant. "That doesn't have anything to do with real men, sis. That's just part of being a human being. Even if I were your *sister* I'd do the same. What I want to know is, if you *weren't* my sister, would you consider me a real man?"

"Oh." Molly averted her eyes. "I suppose I would."

Chase swallowed against his instant disappointment. "Is that a yes or no?"

"It's a yes." Molly looked up at him again and smiled, cheerful and reassuring. "Granted, you do spend a lot of your time writing, and you can be fussy about what you eat…and you aren't exactly the tidiest person in the world. I don't know if you're romantic…but you have a great sense of humor and you're lots of fun…and…and—" she snapped her fingers "—and whenever you're here for supper, you put the dishes in the dishwasher and scrub the pots."

Chase blinked. "Scrubbing pots is a quality of a real man?"

Molly nodded. "I'd say so. Real men always do the dishes. Eddie does them most of the time. It's one of the things I love about him." She flushed. "And one of the things that turns me on."

Chase opened his mouth to ask more, but just then his nephews, Andrew and Simon, burst into the room, their hands filled with toy weapons, cars and other action-figure paraphernalia. "It's my turn to be the bad guy, isn't it, Uncle Chase?" Andrew demanded. "Simon got to be the bad guy last time."

Simon shoved him aside. "I did not! You were the bad guy. I had to be the girl."

Chase held up his hands. "In this scene you can both be

bad guys and we'll use pillows for the hero and heroine. That way no one will get hurt.''

The boys yelped approval and raced out to the car. Chase shoved his hands in his pockets and followed. This real man stuff was more complicated than staging a scene. Confident. Vulnerable. Liked to wash dishes:

"Don't concern yourself with Laromee's men," Hunter told Bridgett as they ate beans out of a can. "We can handle them."

"Are you sure?" asked Bridgett.

"Pretty sure," said Hunter. "I'm a little worried about it, but if we plan ahead, we should be able to pull it off." He finished the last spoonful and got to his feet. "You just stay put here. I'll take care of cleaning up the dishes."

"There aren't any dishes," said Bridgett. "We ate beans out of a can."

"Yeah, well, we might need that can again." Hunter carried the can down to the creek and rinsed it off.

Bridgett was still sitting in front of the fire when he returned. He settled down beside her. "There. All done."

She turned two luminous eyes in his direction. "Hunter?"

"Uh-huh?"

"Did I ever tell you that men washing dishes turns me on?"

"Not in so many words." His eyes widened as Bridgett unbuttoned her blouse. "But I'm starting to get the message."

"Aren't you going to start the car?" asked Andrew.

"What?" Chase realized he was sitting in the front seat with the keys dangling from his fingers. He shoved them into the ignition. That scene did have possibilities, but he'd like it a lot better if it were himself and Tara playing it out. He pictured her in his kitchen, with a stack of clean plates beside her. She'd pop open the buttons on her blouse one by one with a can't-wait look in her eyes as he dried the soap off his hands.

Then Cary Grant would stride into the room and sweep her into his arms.

Chase stepped on the accelerator. It would take more than a few clean dishes to attract Tara.

6

TARA HAD BEEN in a number of bachelor apartments, both from her own dating experiences and the work she'd done for *Real Men* magazine. She'd yet to see the perfect place, but she knew that it would be filled with strong masculine pieces. Comfortable footstools. Bookshelves filled with classics. There'd be a bar in the corner, stocked with the best wine…wine that would be served in crystal goblets. The kitchen would be well-organized, filled with every gadget known to man, and the counters would be gleaming clean.

Chase's place was nothing like that.

Tara discovered this Wednesday evening. She'd spent part of the week interviewing men, interviewing Wutherspoon employees and interviewing chefs. On Wednesday, after talking with the owner of a bungee-jumping adventurers, Chase suggested they get together to compare notes.

"We've talked to half a dozen guys now," he reminded her. "We should get together to consolidate our findings."

Tara didn't think spending a whole bunch of time alone with Chase at his place was a great idea, but she couldn't think of a good excuse. "If we're alone together I might attack you" wasn't something she wanted to tell him. Besides, she was curious about where he lived, how he lived, if he lived with anyone.

His place was an unassuming bungalow on a quiet suburban street, with a huge yard. From the outside, it was impossible to tell a famous author lived inside. As a matter of fact, it was impossible to tell that anyone out of the ordinary lived there.

Inside was much the same. The kitchen was a long rectangle, with red square tiles, a wooden picnic-type table at one end and counters covered, predictably, with packages of granola, bottles of vitamins and a variety of tea. He wasn't a stickler for neatness, either. True, the sink wasn't filled with dirty dishes, but apart from that, there was no sign that neatness was a priority.

While Chase hunted around for a pen, Tara took a quick look at the rest of the place. The living room was furnished with odd pieces in various shades of green, brown and blue that had to have been chosen more for comfort than style. There were three bedrooms off a narrow hall—one occupied by a desk, a set of bookshelves and a pile of magazines, another containing just a bed and a dresser that she decided was a guest bedroom and a large square room containing an unmade bed, a chair with a pile of clothes thrown at it and a dresser littered with more male paraphernalia. It was in no way a "bedroom that said *now*." Instead, it screamed, "Pick up your socks."

It was a direct contrast to Gerald Charmichael's condo. He'd taken Tara there Saturday night, after they'd eaten, to finish discussing his long-range plans for Wutherspoon

Outerwear. "I'm not trying to show you my etchings," he'd chuckled. "It would just be easier if we discussed this at my place."

Tara had agreed because it would have been churlish not to, and because she figured it would be a good opportunity to find out more about Stella's chief suspect. She hadn't found out much, except that Gerald had amazingly good taste. His condo, located on a quiet street in one of the more upscale parts of the city, was bright and spacious and filled with manly-looking antiques. It had been spotlessly clean and outstandingly neat. They'd drunk wine out of crystal goblets while he'd talked about his plans for Wutherspoon, and she'd wished she'd meet an eligible younger man just like him.

The eligible younger man certainly wasn't Chase. "Do you collect miniature toys or something?" Tara asked after she'd sat on one. She pulled a toy Ferrari from under her and set it on the table.

"Not exactly, although I do use them from time to time to choreograph scenes." He sat on the other side of the table and handed her a steaming mug of tea.

"You...block out your scenes with toys?"

Chase nodded. "Sometimes. If I can't get it right, I ask my nephews to give me a hand acting it out."

Who helped him act out the love scenes? No, she didn't want to ask him that. She didn't think he'd have any problem finding volunteers.

"If that doesn't work, I might have to look at a real-life version of the model." Chase went on. "That's what I'm doing next week. Jerome arranged for me to fly to Seattle to take a look at an oceangoing yacht." He wrinkled his nose in disgust. "I've been trying to get this rescue scene right, but it's just not working. Hunter can save the girl, but after he does that he can't get off the boat without getting shot. I've written it three ways, and he always ends up toasted. We're both sick of it.''

Tara chuckled at his wry expression. "Let's review what we've got so far. We've agreed that real men are hard to find, punctual and well-dressed.''

Chase aimed a finger at her. "I want to change that one to appropriately dressed. No one wears a suit bungee jumping…and my hero shouldn't have to wear one when he's breaking into a military base.''

Tara gave in. "All right. All right.''

"I also want to change 'Real men don't eat oatmeal.' I love oatmeal. Oatmeal is good for you.''

It probably was but Tara didn't like it. "Does your hero eat oatmeal?''

Chase shook his head. "My hero eats whatever is handy at the time, but that's out of necessity. When you're surviving in the desert or wandering around the jungle, you don't worry about your cholesterol count. If they had the chance, I'm sure they'd eat oatmeal for breakfast as opposed to fried lizard.''

Tara almost choked on her tea. "We're not saying real men eat lizard, Chase! Charlene would have a fit.''

"I suppose, although I think he should know how to fry a lizard.'' Chase drummed his fingers against the tabletop. "How about 'Real men watch what they eat'? People today should pay attention to their diet.''

Tara looked at his flat stomach and healthy complexion then looked away. "I agree. However, they shouldn't be preoccupied with it. It can't be the entire reason for their existence.''

Chase conceded the point. "I can live with that.''

Chase smiled directly into her eyes, and for a moment Tara forgot what she was doing.

"Confident stays in, so does well-organized, although he can't be a neatness fanatic. I once dated a guy like that. He was so well-organized he bought groceries in alphabetical order.''

"What happened to him?" Chase asked.

"We broke up. One trip to the supermarket pretty much did it." She scribbled a note beside neatness. "Intelligence stays in."

"But this 'Real men don't do housework' comes out!" Chase interjected. "Molly says that men washing dishes really turns her on."

Tara felt a small stirring of jealousy. "Who is Molly?"

"My sister." He rested his elbows on the table. "She said that whenever her husband, Eddie, does it, she gets in the mood, although I can't see it. Eddie's a great guy, but I can't imagine him turning anyone on."

Tara pictured some of the men she'd dated washing dishes. Not many of them had volunteered, although Owen had insisted on it. Unfortunately, he'd been going through his "fanatically clean" phase and had washed them all three times in boiling water before putting them in the dishwasher. Watching him obsess about it had not turned her on. However, the idea of Chase, in his kitchen, wearing…oh, maybe just a pair of jeans or perhaps even less, up to his elbows in soapy water. "Fine. Real men wash dishes. I can do something with that." She made a note. "I think we've handled confidence. Real men are confident…but they have a few vulnerabilities as well."

His lips moved into a slow smile. "Perfect."

Tara stared at him for a moment, entranced, then turned back to her list. "What about 'Real men make the first move'?" She chewed the end of her pen while she thought about it. "We haven't asked anyone about that, but I think it should be changed. A man with confidence wouldn't mind if a woman made the first move." She started to write that down.

"It all depends on the move," Chase said slowly.

Tara glanced up, startled. "What do you mean? In your books, the women are always all over the hero and he doesn't mind."

Chase gave his shoulders a dismissive shrug. "Yeah, well, that's fiction. This is real life, and in real life it depends on the move. I don't mind when a woman calls me up and asks me out, as long as what she's suggesting is 'Let's get to know each other,' not 'Let's get together and have sex.'"

Tara didn't believe this. "You don't like sex? Gee, I never would have guessed that from your books."

Chase gave her a look of utter disgust. "I like sex just fine, thanks, but I like to think a woman is interested in me in other ways as well. The 'let's sleep with the famous author' types don't do anything for me."

"I never thought of that," Tara admitted. She eyed him up and down. "Does that happen often?" It was a dumb question. Of course it happened often.

Chase reddened. "It happens. Let's move on. Where—"

"Is that where all those sex scenes come from?"

"No, it is not where all those sex scenes come from," said Chase. "Those come from my imagination—along with a few true-life adventures. But the truth is, the 'let's see how good you really are' types scare me to death. It feels like a test. The last thing you need after a romp in the hay is the woman saying, 'It was okay but not as good as your books.'"

Tara struggled to hide her smile. "Has someone ever said that?"

"No! I'm just as good as my books! But knowing it could happen adds a lot of pressure."

Tara refused to feel sorry for him. "You can always say no, Chase."

Chase held up a hand. "Hey, I'm a man not a saint."

He certainly wasn't a saint, but he sure was a man. Tara

swallowed. "Okay. What are we going to say about this first-move thing? Real men don't like women who make the first move?"

Chase shook his head. "I wouldn't go that far. In some cases, a woman has to make the first move. For men like poor Hubert, I'd say it's an absolute essential. I don't think he'd ever have a date if a woman didn't make the first move, and it would only work if she wasn't subtle about it." He chuckled. "Come to think of it, she'd probably have to send him an E-mail."

Tara laughed along with him. "How about if we conclude that real men don't mind if you make the first move...as long as it's not a move into the bedroom."

"I like that."

"Great. Now then, let's tackle 'Real men indulge your feelings.' I think it should be updated to 'Real men are sensitive to your feelings.'"

"You're just saying that because we interviewed a psychiatrist. Naturally he's sensitive to your feelings. He's sensitive to everyone's feelings. That's part of his job. Normal men don't have a clue what you're feeling unless you tell them. Unless they're my hero. My hero is astoundingly sensitive!"

"Your hero?" Tara snorted. "Your hero is the most insensitive man I've ever heard of. It's a good thing he's fictional or he'd have been booted off the planet by an army of angry women a long time ago."

Chase's eyes widened with indignation. "What do you mean? My hero is great at sensitive. For instance, he knows darn well that the heroine doesn't like to be tied up or kidnapped. If that isn't sensitive, I don't know what is."

"You're right," said Tara. "You don't. A sensitive man would want to know why the heroine is doing what she's doing...how she got to be in the situation she's in...why it's important to her. Your hero doesn't care about that.

Look at Hunter. He went through the entire book without asking Desmonda why she was shacking up with a villain as creepy as Dorian.''

"That is not true," said Chase, shaking a finger. "There was a good half a chapter on how she wanted to avenge her brother's death.''

"Yes, there was, but you told it from her point of view. She never told the hero, and he never asked!''

Chase winced. "Okay, you do have a point there, but—''

"I have lots of points," said Tara, warming to the topic. "Your hero doesn't really care about the heroines. All he does is run around blowing things up, getting beaten up and generally rescuing the world from chaos and anarchy.''

Chase wiggled his eyebrows. "That isn't all he does.''

Tara frowned at him, exasperated. "I'm not talking about sex, dummy. I'm talking about feelings. Your hero doesn't know and doesn't care how the heroine is feeling and vice versa. That's not the way women act. Women don't jump into bed with someone because he's just rescued them from terrorists. They have to feel something more meaning-ful…and he should, too.''

"Like what?'' Chase demanded.

"Well…'' Tara mentally sorted through his books. "Take when they kiss, for example. Is all a man thinks about when he kisses a woman how to get her into bed?''

Chase opened his mouth as if to agree, then changed his mind. "No. When you're kissing someone, you think about kissing them.''

Tara shook her head. "That's not what your hero thinks about. When your hero is kissing the heroine, he's either planning the next battle or looking for a good place to stage it.''

"That is not true.''

"Yes it is. Take a look at *Sunset to Disaster*. The hero is kissing the heroine, and what's he thinking about? How

to break into some compound on the other side of the At-
lantic!''

Chase beamed. ''You have read my books!''

Read them? She was obsessed by them. ''I've read a
couple of them,'' Tara said in a total understatement. ''And
all the kissing scenes are pretty much the same.''

Chase creased his forehead and pursed his lips while he
considered what she'd said. ''Maybe they do have something in common, but...but they can't be that different.
How many different ways are there to kiss a woman?''

It suddenly occurred to Tara that discussing kissing
scenes with Chase was not a good idea. ''I don't know,''
she said, anxious to put the subject to bed. No, beds weren't
a good thing to think about, either. ''I only know what it's
like to kiss men and there are lots of different ways to do
that.'' Some men were great kissers and some weren't. Tara
preferred the slow, gentle kisses that started out as nibbles
and deepened into something else. She thought about nibbling the corners of his mouth and shivered. ''Look, when
you kiss a woman, what are you thinking about? Your next
book? Or her?''

Chase's eyes gleamed. ''I'm not thinking about my book,
I can tell you that. Mostly I'm thinking about her. As a
matter of fact, I can safely say I'm thinking about her.''

Tara sat back, resting her case. ''Then your hero should
think about her, too.''

''You might have a point there.'' Chase swung his legs
up to the bench, rested his back against the wall and stared
up at the ceiling. ''Let's see. In the book I'm writing now,
the hero and heroine have managed to figure out the villain's evil plan. Hero and heroine have a few minutes alone
together.''

His tone was deep and slow and compelling and Tara's
lower body stirred in response.

''He puts his arms around her and kisses her,'' Chase

went on. His eyelids drooped down. "The second his lips touch hers, the mission slides to the back of his mind. Her mouth is hot and moist. He licks his tongue along her bottom lip and she presses closer..." He popped open his eyes. "That's what she would do, isn't it? Press closer?"

"Oh yes," Tara croaked.

"Good." His eyes closed again. "She presses closer, and all he can think about is how it feels to be this near to her...how she tastes, the feel of her hair in his hands and the heat of her body. When he uses his tongue, he's thinking about her. She fills his mind completely until the only thing in existence is her against him, the beat of her heart, the press of her body as he moves his hips against hers. He wants her. He wants to push her against the wall and take her even if ten thousand villains come pouring through the door." He opened his eyes and straightened. "How was that?"

Fantastic. Arousing. Compelling. She wanted to act out that scene right now, with him, in this kitchen. "N-not too bad." If he wrote like that, he'd sell another million books.

She looked at him sprawled along the bench, barely shaved, hair mussed, eyes gleaming at her, a little wicked and a lot sexy and not a single bit like Cary. Kissing him would be like that—not polite and decorous, but heady and sensual and arousing. She could leap on him right now, and find out how he tasted and how he smelled and how it felt to have that rough stubble pressing her cheek. Bad idea. Really bad idea. "It was better than if he was thinking about battle scenes." She returned to her list and struggled to compose herself. "Let's get back to the real men article. We need a number fifty."

"How about real men can load a gun in less than two seconds?" Chase suggested.

Tara threw her pen at him and he chuckled. "Okay. Okay. But you're better off not depending on me for number fifty. I've got a hard enough time dealing with forty-nine of them. You'll have to think of something.''

"Thanks a lot.'' If she hung around him too much longer, she would be putting in "Real men know how to reload,'' or maybe "Real men didn't talk dirty.'' On the other hand, maybe they did. If they knew the effect it had on women, they'd probably do it all the time. She mentally crossed it off her list. She wasn't telling that to any male. It was a dangerous weapon no one should ever tell them about.

THE ZIMLER YACHT was everything Jerome had promised it would be.

Chase prowled around it, imagining his hero in here, trying to get a handle on the action, while Jerome paced restlessly behind him. "Just so you know, this is not the sort of thing agents do,'' he complained. "Agents sell your books. They do not go around finding you boats to look at.''

"You didn't need to come with me, Jer. And I needed to see a yacht. The heroine is tied up in one, and I've got to figure out how to rescue her. It's a little hard to do when you've never been on a yacht in your life.''

"I see your point,'' said Jerome. He followed Chase down the stairs. "How's that book of yours coming anyway?''

"Just fine.'' Chase took a look in one of the bedrooms. "Hunter and Bridgett are busy saving the world.'' The room was small, but adequate. Bridgett could be tied up here. Hunter would come racing down the stairs, grapple with the guard, rescue Bridgett... He'd have to take out a couple of bad guys on the way up and he'd have to do it quick if they were going to leave before the boat blew up.

Or, if they timed it a little better, they could have half an hour alone in here, then get off the boat.

He scowled at the direction this was leading. He hadn't told Jerome the entire truth about his novel. Granted, Hunter and Bridgett were saving the world, but they were fitting it in around an enormous number of sex scenes. Even Chase was starting to wonder, and he was the one writing the book. He wasn't sure why he was doing it, either. Normally his books were filled with adventure, with a little sex on the side. This one seemed to be composed entirely of sex scenes with a little adventure on the side...and even then, when his characters weren't doing it, they were thinking about it.

And when they weren't doing that, they were having conversations, and it wasn't saving the world they were talking about. They were discussing everything under the sun, revealing things about themselves that even Chase was surprised to discover. Bridgett, it turned out, was a tough street kid who was trying to make a success of herself the only way she knew how. And Hunter! Hunter was busy wishing for a family to come home to after he'd been off on one of his "save the world" assignments. He never would have guessed that Hunter was a white-picket-fence kind of guy, but it turned out that he was.

"How are things going with you and Vanna?" he asked, to take his mind off the problems of Hunter and Bridgett.

"A little better, I think." Jerome sounded optimistic. "I bought her a computer and we signed up for tennis lessons." His expression darkened. "She still hasn't canceled that counseling session, though. She won't talk about it, either. Every time I mention it, she looks worried and changes the subject." He lounged against the railing. "What's the word on real men these days? How's the article coming along?"

"I'm getting better at it," Chase said optimistically. "Yesterday we interviewed a bungee jumper, and a guy who owns an art gallery...and I figured out a couple of things about each of them all by myself. The bungee jumper is obviously brave, and likes to take risks."

"Brave and takes risks, huh?"

"Yup. Apparently, real men take risks."

"Oh no!" Jerome looked horrified. "I don't have to take up bungee jumping, do I?"

"No," said Chase. "That would be stupid. Real men aren't stupid."

"But you just said—"

"I said risk takers. But after we talked to the gallery owner, I figured out that he was a bigger risk taker than the bungee jumper. He opened that gallery with no idea if it would succeed or not, but he really believed in himself, so he just crossed his fingers and did it. Tara said that's what made him a real man—he believes in himself and takes risks. The bungee jumper was just an adrenaline junkie."

"That's not much help."

"Tara said I was a risk taker, too," Chase remembered. "She said that when I quit my job and decided to try writing full time, that was a risk." Her eyes had gleamed approval when she'd told him that. He thought about her eyes, and he thought about her hair, and her smile...

"That's great for you, but what about me?" asked Jerome.

"You?" Chase focused back on him and tried to recall what they'd been talking about. "What about you?"

Jerome's shoulders drooped. "I can't think of one risk I've ever taken." He blinked. "Maybe I should take Vanna to Vegas."

"Vegas?"

"Sure." Jerome's round face brightened at the idea. "There are lots of risks there."

Chase didn't share his enthusiasm. "I don't know, Jer. I

don't think losing a few hundred is going to impress anyone.'' Jerome looked so disappointed and so worried that Chase sighed. "On the other hand, I guess it couldn't hurt.''

7

Real men take care of finances. Not too good with those numbers? Never fear, your real man is here. Not only will he balance his checkbook, he'll balance yours as well. He likes taking care of financial matters. And let's face it, he's probably better at it than you are. Sit back, relax and don't worry. He's got it all under control.

—from "Forty-Nine Things You Need to Know about a Real Man," *Real Men* Magazine, April 1949

"NOW THAT was a colossal waste of time," Chase announced.

He stomped out of the offices of Astonishing Adventures, looking more disgusted than usual—and, unfortunately, more delicious. For this interview, he'd left his purple tie at home, instead choosing a casual khakis and loose white shirt look, because, he explained, this time they were going to be meeting a real, real man.

"J. A. Talbot is going to be the best of the bunch," he'd advised. "Just look at this place. Kayaking. White water rafting. Hiking. Fishing. Camping. Now that's my idea of manliness."

Tara hadn't been convinced. In her experience, men who liked the great outdoors were also men who thought a good date was shopping for a new canoe.

That wasn't how Mr. Talbot, owner of Astonishing Adventures, had turned out. Granted, he'd been an outdoorsy-looking guy, but instead of talking about he-man-type activities, he'd spent most of the interview talking about...

"Financial planning!" Chase exclaimed now. "Can you believe that guy? All he talked about was financial planning. The stock market! Mutual funds! What's that got to do with anything?"

"I think that's what economics was all about," Tara mumbled as she struggled to keep up with him. That was one for her article. Real men did *not* walk faster than you did. "Besides I thought his investment plan was interesting."

"His investment plan might have been interesting but he didn't stop there! He not only went over his investment plan, he pretty much went over our investment plans. I couldn't tell if we were interviewing him, or if he was trying to sell us a total investment package."

Tara hadn't been that taken with Mr. Talbot either. She'd been too busy noticing how great Chase smelled and how pleased she was to see him again. He'd only been gone a day, but she'd gotten used to talking to him on a regular basis. That bothered her. So did the way her body reacted when he was around. She'd resolved not to be attracted to another Mr. Wrong and here she was, doing it again. "He does have a point, Chase. People do need to plan ahead these days. Women and men."

Chase scowled at her. "Don't look so smug! You didn't come out as a star in there. It didn't sound to me as if you do a whole bunch of planning ahead either."

"I don't," Tara confessed. "I have a hard enough time planning for next month. But we aren't talking about me. We're talking about the type of men women like and women like men who plan for their future."

Chase stopped walking. "Hunter can't do that. There's no retirement plan for men who risk their lives on a daily basis."

"He should at least think about it," said Tara. "Today's real men should be concerned about their future." She should be concerned about her future, too. She had to start seriously looking for Mr. Right.

"Keep quiet," Hunter ordered. He crouched down in the bushes and carefully parted a few branches to get a look at the place.

"Do you have a plan?" Bridgett whispered into his ear.

"Of course I have a plan," Hunter growled. "Break into Laromee's headquarters. Find the schematics and get the hell out of there without getting shot."

Bridgett didn't look impressed. "That's not what I meant. I mean a financial plan for the future."

CHASE STUDIED the words he'd just written, then erased half of them. This was not a good time for Hunter and Bridgett to discuss finances. On the other hand, it might be a good time for him to discuss finances.

He picked up the phone and dialed. "It's me," he announced when Jerome answered. "I need to ask you something."

"This better be good," said Jerome. "I'm leaving for Vegas in a couple of hours."

Chase shrugged that off. "It's important, Jer."

"What is it?"

"Do I have a retirement plan?"

Jerome's sigh would have knocked over a chair if they'd been in the same room. "How in hell would I know if you have a retirement plan? I know I have a retirement plan. I don't know if you have one or not, and it's not something I should know. I'm your agent, not your financial planner.''

Chase ignored the last part of Jerome's diatribe to focus on the first. "You have a financial-planning strategy?"

"Yeah, I do. Why?"

"It just doesn't sound like something you'd do, that's all." Chase swung his feet up onto his desk. "Does Vanna know about it?"

"I imagine so…at least I would think she does." Jerome's voice sharpened. "Why? Do you think she should?"

"You should discuss it. Real men should be concerned about their future."

Jerome chuckled. "That lets you out, pal."

"No, it doesn't," said Chase, feeling smug and virtuous. "I'm thinking of registering in a financial-planning seminar."

"You are not!" said Jerome. "You never think about stuff like that."

"I am now. I was talking to J.A. about it and he mentioned this seminar. I think I should go."

"I don't believe this," said Jerome. "I do not believe that you…you who never know how much money you're supposed to get from royalties, who doesn't know how much money he has in the bank or if he has any…is talking about financial planning."

"I'm not just talking about it. I'm doing it. We're interviewing a financial planner later this week and I'm going to ask him about it." Chase glanced at his computer screen. "And Hunter is going to get into it as well."

"Hunter!" Jerome sounded alarmed now. "What do you mean Hunter? You're not going to start sending your hero off to financial-planning seminars, are you?"

"Uh-huh."

"Is there an explosion there or something? A clue?"

"No!"

"Gee, that should add some excitement to your story," Jerome drawled. "Hunter attended a financial-planning seminar. I know I couldn't put a book down with a sentence like that in it."

"Get stuffed," Chase said cheerfully. "Have fun in Vegas." He hung up the phone and returned to his story.

There was a slight noise in the hallway. Hunter crouched down behind the desk and motioned Bridgett to do the same. He wasn't worried about the guard. He could take him out. He just didn't want anyone knowing they were there.

He took another look around the room. There was no sign of their presence. The desk drawers were closed, the safe locked, the newspaper... He slid the newspaper off the chair and quietly flicked to the last page.

"What are you doing?" asked Bridgett.

"Just thought I'd take the opportunity to check my investments." Hunter scanned the page, then replaced the paper, taking care to make sure it was in exactly the same position. "Remind me to give my stockbroker a call when we get the chance."

TARA HAD RESOLVED to put Chase's kissing scene out of her mind. When that didn't work, when every time she closed her eyes she recalled him sprawled against the kitchen table talking about Hunter kissing Bridgett, she did the next best thing. She told Stella about it.

"You should have heard him," she confessed as she put together the meal she'd invited Stella and Matthew to share with her. The six-year-old was in the den watching television. "It was the most erotic sex scene I've ever heard. He sat there talking in his deep voice and I almost lost my mind. It was all I could do to keep myself from ripping off his clothes."

"That might not have been a bad thing," said Stella. "You would have gotten some interesting material for that article."

Tara paused in the middle of cutting up veggies. It wouldn't have been bad. It probably would have been good, maybe even great.

She chopped up a piece of celery. This was Chase Montgomery. Even if he was interested, and she wasn't sure he was, she couldn't sleep with him. He was so not her Mr. Right. She'd be doing it strictly from lust and that would be wrong. "I'm not sleeping with Chase for the sake of an article. I'm sure I've told you that."

"I just thought you might change your mind. And speaking of articles, what did you find out from Gerald the other night?"

"Only that he's got a great condo." Tara returned to her chopping. "It's one of the best-decorated places I've ever seen. If I'd seen it when I was writing 'His Place or Yours' I would have definitely recommended his."

"How would you have put that?" Stella wondered. She sprawled in a chair in Tara's kitchen, her blue-jeaned legs stretched out in front of her. "When spending the night with a murderer, be sure to check out his pad before deciding where you are going to do it?" She paused. "You didn't actually 'do it' with Gerald, did you?"

"Good Lord, no. He's old enough to be my father. All we did was discuss his business." Tara cut a tomato into small pieces to put into the salad. It was too bad Gerald wasn't a young, unattached male. If she could find one like him... "And he's not a murderer, Stell."

"He might be," Stella objected. "His apartment sounds expensive and so does his furniture. He could have bumped off poor Franklin to get the bucks from Wutherspoon's."

"I doubt it. He got most of the furniture secondhand and refinished it himself."

Stella narrowed her eyes into her suspicious-detective expression. "Is that what he told you?" Tara nodded and she made a face. "Do you think we should simply take his word for it?"

"For heaven's sake, Stella, I'm not going to investigate the man's furniture! I'm sure he has nothing to do with Franklin's death. He's got such good taste."

"There's no rule that says someone with good taste wouldn't bump off his uncle."

Tara tossed the tomatoes into the bowl. "There's no proof his uncle was bumped off at all."

"Maybe there isn't, but...but I still think something fishy is going on. Even if Gerald didn't do it, it could very well be someone else did."

"Like who?" Tara invited. "I've talked to almost everyone in the place, and I haven't come up with anyone."

"How about Mrs. Glasier? I heard that she had an argument with Franklin a few days before that dinner."

"She told me that herself." Tara opened the fridge and hunted around for the cucumber. "But all they argued about were the new fall jackets. She wanted to add some pink but he hated the idea." She pulled out the cucumber and made a face at its wilted appearance. "I don't think they fixed my fridge, after all. It still doesn't seem to be keeping things cold."

"It was built in 1902, Tara. They hadn't even invented cold yet." She tapped her fingers together. "I guess you're right about Mrs. Glasier. She ordered roast beef, although she thought she was ordering lamb." She reflected on that for a moment. "What about Marvin Singleton? He's the man in charge of new development. Have you spoken with him yet?"

Tara thought of skinny, wimpy-looking Marvin and nodded.

"Maybe it was him. According to Stanley, he was unhappy because Franklin didn't like the new slogan he came up with."

"You mean 'Wutherspoon's. Wear it or you'll be cold'?" Tara shuddered. "He mentioned that to me, too, and I agreed with Franklin. Besides, I don't think Marvin would bump off Franklin because he had good taste."

"You can never tell what will push some people's buttons. And I don't know what Marvin ordered. He says he can't remember." She eyed the plates of food Tara was preparing. "Speaking of ordering, is that all we're having for dinner? Fruit and salad?"

Tara nodded. "I'm afraid so. The stove is on the fritz and all I know how to make without a stove is salad and fruit."

Stella sighed. "I thought with all those interviews you were doing with chefs, you'd have come up with some great recipes by now."

"Well, I haven't." Tara set the plates on the table. "I'm not supposed to be gathering recipes. 'Food That Puts Him in the Mood' is supposed to be a more general article. I'm meeting with Dr. Crenshaw up at the university. He's going to tell me which food have a psychological effect on the body."

"Good," said Stella. "When you find out, you can serve some to Chase and have a few bites yourself."

Tara paused to stare at her friend. "What is that supposed to mean?"

Stella gazed back at her in wide-eyed innocence. "Hey,

you've got to admit it's a little weird. Here you are, spending tons of time with a guy who writes some of the best sex scenes I've ever read, and you aren't taking advantage of the opportunity. It sounds like all you talk about is work."

Tara flushed. "That's all we're supposed to be doing, Stell."

Stella rolled her eyes, and Tara gave up and went down the hall to call Matthew for dinner. Stella was wrong. She didn't need food to put her in the mood either. All she had to do was look at him and she was in the mood. And work wasn't all they talked about. Chase told her about his family, and that his father had died when he was young, and how his mother had worked to take care of them, and how glad he was that now he could take care of her. She told him about her family, and some of the assignments she'd worked on, and how she wanted to get into more serious work.

After they'd interviewed the private detective, she told him about Wutherspoon Outerwear and Stella's Franklin Files.

"I think the women who said private detective were thinking about TV private detectives," Tara told Chase over a cup of tea in another trendy little teahouse that he said served the best cup of tea in Chicago. "I'm sure they weren't thinking about Mr. Nightingale."

"I hope they weren't." Chase took a long, grateful sip. "If you looked in the dictionary under *seedy,* you'd find his picture. And that office…" He shuddered. "I've never seen a place like it. That's one thing we learned from him. Real men might like animals, but they do not keep cockroaches as pets."

"Stella is going to be so disappointed. She was hoping I'd get some investigative ideas from him."

"Why does Stella need ideas?" Chase asked, so Tara told him.

"She's convinced that there's a murderer lurking around Wutherspoon's and nothing I can do convinces her otherwise." She stirred brown sugar into her tea. "Now she's busy cross-referencing people to what they ordered and what they tasted at the employee thank-you dinner. You should see it, Chase. It's a huge chart!" She shook her head. "If she's not careful, I'm afraid she could lose her job."

"If she's not careful, she could lose a lot more than her job," Chase muttered.

"What do you mean?"

"What do I mean?" Chase glared at her. "What do you think I mean, Tara? Stella is going around looking for a murderer. If she finds one, he or she is not likely to be grateful she did."

Tara hadn't thought of that. The idea of someone at Wutherspoon's being a criminal had seemed so far-fetched that she hadn't considered the ramifications. "There's nothing to worry about. There hasn't been a murder, so there can't be any murderers."

Chase's dark eyes still showed concern. "I hope you're right. Murderers aren't nice people, you know. I met one once, and let me tell you, he was not a nice person." He shuddered. "He scared the bejesus out of me."

"When did you meet a murderer?"

"A couple of years ago. I was writing *Midnight Storms* and I wanted to know what a cold-blooded killer looked like, so I got Jerome to introduce me to one." He made a face. "It was not a fun experience. I was glad he was on the other side of the steel bars."

Now he was scaring her. "That eliminates all the people at Wutherspoon Outerwear," Tara assured both of them.

"I've met all of them, and none of them look like cold-blooded killers."

Chase gave her an odd look. "Harry didn't look like a cold-blooded killer, Tara. He looked like everyone else. That was what was so scary about him."

A thousand goose bumps invaded Tara's body and she shivered. If either Stella or herself did run across a murderer, they could very well need the services of a real, Cary Grant-type man. She just hoped she met him before that happened.

8

Real men don't deal well with children. Don't invite
those nephews over if you want to impress a real man.
Oh, he adores his own children, but he doesn't understand them, and he simply doesn't relate to those
of others. He wants scintillating conversation, not di-
apers and runny noses.

> —from "Forty-Nine Things You Need
> to Know about a Real Man,"
> *Real Men* magazine, April 1949

ON FRIDAY AFTERNOON, Tara met the photographer and
went with him while he took the required pictures at Wutherspoon Outerwear.

Tara had already sorted through a stack of "before" pictures that Angie had supplied. She and the photographer
studied the best ones, and chose similar locations for the
"after" pictures, including a few with Angie to add some
cheesecake appeal.

Gerald caught up with her as they were packing up. "We
got everything we needed," she told him. "It's going to be
a great article. I'm sure it will attract a lot of interest."

Gerald looked pleased. "That's wonderful, Tara. Wonderful. We can't thank you enough."

Tara mentally squirmed. Here he was thanking her, and
she'd been busy trying to find out if he was a murderer.
"No problem."

"I certainly appreciate it." He took a step closer. "Listen, I know it's short notice, but I was wondering if you were free tonight? We could go out to dinner...and maybe take in a play. It would be my thank-you to you for all this free publicity."

Tara closed her eyes against the rush of guilt. "I'd love to, but I'm afraid I can't. I promised Stella I'd watch her son for her this evening." *While she quizzes another one of your employees about you.* She was going to talk to Stella tonight and put a stop to this. "But if you'd like to come over..."

A look of distaste crept up Gerald's face. "Why don't we make it another evening?" he said quickly. "I'm not that great with children...and I'd like to make it a special occasion. I'll give you a call next week."

"All right," said Tara, a little disappointed by his attitude. She shouldn't be surprised though. He was an older version of what she was looking for. The younger version would certainly feel differently.

That evening, she tackled Stella as soon as she stepped in the door to drop off Matthew. "We have got to put an end to this, Stella. You can't go around accusing that nice man of murder. It's just not right."

Stella tightened her lips into a mutinous line. "I'm not accusing anyone of anything. I'm just trying to find out what happened."

"I still don't think it's a good idea." Tara lowered her voice so Matthew wouldn't hear her. "Besides, it might be dangerous. I told you what Chase said..."

Stella pooh-poohed that with a wave of her hand. "Chase has a vivid imagination, which is only to be expected from a writer. Besides, I'm not doing anything dangerous. I'm looking for someone who mixed a little fish with Franklin's dinner, that's all. That won't work on me. I love fish." She flashed a reassuring smile. "I'm not even meeting with a suspect tonight. I'm just going to meet with Mr. Sweeny."

Tara struggled to put a face to the name. "Who is Mr. Sweeny?"

"He owns Sweeny Cleaning Services. Stanley suggested that he might know something. After all, janitors sometimes know all the secrets in the company. And I'm not going to be alone with him. Stanley is coming with me. He can handle anything." She kissed Matthew goodbye and flew out the door.

Tara closed it after her, and leaned against it. She'd met Stella's Stanley, and she'd been less than impressed. Granted, he was good-looking, in a blond, beach-boy kind of way, and he'd certainly oozed charm. He'd told her confidentially how thrilled he was that she was working on this, and how much he admired her for doing so...but there was something about his smooth, salesman manner, and the way he'd squeezed her hand that she hadn't liked. She wasn't clear on his motives but she had a strong suspicion it had more to do with Stella's sexuality than it did with a murder investigation. There wasn't much she could do about it, though, and there wasn't much she could do about Stella's murder investigation either. She just hoped her friend wouldn't get herself in a big mess of trouble.

Matthew tugged on her skirt. "Can we watch a movie?" he asked. "I brought a real scary one this time."

"Sure." Tara followed the six-year-old into the den and switched on the VCR. After a few minutes of watching, she realized that Matthew hadn't been kidding about the movie. It was darn scary. She and Matthew huddled together as the heroine, a wimpy blonde whose main talent was her ability to scream, was about to open the door, where the crazed, knife-wielding guy waited in bone-chilling silence for her arrival. The hero, a non-real man whose claim to fame was that he was never around when the heroine needed him, was naturally nowhere in sight. The heroine opened the door, Mr. Knife raised his hand…and the television, as well as all the lights, flashed and died, leaving them in semidarkness.

"What's wrong?" cried Matthew. He grabbed her hand and squeezed hard.

"Maybe my lightbulb burned out and my television went on the fritz at the same time," Tara suggested optimistically. With Matthew determinedly attached to her, she went into the hall and flicked the light switch. Nothing happened. She wandered through the apartment, trying every switch in the place, but none of them worked. Either every lightbulb she owned was burned out, along with her television and every other electrical appliance in the place, or… "It looks like there might be a problem with the electricity," she told Matthew.

His eyes rounded with alarm. "You mean none of the lights work?"

"I don't think so." Tara phoned the building manager. "You're the third person who's reported it," he told her. "I don't know what's wrong, but it's going to take a while to get the problem fixed."

"It doesn't look good," Tara told Matthew when she hung up.

"Oh no." Matthew looked as if he was going to cry. "I don't like the dark. I don't want it to be dark."

"Don't worry." Tara took him in her arms. "I'll think of something."

Matthew shuddered against her. "Think fast. I'm scared of the dark."

Tara wasn't too impressed with it herself, especially after watching that movie. She was hunting down candles and flashlights, and trying not to think of Mr. Knife, when the phone rang. She stumbled through the darkness looking for it, hoping it was the building manager with good news. It was Chase, sounding harried and distracted. "Sorry to bother you, but I need to ask a favor."

Even though she knew very well that Chase didn't know anything about electricity, and wouldn't know what to do in this situation any better than she did, Tara still found his deep, warm voice both comforting and reassuring. "Go ahead."

"Did you say your friend Stella had a six-year-old?"

"Yes, I did. Matthew. As a matter of fact, he's here with me right now."

"He is?" Chase's tone grew suspicious. "Why? His mother isn't out accusing someone else of murder, is she?"

Tara winced. "Not exactly, no."

"Good. In that case, can you bring Matthew over here?"

Was she missing something or was this an odd thing for a man of thirty to be asking. "Why?"

"Because I need him," Chase said impatiently. "We've got an emergency situation here. I'm trying to choreograph a helicopter-rescue scene and I don't have enough people! Andrew's trying to be the pilot and the bad guy, and Simon's trying to be the hero and another bad guy, and they both end up having fights with themselves. It's just not working."

Tara hesitated. Taking Matthew to play cops and robbers with an off-the-wall writer might not be Stella's idea of a good activity. On the other hand, it was a lot better than spending the evening sitting in the dark. "I'll be right over."

Less than half an hour later, she was ensconced in a chair in Chase's living room. All the furniture had been pushed back against the walls, leaving a large square of space in the middle that Chase had populated with four kitchen chairs, arranged to resemble the inside of a helicopter. Chase was perched on the arm of the sofa, studying the scene with intent seriousness. "Okay," he said. "In this scene, the good guy and his date try to capture the helicopter to escape. The good guy gets away, but the date gets captured. Simon, you can be the pilot. Andrew, you're the bad guy—"

Simon tugged on his arm. "It's my turn to be the bad guy."

"Okay, Simon, you're the bad guy. Andrew, you can be the pilot." He turned to Matthew, who was studying the scene with wide-round eyes. "How about if you're the hero?"

"Okay," said Matthew.

"I don't want to be the pilot, either," Andrew complained. "All the pilot does is get hit on the head. I want to be one of the bad guys."

Chase stood back, stroking his chin. "Well, there are supposed to be two bad guys...but I do need a pilot..." He looked at Tara hopefully. "I don't suppose..."

"Sure," said Tara. "Why not?"

"I DON'T BELIEVE YOU," Stella said when she came to pick up Matthew. "You spent the evening with Chase and all you did was play helicopter games? That's either really sick or really weird."

"It isn't really anything," Tara whispered so she didn't wake up Matthew, who had fallen asleep on her couch. The electricity had, thankfully, been restored while they were out. "We were just helping him choreograph a couple of scenes. It was fun, too. And Chase told me I was the best helicopter pilot he'd ever had."

"There's a compliment for you," Stella said dryly. "I

gather you didn't get around to any sex scenes…unless the hero and the pilot had something going on.''

"Of course there weren't sex scenes! I would not subject your son to anything like that!'' It hadn't even come up. She'd spent the entire evening either stretched out on the floor trying to look unconscious, or pretending to fly a helicopter, while Andrew and Simon took turns thwacking her on the head, and Chase watched, criticized, took notes and rearranged them so they could start all over. It had been lots of fun, but it wasn't the type of evening she intended to spend with her dream man. They would dine out, not order takeout vegetarian pizza, and eat in style, not on the floor of the living room, and spend the evening making intelligent conversation, not playing cops and robbers. It didn't sound as if it would be as much fun, but that was her plan. "How did your interview with the janitor go?'' she asked to take her mind off it.

Stella shook her head. "Mr. Sweeny doesn't know anything except that Franklin threw out a lot of paper and once used green notepads instead of yellow.'' She sighed. "Stanley was so disappointed. He thought Mr. Sweeny might provide a useful clue.''

"Too bad for Stanley.''

"Don't worry. We'll figure this out yet.'' Stella started gathering up Matthew. "Are there ever going to be sex scenes?''

"What?''

"You and Chase.''

"No,'' said Tara. "Absolutely not. I'm going to find Mr. Perfect Real Man, remember?''

"Right,'' said Stella, who didn't look convinced.

Tara wasn't sure she was convinced, either, especially after they interviewed Ephram Enright. Ephram was a smooth, sophisticated real estate agent, who was on the list,

Tara suspected, because he simply oozed charm. "Social ability," he announced when Chase asked him about the qualities of a real man. "That's important these days. Men have to have the ability to socialize. It's good for their career…and for their love life, as well."

Tara watched in silence while he made other points about maturity and commitment and Chase took notes. Chase had on his "interviewing outfit"—black khakis, gray shirt, darker gray sports jacket, and despite his outrageously red tie, he looked as good as Ephram.

Okay, he looked better than Ephram. Not that there was anything wrong with Ephram. With his dark eyes and square, even-featured face, Ephram could almost be considered handsome, in the classical sense. He worked out at the gym three times a week, he'd explained. "I've met a number of my clients there," which had made Tara wonder if he brought up real estate while he was lifting weights. He was also well-dressed. "Clothes spell success," he told them. "A poorly dressed real estate agent would not inspire the confidence needed in this line of business."

There wasn't one thing wrong with him, except he did nothing for Tara. There was no reason for her not to be attracted to him, but if he asked her out, she'd probably refuse. However, if Chase asked her out, she'd leap on him. What happened to growing up and finding a mature, lifetime companion? It was hard to stick to a resolution like that around a man like Chase.

"YOU SOUND MISERABLE," Stella accused later in the week when she phoned to pass on her latest "inside source" information. "Don't tell me something else in your apartment has fallen apart?"

"They're still having problems with the electricity," Tara admitted. "It keeps going off and on. And the floorboards keep coming loose. Every time Chase nails them down, another one pops up."

"Chase nails your floor?"

"He worked construction for a while." After tripping over a loose board, he'd astonished her by dropping in, unannounced, with hammer and nails, looking exactly like a construction worker. "I might not know how to fix plumbing but I can pound a nail with the best of them," he'd explained. He'd fixed the floor, made a number of unflattering comments about the apartment and complained about the way she made tea while she'd reminded herself over and over how her perfect man wasn't one who wore a white T-shirt and grubby jeans, no matter how good he looked in them. "I've written part of the article about Wutherspoon's and I don't like it," she continued. "And I've seen so much food for 'Food That Puts Him in the Mood' that I'm sure I've gained weight."

"You have not," said Stella. "I've seen you. You haven't even developed hips yet."

"Chase thinks I have. He mentioned it the other day. I decided then and there to add 'Real men don't notice if you've gained weight' to my list of qualities."

"Ah," said Stella wisely. "Now we come to the crux of the matter. Chase."

Tara opened her mouth to deny it, then changed her mind. "You're right. He is the problem. I'm not sure I'd recognize a real man when he walked into the room, because I'm so obsessed with Chase."

"Why don't you do something about it?"

"I am not going to do anything about it," Tara insisted. "At least not the something you are suggesting."

"It's just an idea. Listen, I've got some interesting news here." Stella's voice grew excited. "One of the salesclerks heard another clerk say that she thought Franklin was cheap. What do you think of that?''

"Not much," Tara mumbled.

"Well, I do. Stanley and I are going to quiz them separately. Then we're going to put our heads together." She paused. "I don't suppose you can watch Matthew again tonight for me, can you? Stanley's coming over and he's nervous around children."

"Oh he is, is he?"

Stella sighed. "He's a man, Tara. Men don't like other people's children. It says so in that article."

"That article was written in 1949. Today's men are supposed to like children. You should see Chase with them. He's terrific." She grinned as she thought of Chase dashing around his living room playing cops and robbers. "Of course, I suppose that could be because he's something of a child himself."

"Whatever. Did you say you could watch Matthew?"

"No," Tara said regretfully. "I'm afraid I can't. I've got a date."

"With Chase?" Stella guessed.

"Good heavens no. Chase and I aren't on dating terms. Besides, he's in Seattle. I'm meeting Lowell Thomas. He's one of the men for my article, the environmentalist."

"What kind of environmentalist?" Stella demanded. "Do you mean the kind who goes around talking about the great outdoors or the other kind?"

Tara gave the phone a quizzical look. "What kinds are there?"

"The good kind and the bad kind," said Stella. "I dated both before I married Bill. The good kind just talk about the great outdoors. It's interesting, sort of like watching the Discovery Channel. The other kind want to do weird outdoorsy things, like winter camping. Have you ever tried that? You go out in all this ice and snow and cold and build an igloo. Then they expect you to sleep in it. There isn't even any electricity. That is not a date, Tara. It's an endurance test.''

Tara covered the phone to hide her giggle. ''We're not going winter camping, Stell. I'm just having dinner with him. Besides, maybe I'd like winter camping. I didn't mind hiking.''

''When did you go hiking?'' asked Stella.

''The other day. Chase needed to do this 'hide in the forest' scene, so we took his nephews out into the forest and hid from one another.''

''Now there's the recipe for a fun date,'' said Stella. ''You, Chase, two boys and a bunch of wildlife all hiding from one another.''

''It was not a date!'' It had been a good time though. She shook her head. Playing in the bushes was not her idea of a perfect date, either. There was no way Mr. Right would ever even suggest it.

''And speaking of dates,'' said Stella, ''where is this environmentalist taking you?''

''I'm not sure.''

''Well, if you see any snow, start worrying.'' She paused. ''Is Chase going to be there, too?''

''No,'' said Tara.

''Why not? Aren't you and Chase supposed to be doing this together?''

''Yes. But Lowell called and asked if we could meet for dinner, and I thought it might be a good idea. It would give me a chance to form my own impression.'' And if Lowell had real man potential, she could follow up on it instead of obsessing about Chase.

UNFORTUNATELY, although Lowell was the good kind of environmentalist, didn't mention winter camping and was as fascinating to listen to as the Discovery Channel, Tara couldn't summon up much interest in him. She couldn't summon up much interest in the horticulturist either, who insisted real men liked plants, or the chiropractor, who confirmed that real men should take care of their bodies.

"At least we're getting through this list," she told Chase during another "take stock" session at his place after they'd spent two hours with a classical guitarist whose dark eyes and soulful expression had indicated he'd be great at romance but had no talent for much else. "We've only got eight or nine to go. The dentist, the archaeologist—"

"Don't forget the environmentalist," Chase put it. "Lowell somethingorother. Have you scheduled anything with him, or do you want me to—"

"Oh, we don't have to meet with him," Tara said carelessly. "I've already talked to him."

"You have?" Chase's eyebrows came down. "When did you do that?"

"A couple of nights ago." Chase's lips tightened and she fought the feeling that she'd done something wrong. "He called and invited me to dinner."

"Dinner?" Chase's glower intensified. "You had a *date* with the guy?"

He made it sound as if she'd robbed a bank with him. "It wasn't really a date. It was an interview."

"An interview during which food was served," Chase corrected.

Tara nodded.

"And the difference between that and a date would be…?"

Tara squirmed. "A date is just different!" She pawed through her papers in a desperate attempt to change the subject. "Here's my notes about him."

"Where did you go for this non-date date?"

Tara looked at his disapproving face and wondered. "A restaurant. Nothing fancy. Lowell said—"

Chase folded his arms across his chest. "Had you met this guy before you made this *date* with him?"

Tara gave up. "No, I hadn't. I told you. I called him to schedule the interview and he suggested—"

Chase's voice rose. "You mean you went out to dinner with a perfect stranger?"

"It wasn't like that!"

"It sounds like that's exactly what happened." He shook a finger at her. "That's not a good idea. A woman shouldn't go out with a man she knows nothing about. This guy could have been a serial killer."

"He wasn't!"

"You didn't know that when you went out with him, did you?"

Tara clenched her teeth. "I never asked him, if that's what you mean. It's not on my list of interview questions."

"Maybe it should be," Chase suggested unreasonably. "Apart from that, we're *supposed* to be doing this together. We can't do it together when you go around doing it separately."

Tara threw up her hands in surrender. "All right. All right. I don't know why you're making such a big deal about it, but if it bothers you that much, I won't do it again. I just thought it would save time."

"I have lots of time. We're not going to miss this deadline, and one thing I don't have time for is scheduling a second interview with someone when you've already done the first one."

Tara gaped at him, stunned. "You're going to interview Lowell again?"

"I have to. Otherwise I can't confirm or deny your findings."

"Can't you just believe me?"

"No, I can't." Chase looked surprisingly grumpy. "That wouldn't be responsible journalism."

"I guess not," said Tara, although she thought he was being completely irrational. She made another mental note. Real men did not fall off the deep end about nothing.

Hunter eyed Bridgett's long, figure-hugging, low-cut sparkling blue gown. The slit on her right showed far too much thigh, and the low bodice showed too much of everything else. "Where in hell do you think you're going?" Hunter demanded.

Bridgett gave him an arch look. "Hamilton Wells is going to be in the casino this evening. I'm going to find out what he knows."

Hunter bit back an oath. The thought of Bridgett in the same room as that sleazy character made him physically ill. "I don't think that's a good idea."

"We need the information, Hunter. If I can get him talking, he might just tell me something useful."

"HAVE YOU EVER BEEN jealous?" Chase asked Jerome when they met for a drink the next evening. According to Jerome, the trip to Vegas hadn't been a success.

"We had a good time," he reported. "But we're still scheduled to see that counselor." To top it off, Vanna was out with her mother, which had made Jerome more despondent than ever. "It's a sign, Chase. When a woman starts spending time with her mother, it means divorce is only a court appearance away."

Chase was doing his best to cheer up Jerome, which

wasn't easy because Chase didn't have a lot of cheer in him to throw around.

"Of course I've been jealous," Jerome responded. "At one time or another I suspect everyone is." He looked at Chase with outright curiosity. "Why? Are you trying to make your hero jealous?"

"No." Chase rolled his glass of bottled water between his palms. "It's Tara. She interviewed some environmentalist the other day by herself."

Jerome shrugged and took another sip of his martini. "So what? Interviewing separately seems like a good way to get this done."

Chase couldn't believe his friend. "They had the interview over dinner, Jer!"

"Ah." Jerome nodded wisely. "That's what bothers you about it."

"Yes, that's what bothers me about it!" Chase snapped. "We are supposed to be doing these things together!"

"And you don't like the idea of her dating some other guy."

"No, I don't!" Chase frowned at the dark wooden table. "It bugs the hell out of me. She wouldn't have dinner with me, but she'd have dinner with an environmentalist. An environmentalist, Jer! What in hell does a woman see in an environmentalist? All they do is go around...environmentalizing!"

Jerome held up a hand. "Hey, the environment is a hot topic these days. I wonder if Vanna is interested in the environment? Maybe I should, uh, buy her a rain forest or something."

"I'm in favor of the environment," Chase went on in an aggravated tone. "If we didn't have it, where would we live? But that's not the point. The point is, she told me she'd had dinner with this guy and I wanted to punch him."

He sat back and took a long swig of water. "I think I might be jealous."

"I think you might be jealous too, but can't say as I blame you. I'd be jealous if a woman I was sleeping with started dating someone else."

"I'm not sleeping with Tara," said Chase.

Jerome froze with his martini halfway between the table and his mouth. "What do you mean you aren't sleeping with her?"

"I mean I'm not. Why would you think I was?"

"I just did, that's all." Jerome kept eyeing him while he drank. "You spend a lot of time with her. You're always talking about her. I just naturally assumed...I mean, she's a woman and you're you and..." He blinked. "Are you sure you aren't?"

Chase got a rush just from thinking about being naked with Tara. "Believe me, Jer, I'd know if I was sleeping with Tara."

Jerome seemed completely flummoxed. "Well, why aren't you?"

"It's not like that with her." Somehow, he'd moved Tara from the list of women he'd like to be with to the list of women he'd never be with. It wasn't an extensive list. So far, it included his mother, his sister, Jerome's wives—all four of them—and Tara.

Jerome blinked a few times. "Why isn't it? The way you talk, it sounds as if you're interested in her."

Chase thought of her green eyes...her big smile...her soft curves...the flush on her cheeks after a game of helicopter. "I am interested, but I'm not her type. She wants the Cary Grant type. Would you call me the Cary Grant type?"

Jerome eyed him and chuckled. "Nope. You're more like Jim Carey, or, uh, Robin Williams." He snapped his fingers. "I've got it. You're one of those guys who kept smacking each other. The Three Stooges. That's your type."

Chase scowled. "You are not helping."

"I'm just telling it as I see it. But you never know. Women can change their minds." He took a long swallow of his drink. "Look at Vanna. She used to like the Jerome type and now she doesn't."

"Yeah, well, I don't think Tara's going to fall for the Chase Montgomery type." Chase slumped down. The computer geek, the neat guy, and all the men they'd met hadn't made the cut.

Jerome sighed and settled back. "Let me think about it. Maybe I can fix your life even if I can't fix mine." He drummed his fingers on the tabletop, thinking. "Did Tara fall for the environmentalist?"

Chase considered it. She hadn't said much about the tree lover except that he liked women who were good sports and didn't cut down trees. "I don't think so."

"Great. You've still got a chance." He snapped his fingers. "I've got it. Why don't you try something romantic? You know. Candles. Wine. That sort of thing. You did tell me that real men are romantic."

Chase shuddered. "That isn't me. I'm no good at that kind of thing. Besides, Tara told me romance is in the head. What one person thinks is romantic, the other person might not. For example, Molly thinks Eddie is romantic when he does the dishes. I can hardly wash a bunch of dishes in front of Tara."

"Tell me about it," said Jerome. "I washed the dishes the other night, and both the maid and Vanna thought I'd lost my mind."

THE NEXT EVENING, Chase took Lisa out to dinner.

Lisa was a friend of Jerome's wife, Vanna. "She wanted

me to set up Lisa with someone," Jerome reported mournfully. "I didn't know if real men do stuff like that, but right now, if Vanna asks me to do something, I do it. And since you don't have anything going on with Tara..."

"I don't know if real men are wimps, Jer," Chase responded, but he couldn't say no to Jerome. Besides, according to Jerome, Lisa was crazy about his books, which made him think maybe she'd be crazy about him. Right now, that wouldn't be a bad thing.

Unfortunately, he wasn't crazy about her, or anything else about the evening. He took her to a Moroccan restaurant that Jerome had recommended, which turned out to be a disappointment because there wasn't much on the menu he wanted to eat. Lisa was a bigger disappointment. She was almost a clone of Vanna, with the same pencil-thin figure, the same brunette hair she kept flicking around in a manner that Chase found irritating because he didn't like hair in his salad, and the same way of making conversation that revolved around the last play she'd seen and a number of books he hadn't read.

"Tell me, Lisa," he asked as he picked a brown strand out of his broccoli. "What's your idea of a real man? Do you think my hero is a real men?"

"Of course," Lisa said promptly. "I think your hero is wonderful." She giggled. "Not that I'd marry him, but I'd certainly sleep with him."

The way she eyed him indicated that she felt the same way about him. "Why not?" Chase asked, trying to stifle his irritation with her. He didn't understand it. She was well put together, and she was making it clear that she wouldn't mind spending the night with him. The idea did nothing for him.

"He isn't the kind of man women marry," Lisa explained. "I mean, he's exciting and handsome, and from the sound of things, great in bed. But I doubt he'd take out the garbage."

"Garbage?" Chase asked, confused. Was this something else for his list? "Real men take out the garbage?"

"Real men you marry do," said Lisa. "I would never marry a man who wouldn't take out the garbage. My sister did that, and all she does is take out the garbage. Of course, she married a man from Cleveland, so what do you expect?"

"I don't know," said Chase. "I guess either real men don't come from Cleveland, or real men take out the garbage."

He watched Lisa flick back her hair, and decided a night with her was out of the question. She would do exactly what Arla and all the others had done—dump him after a few weeks, which probably wouldn't bother him a bit. Right now, the only woman he was interested in was Tara.

There was no other solution. He was simply going to have to give romance a try.

9

Real men are natural romantics. It's instinctive!
There's nothing your real man likes better than a romantic evening, with candles and flowers and you.
——from "Forty-Nine Things You Need
to Know about a Real Man,"
Real Men magazine, April 1949

"IT'S NOT JUST the food that puts you in the mood," Armand explained. "It's the ambience."

He stood in the kitchen of Armand's Fine Dining—a
short, round man with a white chef's hat half covering his
forehead and a wide white apron covering the rest of him.
"Come with me and I'll show you."

He led her out of the kitchen into the quiet elegance of
the dining area, where waiters were scurrying around, preparing for the upcoming dinner hour. "Now this…this is
the sort of place you take a woman to if you have romance
in mind."

"It's lovely," Tara said inadequately. She took in the
soft green plush cushions, the well-separated tables set up
in dark corners, the silver wine cooler placed beside each
table. Armand was right. This was the way to wine and
dine a woman. It was the sort of place a man like Gerald
would choose. She could almost picture a younger version
of him sitting here, attired in a well-fitting suit, looking
urbane and at home.

On the other hand, the thought of Chase in here made

her snicker. He'd have a conversation with the waiter about the tea, insist on ordering something that contained no fat.

"This is the way to win a woman's heart," Armand continued, making an expansive gesture with one arm. "And for the meal…there has to be fish."

"Fish?"

"That's right." Armand nodded one decisive nod. "There's nothing like fish to put a woman…or a man in the mood. A nice linguine with shrimp and crab sauce. Or lobster. If a man encourages you to have lobster, watch out. He's got something besides a quiet evening in mind."

Tara shuddered. "That sounds, uh, wonderful." She followed him back into the kitchen. "But it wouldn't do anything for me. I don't like fish, so I'd never order anything with fish in it."

Armand patted her shoulder. "That doesn't mean anything. I can create a dish that doesn't even taste like it's got fish in it. Take my Volaise à la Grecque. You'd never know about the lovely oyster sauce just by reading the name. We do mention it on the menu, but it's in small print." The good humor faded from his face. "That's going to change, though, after what happened a couple of months ago. I've told all my waiters to make certain everyone knows the ingredients."

Tara eyed him curiously. "What happened a couple of months ago?"

"It was terrible." Armand's shoulders fell. "A man with a fish allergy…" He turned away.

Tara stared at him in astonishment. It had never occurred to her to ask Stella where they'd eaten on that fateful night. "You don't mean Mr. Wutherspoon, do you?"

"That's right." Armand picked up a whisk and started whipping egg whites at a rapid rate. "That was not anyone's fault though. Someone ordered it. I made it."

Tara's heart stopped. "Are you saying that someone at

Wutherspoon's Employee Thank-You Dinner ordered the Volaise à la Grecque?"

"Of course!" Armand said indignantly. "It's one of our special dishes. However, it had nothing to do with Mr. Wutherspoon's death. He wasn't the one who ordered it."

"I, uh, don't suppose you know who did?"

"No, I don't. But I am positive it was not Mr. Wutherspoon."

TARA DROVE HOME without noticing the traffic while she mulled over Armand's information. Could Stella be right about this? At least one person had ordered Armand's special dish. That didn't mean there was a murderer, or even a murder, but it did make Stella's theory more plausible— depending on who had ordered that Volaise à la Grecque, of course. Who could it have been?

She called Stella as soon as she got home. "No one mentioned Volaise à la Grecque," Stella admitted. "But I bet it was Marvin! I told you he was a good suspect! Oh, I can't wait to tell Stanley about this!"

"We shouldn't leap to conclusions," Tara cautioned although she shared Stella's excitement.

Her euphoria dissipated somewhat when the building manager stopped by a few minutes later to inform her that the power was going to be off again. "I don't know how long it will take," he advised. "But I wouldn't plan on doing any cooking."

"Terrific," Tara muttered. She was almost too excited to eat but the idea of sitting alone in a dark apartment wasn't appealing.

She changed her clothes in her rapidly darkening bedroom, and was trying to work up some enthusiasm for a cold salad when Chase phoned. "I am calling to invite you over for dinner," he explained.

Tara eyed her nonfunctional stove. "Why?"

Chase's voice came right back at her, tinged with exasperation. "What do you mean why? Because I want you come to dinner. What other motive is there?"

"You could be trying to lure me over there to help you choreograph another scene."

"I could be," Chase agreed. "But I'm not."

"Honest?"

"Honest," Chase promised. "There will be no acting out of any sort. Just you and me and food."

Tara didn't believe him, but salad and a bowl of granola, or take-out vegetarian pizza was better than what she could put together. "All right."

When she arrived at Chase's house forty minutes later, though, she discovered that salad and a bowl of granola weren't on the list. Neither was take-out vegetarian pizza, or take-out anything. The place was spotless, the table was set as nicely as a picnic table could be set, and Chase was in the kitchen, wearing clean, well-pressed khaki pants and a short-sleeved white golf shirt. "I'm making spaghetti à la Chase," he told her as he poured her a tumblerful of wine. "There's no meat, but there are enough tomatoes to give you your vitamin requirements for a month."

It sounded delicious and it smelled delicious and he looked delicious. Tara leaned against the counter and watched him cook while she told him her news. "We might just solve this. Isn't that exciting?"

"I don't know if exciting is the word I'd choose." He narrowed his brows together. "I don't think you and Stella should be going after a murderer. If you've got reason to suspect anyone, you should contact the police right away."

Tara was a bit disappointed in his reaction. That's not what Cary would have said. He would have said, "let's go get him," and come up with some wonderful ideas on how to do that.

Chase was not Cary. She watched the movement of his

arms and the easy way he moved around the kitchen, and wished fervently that he was. "Can I do anything?" she offered, hoping that peeling carrots or some other chore would take her mind off him.

Chase shook his head and gestured toward the living room. "Make yourself comfortable. I'll finish the salad and join you in a minute."

"Okay." Tara watched him return to his cooking, then wandered into the living room. It had experienced a good tidying as well. So had the bathroom, and when she'd finished in there and took a quick peek into the open door of his bedroom, she discovered that his bed was made, the clothes put away and not a single sock was in sight. It didn't look like any of her "Bedrooms That Say *Now*," but for him a made bed was pretty close.

She returned to the living room and paused at the doorway to take stock. Clean house. Great-smelling meal— which, according to everyone she'd talked to, was one of the important things to "put you in the mood"—a nicely set table. If this were any other man, she'd suspect he was trying to seduce her.

But this wasn't any other man. This was Chase. Chase's idea of seducing someone was probably "Do you want to have sex?" Still, it was out of character for him. Maybe he was making a move. The idea of another notch on Chase's belt wasn't what she wanted. She should make up an excuse and leave.

She went back into the kitchen. Chase was standing in front of the stove stirring the sauce, his hair curling from the steam rising from the pot. Tara took in the wonderful smell and her stomach growled. Chase might not be trying to seduce her, she told herself. People cleaned up their houses for a lot of other reasons than that they wanted to seduce a woman. She'd look like an idiot if she ran out screaming now. She could make a graceful exit later.

He looked up and smiled, slow and sexy and inviting, and Tara had to force herself to breathe. Maybe she wouldn't make that graceful exit, after all.

The phone rang, shattering the moment. Chase mumbled something under his breath and went off to answer it while Tara regrouped.

She'd taken over stirring the sauce when Chase returned. "There's been a change in plans," he announced as he took the spoon away from her. "Molly's got to go to a meeting at the school, and Eddie isn't going to be able to make it home for a while. She wants to drop the kids off." He looked as disappointed as she felt. "It should be for only an hour or so."

"No problem," said Tara. The kids were a good idea. With them around, nothing would happen. He wouldn't make a pass at her, and she wouldn't make a pass at him.

Chase pushed his fingers through his hair. "I didn't plan on having them here, but Molly—"

"It's fine. Really." She shook a finger at him, teasing. "Although I don't believe you. I suspect you planned this so we could act out another scene for you."

Chase's scowl told it all. "That's not how it is."

But that's how it turned out. They ate spaghetti while the two boys watched television in the den, but as soon as they were finished, Andrew and Simon were back, pleading for a chance to act out another scene. Chase refused. "We're done with the helicopter. I've already written it."

"Don't you have anything else?" Simon begged, his sweet, round face a direct contrast to what he was suggesting.

Chase shook his head. "No. Except for the escape from the yacht, and we don't have enough people for that."

"Let's call Matthew," Andrew chimed in. "Maybe he can come over."

Eventually that's what they did. Stella was delighted with

the opportunity to get out for a little while, and Matthew was delighted to be the bad guy.

It was well after ten when Chase finally called a halt. "That's enough for now. You guys go watch TV for a while."

The boys grumbled but headed off to the den. Chase made them both tea, and they carried their cups into the living room. Tara curled up on one side of the sofa, with Chase at the other. The game had taken her mind off his bod, but as he sprawled on the sofa, with his white shirt untucked and a spot of spaghetti sauce near the right pocket, it all came back to her.

She searched for some topic…anything…to get her mind off his body, and off her body, and away from how much she wanted to be with him. "That scene," she asked in desperation. "The one we were just choreographing. How does it end?"

Chase relaxed back, easy and comfortable. "Let's see. Hunter rescues Bridgett. They get to the island." He winked. "Then, of course, Hunter and Bridgett get together."

"I see," said Tara, trying hard to ignore the feeling that it might be a great idea. "They've almost been killed so naturally they jump into bed."

Chase chuckled. "It isn't exactly a bed. This is an island, remember? They jump into the sand. But it's pretty much the same thing." She frowned and he held up a hand. "Hey, it was your idea."

Her idea? "I don't remember ever suggesting anything like that."

"Well, you did. Talking to you made me realize that if something like that happened—if the woman Hunter cared about was in desperate danger—when it was over, they'd want to be together."

That didn't sound bad. As a matter of fact, it sounded like something she might suggest.

"Want me to read it to you?"

"Well, uh..." Reading one of Chase's hot sex scenes might not be a good idea right now.

"I'll get it," said Chase.

Tara opened her mouth to object, but Chase had already disappeared down the hall. Tara hesitated for a moment, then settled back and waited for his return. What the heck. She'd read these scenes before and she hadn't gone berserk. Surely she could control herself through another one. Besides, she was curious about how he'd put it together.

Chase returned to the living room, papers in hand. "You'll have to read the old version," he complained. "The printer is on the fritz so I can't print out the new version. It's just the toner cartridge. I know how to fix it but it'll take an hour." He started to hand her a page. "First you read this and then..." He pulled it back from her fingers. "No, that's not right. It's this one and then..."

"That's okay," said Tara. "I can..."

"It'll be easier if I just read it to you." He sat down. "I can follow my notes a lot better than you can."

Tara recalled listening to him recite the kissing scene, and shook her head. "You don't have to do that. I can read it, um, another time."

"I don't mind." He sprawled into the chair, legs stretched out in front of him, and picked up the pages. "Every story should be read out loud at least once anyway."

Tara swallowed. Having Chase read a sex scene to her was not a good idea. As a matter of fact, it was a bad idea.

"Here's the lead-in." Chase started reading. "Hunter raced down the stairs, dodging bullets as he went, while a mental clock in his head kept the countdown. Thirty. Twenty-nine. Twenty-eight..."

Tara closed her eyes as he took her through the scene, with Hunter frantically searching for Bridgett while bad guys searched for him. He went through every possible emotion, from sickening fear that Laromee had disposed of her, absolute fury at the idea and, finally, desperate relief when he found her. By the time the hero and heroine had leaped into the water, Tara was totally caught up in the story. "Laromee's boat exploded!" she exclaimed when he read her that paragraph.

"Uh-huh." Chase scowled. "But Laromee's not on it. The creep took off just in time." He thumbed through the pages. "Where were we? Oh yes. Hunter's got Bridgett. The boat is toast. They swim to the island and crawl onto the shore. That's when the love scene starts. Ready?"

"I can't wait." She pushed aside every thought of playing with fire.

"Okay." Chase settled back and started reading in his dark, rich voice. "Hunter put his arms around her, and held her. Her head sank into his shoulder, her body, still wet from the water, pushing against him as if she couldn't get close enough. Hunter's grip on her tightened. He didn't intend for anything to happen between them. There was still a missile out there he needed to get his hands on, a villain to capture, and a number of the villain's men still on the loose. This was no time to be doing anything except planning their next move. He'd do that in a minute. Right now he just wanted to hug her, to feel her against him, to reassure himself that she was all right. He felt her lips press against his neck, warm and soft, and something inside him snapped. The chill of the ocean fell away, replaced by searing heat. It was her. He was hot for her, hotter than he could ever remember being. He lowered his head and took her mouth. She squirmed against him, kissing him back with desperate passion, as if she couldn't get enough of him. He kissed her again and again, hot, open-mouth kisses, fitting her against his body, pushing into her heat, inflamed by her gasps of passion. She pushed him back a little and looked him straight in the eye. 'I want you, Hunter. I want to make love with you. Right now.'

"Hunter hesitated. A small voice of reason whispered in the back of his brain. This was not the time or the place.

"Bridgett yanked off her black turtleneck sweater and fumbled with the clasp of her bra. The clasp came free, and two luscious breasts tumbled into his view. Hunter stared at them, then at her. To hell with it. He didn't care about anything else. He needed her now. He shoved aside the material, fastening his mouth around a nipple. 'Oh yes, baby, yes.' Her hands moved over his face, behind his head, into his hair.

"He rolled, pinning her under him, then sliding down her soft, hot body, tugging away her clothes, tasting her, licking first a nipple, then her lips, while his fingers kneaded her breasts. She squirmed, moaning under him. Her hands were on his bottom now, urging him closer. Her hips arched upward, and he struggled for control. 'Give me a minute, baby.'

"'No. Do it now.'

"'Not yet.' He slid lower, yanking off the rest of her clothing, cupping his lips over her moist heat. The taste of her, the scent of her arousal, her twisting, squirming body, were driving him over the edge. He touched her with his tongue, and she moaned out loud. He wanted to hear that sound again and again. He eased apart her legs and...''

Chase set down the manuscript, took off his glasses and rubbed the bridge of his nose. "This isn't working, is it?"

Tara practically slid off the couch. Wasn't working? What wasn't working about it? She was hot and cold at the same time. Her blood was filled with it, her head pounding with thoughts of Chase doing to her exactly what Hunter had done to Bridgett. If it worked any better, the heat from her body would set fire to the couch. "Well," she said, trying to form words out of the haze and lust occupying her brain. "I...uh...wouldn't say that."

Chase was still frowning at the pages. "There's something just not right about it. The way it starts is confusing. Maybe they shouldn't be in the sand. Maybe they should be sitting near the cool stream flowing down from the mountains...or a waterfall. Plus, he's still got his clothes on." He frowned at his prose for a few minutes, then abruptly slid to the floor. "Let's try acting it out."

Tara didn't move. Was he suggesting that they...?

Chase patted the floor beside him and gave her a quizzical look. "What's wrong?"

The noise from the television drifted down the hall, accompanied by boyish sounds of laughter. Chase wasn't suggesting anything outlandish. He was only trying to get the action at the beginning right, that's all. "Nothing," said Tara. She slid down to sit beside him.

"Don't just sit there," Chase instructed. "You just swam across an ocean. You're exhausted. And you can't lean against the sofa, either. We're in the sand, remember? There's nothing to lean against except him."

Tara scuttled closer to him, and he put an arm around her, his attention firmly on his manuscript. "That's better. Oh, and you've got a bandage on your arm." He scribbled on the page, while she tried to ignore the heat between her legs, and the proximity of him, fitting next to her, holding her. "I'd forgotten about that arm. He'll have to be careful about that. Now, let's see. He's holding her. They're both on the ground...dada...dada...dada...that's okay...and this...yeah, that's okay, too. Now we get to this part..."

"What part is that?" Tara asked, striving not to sound as breathless as she felt.

Chase grinned down at her. "The part where he kisses her. It goes something like this."

He kissed her.

His lips were soft and his mouth was hard, and it was a good thing they were sitting down because if they'd been standing she would have collapsed from the sheer pleasure of being held against him like this, while he rubbed his lips across hers and took her tongue in his mouth and held her tightly against him so they were touching toe to toe, hip to hip, breast to chest. She made an inarticulate sound of pleasure and her arm came up...slowly because the back of her brain remembered that it was supposed to be hurt...circling his neck, holding it in place so she could keep on tasting him and smelling him and feeling him. He sucked on her bottom lip, nibbled at her tongue, then tasted his way across her cheek, finally burrowing his head into her neck. "I don't think I've got that right," he growled into her ear.

Tara gasped in a breath. "What?"

"Let's try it again." He moved, shifting so his back was resting against the sofa, hauling her with him, ending up with her sprawled between his legs. He held her hips against his with one hand, while the other raised her chin. Then he was kissing her again, hard and heady, and Tara leaned into it, both arms around his neck now, thrusting her breasts against his chest, feeling the heat from his hard erection between her legs. How she wanted him. She wanted...

The sound of the doorbell, followed by the pounding of feet racing down the hall had them scrambling apart. "My mom's here," Matthew called out.

"So's ours," Andrew shouted. "Uncle Chase? Where are you?"

"Right here," Chase called back. He shoved his hand through his hair, took a couple of breaths and slowly pushed himself to his feet. "Don't move now. Just stay put. I'll take care of this."

Tara couldn't move. She slumped back against the sofa

in a heap of bone and muscle, gasping for air, while in the background a woman—Molly, she recognized from the voice—murmured thank you, and another woman—Stella this time—did the same and then she heard her name. "Is Tara still here?"

Tara staggered to her feet. She was still here and she shouldn't be, because after Molly left and Stella left and the boys left she'd be alone with Chase and then who knew what would happen? Okay, she did know what would happen and it would not be a good idea. She closed her mind against the remembrance of the feel of his mouth and the ache in her body, gulped in more air and tottered down the hall. Molly and her brood had left. Stella was still there, thanking Chase, talking to Matthew and casting curious looks over both their shoulders. "Oh, there you are," she said when she saw Tara. "I wanted to thank you for taking care of Matthew this evening."

"No problem," said Tara. "It was fun. Really." She looked around for her coat. "I should be going as well. I—"

"No, you shouldn't," said Chase. "You can't go now." He dropped an arm across her shoulders and caressed a hand along her arm. "I still need help with my research."

Her body leaped at his touch. Tara leaned against him and smiled brilliantly at Stella. "That's, uh, what we were doing. I'm helping him with his research."

Stella looked from Tara to Chase, then back to Tara again, and winked. "Right. Research. You just have a good time with that." She took Matthew's hand. "Come on, Matthew. You're too young for that kind of research."

She went out the door and closed it behind her. Tara looked up at him. "It is late. I—"

"It's not that late, and besides, what about my book?" He dropped his arms onto her shoulders. "Do you want to be responsible for another poorly written, poorly construed scene?"

Tara looked into his dark, passion-filled eyes and gave up. So he wasn't her ideal man. Right now, that didn't matter. "No, I don't."

Chase drew her closer. "Good." He kissed her again, hard, hot kisses that drew the air from her lungs and filled her body with that exquisite heat, and she was just barely aware that they were moving until she felt a wall against her back and opened her eyes and discovered she was in his bedroom. The sight of the bed—his bed, Chase Montgomery's bed—reminded her of what she was about to do. "Oh," she said. "I, uh, thought we were supposed to be on a beach."

Chase grinned, slow and sexy. "This is the beach. Don't you have any imagination?"

He pressed her back harder against the wall, pushed a leg between her trembling thighs and started unbuttoning her blouse. "Let's skip to the part where she's got her clothes off."

"You could always use your imagination."

"To hell with that idea," said Chase.

His thumb grazed her nipple through her bra and she shuddered with pleasure. "You're right. To hell with that idea."

Then he was peeling off her blouse, dropping to his knees to tug down her slacks. "That's a better outfit for this scene."

His eyes were so dark they were almost black, and she gasped out his name. "Chase."

He slid a finger inside her panties. "What?"

"Nothing." She leaned against the wall for support and widened her legs. He stroked her, pressed his mouth against her panties, his warm breath arousing her as much as his touch. He licked his way up, unfastening her bra, sucking on her breasts, and finally taking her mouth before abruptly yanking his away and pulling her over to the bed. "Just a minute," Tara objected as he came down beside her and it suddenly occurred to her that she was the only person in the room in her underwear. "Just a minute. What about you? Shouldn't you...?"

"I'm supposed to be fully dressed, just wet." He nuzzled her neck. "We're going to imagine wet right now."

Tara couldn't imagine anything with his mouth on her. She held him and kissed him back, then pushed him aside. "I know how he gets his clothes off."

"What?"

"For your book. I know how he gets his clothes off." She grabbed his shirt and tugged it upward. "It's like this."

"You mean she rips them off?"

"Exactly," Tara confirmed, but in the end they both had to do it, which made her wonder how Bridgett would ever get Hunter's clothes off if they were wet. Then she was holding him between her palms, and he was groaning and stroking her, and finally rolling away so he could yank open a drawer. "Real men take care of birth control," he suggested as he settled back beside her. "Do you think we should add that to the article?"

"We'll just say that real men are responsible." Then he moved into her, and for the rest of the night she forgot all about every other man but him.

10

Real men want commitment! Is playing the field your cup of tea? Don't tag up with a real man then, darling. When a real man falls for you, he falls for you. He'll be the one rushing to the altar.

—from "Forty-Nine Things You Need to Know about a Real Man," *Real Men* magazine, April 1949

"What are we going to do now?" asked Bridgett.

"Don't concern yourself about it," Hunter advised. Bridgett looked terrific this morning. She was still wearing the sweater he'd put on her last night, but he knew darn well that she was naked underneath. "I've determined our position, used the transmitter I stole from the boat to call for reinforcements and scrounged up some fruit for breakfast," he told her. "I even managed to grind up a few leaves for tea." He checked the fire. "Good thing we saved that can from the beans. I used it to boil the water."

"That's terrific." Bridgett came up beside him. "You're terrific."

She swayed against him and Hunter groaned. "Reinforcements should arrive in less than an hour, honey. Then we'll be back on Laromee's trail."

"Then what?" asked Bridgett. "What are you going to do after we capture him?"

"Good question," said Chase.

He yawned and rubbed his eyes. What would they do after this was over? His other books ended with the villain vanquished, and the hero and heroine getting naked and horizontal. Naked and horizontal reminded him of himself and Tara last night. It turned out he was a lot better at romance than he'd thought.

He stretched back in his chair, clasped his hands together and smoothed them down the back of his neck. He felt great this morning. He was almost finished the story, and, after the night he'd spent with Tara, he figured he'd got the real man thing aced as well. Now if he could just find the right ending for Hunter and Bridgett.

He'd tried three versions and was in the middle of deleting the fourth when Jerome arrived. "I've read the first part of your manuscript," the agent said as he plunked a stack of paper onto the kitchen table. "It's not bad. A little different from your usual style but not bad. When are you going to be finished?"

"Soon," Chase promised. "Or maybe never, if I can't figure out the ending."

"You'll figure it out." Jerome sat down across from him at the table. "Just don't kill yourself doing it. You look exhausted. Have you been up all night writing again?"

"Sort of." He had been up most of the night and he had been working on a scene or two. He smiled as he recalled the scenes. Darn good ones if he did say so himself. They were going to choreograph another one tonight, and then another one tomorrow night, and the night after that...and on into eternity. He froze as he realized something. He didn't just want a few nights with Tara. He wanted all the days and nights there were. Which was exactly what Hunter wanted with Bridgett. "Can I ask you something, Jer?"

"Sure." A shadow crossed Jerome's face. "As long as

it has nothing to do with women.''

"Oh no," said Chase. "Haven't you and Vanna sorted things out yet?"

"Nope." Jerome made a face. "I've done everything I can to prove that I'm the one for her, and she's still got that counseling session scheduled. Plus, ever since our trip to Vegas, she's been leaving all this literature lying around about Gamblers Anonymous." He dropped his head onto a hand. "I don't suppose you've got any other brilliant ideas I can try? So what did you want to ask me?"

"Well..." Chase hesitated, wondering how to put it. "My question is sort of about women, but I think it might be one of the few things you know about the subject."

Jerome snorted. "I doubt it, but go ahead."

"How did you propose?"

Jerome's eyes widened, and for a moment he looked completely stunned. Then he chuckled. "Which time?"

THE TELEPHONE WAS RINGING when Tara arrived at her apartment. She fumbled with her key, finally got the door open and managed to catch it on about the ninth ring. "Hello?"

"It's about time you got home," Stella said, sounding a little hysterical. "I've been going out of my mind here. Where have you been?"

Tara tugged off her coat. "Picking up the proofs of the Wutherspoon photographs." She'd been an hour late for that meeting. "You'll have to see them. They're not bad."

"Never mind about that. I want details, Tara. Details."

"About what?" Tara asked innocently.

Stella sighed a huge, impatient sigh. "About last night, dummy! You know. The research you were helping Chase with."

"Oh, that," said Tara. She'd made a conscious effort to

void thinking about Chase and the night they'd spent together, after leaving his place this morning. "Well, um, I was just helping him with a scene from his book." Okay, here had been more than one scene. After the beach scene, they'd tried a shower scene, a kitchen scene while they were looking for food and a really erotic rescue scene on the sofa.

"Was it a sex scene?" Stella asked.

Tara closed her eyes. "You could say that."

"Go on. Go on. Was it a great sex scene?"

"It was an outstanding sex scene," Tara admitted.

"He *is* as good as his books, is he?" Stella asked with some satisfaction. "I thought he would be. I'm so happy for you. When are you seeing him again?"

"I don't know. We're scheduled to check out an orthodontist this afternoon, but—"

"A what?" asked Stella, sounding puzzled.

"An orthodontist." Tara carried the phone into the living room to check the floorboards. Sure enough, another one had lifted. Darn. "Apparently four out of five women identified their orthodontist as a good example of a real man."

"Where do they find these women?" Stella wondered. She lowered her voice to a whisper. "Listen, I've got some bad news here. Marvin ordered the Volaise à la Grecque all right, but he didn't know what it was. He didn't even read the menu. The waiter suggested he order it. Mrs. Grisly heard him do it. Can you imagine? Who goes to a French restaurant and orders that way?"

"Apparently Marvin," said Tara. So much for her skills as a great investigative reporter. "I guess this means Franklin's death was an accident after all."

"Yeah." Stella's tone was glum. "I was so sure I was right, but I wasn't. Darn, huh?"

"Yeah, darn," Tara said absently. She hung up the phone, disappointed, and, surprisingly enough, a little relieved. At least she didn't have to worry about Chase's "dangerous" warning anymore.

Chase! She leaned back against the counter and thought about Chase and his long-legged body, how he'd looked when she'd stripped off his jeans, the dark passion in his eyes when he'd finally entered her. He wasn't just good in bed. He was great in bed.

Unfortunately, that's all he was.

She dropped onto the sofa and pulled out the photographs from Wutherspoon's. There were a few good ones of Angie in front of the tent display, a few of the leather underwear that had her smiling and a couple of excellent ones of Gerald, looking suave and debonair and a lot like Cary Grant.

And nothing, nothing, nothing at all like Chase. Tara let the photographs slide out of her fingers, onto her lap. There was no doubt about it. Last night had been a major mistake and she should have had more sense. Yes, it had been great, and yes, she was fond of him, but he was in no way, shape or form the perfect mate she'd envisioned for herself. He wasn't elegant, he wasn't sophisticated and his idea of a good time was to play with his nephews. He had little sense of decor, hardly any sense of style and he knew next to nothing about romance, or how to wine and dine a woman. He ate oatmeal and drank tea and although he was a good example of today's man, she knew very well that she had no future with him, and she had no business sleeping with him. Not only was it morally wrong, it also might give him ideas and she didn't want him to get ideas. If the possessive gleam in his eye this morning was any indication, he'd already got some ideas, although they were mostly ideas about how they'd spend the night.

She thought about the press of his body and closed her eyes. No. She was not doing that again. And she probably didn't have to worry about a man like Chase getting other kinds of ideas because he wouldn't. Men like him weren't into commitment and maturity and all the other things she was looking for in a mate. However, it would be better if she put a stop to this now, before she was the one getting ideas.

BY THE TIME Chase arrived to pick her up for the orthodontist interview, she had her entire speech planned and rehearsed. The speech part shouldn't have been difficult. She'd written both "Diplomatic Dumps" as well as "Lively Lines for Leaving," plus she'd broken it off with a number of men, so she knew what to say. Most of them hadn't been too upset. A few had been astonished, as if they couldn't believe anyone would break up with them, and the rest had almost seemed relieved. That's probably how Chase would feel. He'd probably be relieved to hear that she wasn't expecting anything after their night together.

She shoved aside the suspicion that this was not the way Chase felt, and wasn't the way she felt, either, and concentrated steadily on all the reasons she was doing this.

She almost changed her mind when he bounded into her apartment a little before two. He had on his standard interview outfit—with a yellow tie this time—and he looked too delicious to be believed.

"Hi, there," he said in greeting, gave her a quick kiss, which she tried not to enjoy, and glanced around her apartment. "How are things here? What's broken this time?"

"Nothing." She forced a smile. "Everything's working today. Listen, I've rescheduled the orthodontist. He's free tomorrow afternoon, if that's all right for you."

"Sure. That will give me all day to brush my teeth." He grinned at her, a grin that faded after a moment. "You look a little pale. Is something wrong?"

"N-not really." She cleared her throat. "I was just, uh, thinking—"

"I've been thinking, too," said Chase. "And I think you should bring along a change of clothes. We've got an early appointment with the weatherman tomorrow."

Tara swallowed. "I don't think I can make that. Do you think you could do it yourself?"

His forehead creased into puzzled. "I suppose. But you can still leave from my place to wherever you have to go."

Tara twisted her hands together. "I don't think that's a good idea. As a matter of fact, I don't think it's a good idea for us to see each other again. At least not socially, I mean."

Chase couldn't have looked more stunned if he'd been hit by a grenade. "What?"

"I just don't think it would be a good idea. I mean, uh, I enjoyed being with you and everything, but…um…we shouldn't make a habit of it. After all, all we're doing is writing an article together. After we finish that, we'll be, uh, finished."

All the expression drained from his face, leaving it cold and blank. "Finished?"

"Yes." Tara cleared her throat. "As a matter of fact, it might be better if we split up the rest of the list." She picked up a piece of paper from the living-room table. "You've had lots of practice interviewing, so there's no reason for us to do it together. You can do your part and I can do my part and, um, well, I just think it would be better if we did it that way."

Chase blinked twice, then stretched out a hand, took the paper from her and stared at it. "I get the weatherman and the orthodontist, do I?"

"Yes. And I'll take the archaeologist and the corporate president."

His lips twisted. "You think they might be a better bet than me, do you?"

He looked so stunned and so hurt that Tara could have kicked herself. This was her fault. "No, no, that's not it at all, I…"

Chase shoved a hand in his pocket and slouched against the door frame, watching her. "You're not doing this right, you know."

"What?"

"You're supposed to tell me that although we've had a lot of good times, and I'm a special person, you think we'd be happier seeing other people. Then I agree with you because I usually do agree." He looked down, then up and straight at her, his dark eyes filled with misery. "Unfortunately, in this case, I don't. I won't be happier seeing anyone else." He shrugged. "Sorry, but I won't."

Tara winced. "I am sorry. I didn't mean—"

He chuckled, dry and humorless. "You don't have to explain, Tara. I know how this scene goes." He opened the door to leave. "As a matter of fact, I'm a master at it."

"Yeah, it's over," Hunter assured Bridgett. "Laromee's in jail and I don't see him getting out for a long, long time. The missile is safely back in the hands of the government." Now he could concentrate on the one thing he'd been wanting to concentrate on ever since he'd met her. "Now we can talk about us."

Bridgett faced him, her blond hair flying loose in the breeze. "There isn't any us, Hunter, at least, there isn't going to be."

Hunter narrowed his eyes. "What are you talking about? We've got a good thing going here. You're one hell of a woman, and—"

"And you're one hell of a man." She put her hand on his arm. "I do care about you. But you're not the man I want to spend the rest of my life with. You're just not husband material.''

Hunter felt as if he'd just been thumped by Laromee's thugs all over again. "Come on, baby, you don't mean that."

"Unfortunately, I do." Bridgett's round blue eyes filled. "I need someone who will stay at home nights, help take care of the children, carry out the garbage…handle our finances…bring me flowers once in a while…and fix our computer when it breaks. That's not going to be you."

"You don't know what you're talking about," Hunter growled, although he had a strong suspicion she was right.

"I think I do, and I think you know it. That's the kind of man I need, Hunter, and someday I'm going to find him."

Hunter couldn't think of one thing to say that could conceivably change her mind. Finally he bent forward and touched his lips to her cheek. "I hope you do, baby."

"I will." Her eyes filled with tears and determination. She'd do it, too. Anything Bridgett set her mind to, she'd get.

She turned and walked down the pier, toward the fading sunset. Hunter stayed where he was, watching her until she was out of sight. He'd taken a few bullets in his time, broken his leg in that damn helicopter accident, but he couldn't recall an event that hurt this much. She wasn't just leaving. She was taking his dreams with her.

Finally, when it was almost dark, he turned and walked back toward the boat, a lonely figure, with only his gun and his conscience for company.

"I'VE GOT GREAT NEWS," Jerome announced when he dropped by Chase's place a couple of weeks later. "Vanna and I went to the counselor."

Chase sourly eyed Jerome's cheerful demeanor. "That's good news? I thought counseling was the end of your marriage."

"Well, it isn't." Jerome settled onto the sofa, the living picture of a contented man. "It turns out that the reason Vanna wanted to go to a counselor is that she wants to have a baby."

Chase tried to put "motherly" in the adjectives he'd use to describe Vanna. It didn't go along with "fashion-conscious" and "sophisticated." "She does?"

"Uh-huh." Jerome grinned. "She didn't know how I would take to the idea. She was scared. She figured someone with my track record would be worried about responsibility and the level of commitment required to have a family."

Chase nodded. Man-about-town Jerome didn't strike him as the family-man type. "I can understand that."

"Well, I can't! I love responsibility and commitment. As a matter of fact, they're my middle names."

"You're middle name is Daxton."

"It doesn't matter. I like the idea of having a family. It took me a little while to convince Vanna and the counselor that I really meant it, but when I did, Vanna was fine." Some of his elation faded. "Then she insisted we spend the rest of the session discussing my weird behavior recently. She thought I was having a nervous breakdown or something." He shook his head. "Women. Who knows how they think?"

"I sure don't," Chase grunted. No, that wasn't true. He knew exactly how one woman's mind worked.

Jerome shot him a concerned look before continuing in

a relentlessly cheerful tone. "I've got more good news. Your editor called, and he's delighted with your book."

Chase tried to summon up some interest in the manuscript he'd finished a few days ago. "Good."

"According to Wendell, it's more than good. He said this is the best work you've ever done. Better sex scenes, better plot and better characters. He's confident it's a bestseller, and he's working on selling the movie rights even as we speak."

"Great." Chase sank lower in his chair. At least he could invent a hero who was a real man even if wasn't one himself.

Jerome cleared his throat. "I also spoke with that woman from *Real Men* magazine. Charlene. She said she adored the article and thought you'd done a splendid, splendid job and she's incredibly grateful."

"Oh yeah?" So Tara had finished it, had she? He'd interviewed the two men on his list, decided they were both well-dressed, intelligent, had good teeth and great senses of humor, and faxed the information to Tara. Maybe she'd hook up with one of them, if she hadn't already hooked up with one of the characters on her list. He thought of her with someone else, and his misery deepened.

"Charlene did mention something about it not being finished, though. Something about the fiftieth one not being quite right..."

"That's no surprise," Chase grumbled. "Tara is probably busy thinking up a few million other things she wants in a man." They'd all be qualities that he didn't have, too. He wouldn't be surprised if she'd decided she wanted a man who could dance the fox-trot, disarm a missile, rebuild a car engine and cook a gourmet meal, all while wearing a tux.

Jerome studied Chase. "What's the matter with you? You've been moping around ever since you and Tara—"

"Of course I've been moping around," Chase growled. "She dumped me, remember? What do you expect me to do? Laugh and sing and take up with another woman?"

"That's what you've always done before."

Chase blinked. Jerome was right. That was what he used to do. He'd been ditched by plenty of women and it had never bothered him. Then again, it had never felt like this before either.

He shoved a hand through his hair, absently noticing its length. It was time he got a haircut. After all, real men were perfectly groomed.

He scowled at that. Darn Tara anyway! He never used to think about things like that before he met her. Now, he thought about all kinds of dumb things and he did dumb things as well. Just the other day he'd changed the toner cartridge in the printer! Before her, he had to get someone in to do that for him. He could also write a book on manners, knew more than he needed to know about men's fashion, and had even read *Moby Dick* because Tara had once mentioned how much she liked it.

But deep inside he knew that no matter what he did, he was never going to get Tara to feel the way about him that he did about her.

He was still crazy about her, too. He hadn't known he could feel this miserable, but it turned out, he could. There didn't seem to be anything he could do about it either. When he'd first walked out of her apartment, he'd been furious. Furious with her for calling it off, and furious with himself for being dumb enough to get into that situation in the first place. He'd known what she wanted in a man, and he'd known he didn't qualify. He should have left well enough alone. He resolved to put her out of his mind.

Unfortunately for him, love didn't work that way. Chase couldn't believe he could miss someone as much as he missed Tara. He thought about her at least once a second.

Every time the phone rang he hoped it might be her, with another dumb suggestion about what a real man was like. When he was proofreading his book he thought of her, of how she'd looked playing helicopter, of the way her eyes sparkled when she smiled, or the flash of her hair in the sunlight, or how she'd felt moving under him.

"You've got it bad, don't you?" asked Jerome.

Chase focused back on his friend's wide, sympathetic eyes. "Yeah, I do," he admitted. "You must have been through this before. When am I going to stop feeling like this?"

Jerome winced. "The way you look I'd say quite a while."

Chase dropped his head back and stared up at the ceiling. If he had to feel like this for another day he'd be insane. *Quite a while* sounded like a death sentence. "Hunter is lucky," he grumbled. "In his next book, he'll have forgotten all about Bridgett."

"Hunter is fiction," said Jerome. "Unfortunately for you, you aren't."

Chase lifted his head high enough to see his friend. "Yeah, well, as it turns out, I'm not real either." At least, not real enough for Tara.

TARA WAS STILL STRUGGLING with number fifty.

She sat in her kitchen, with her papers spread around her, hoping for inspiration. "How about 'Real men are talented'?" she muttered to herself. No, that was covered in intelligent, successful and creative. "Or maybe, uh, 'Real men like dogs.'" Nope. Animals had taken care of that. Of course, there was always "Real men can reload in less than five seconds," or Chase's other favorite, "Real men eat lizard."

She smiled briefly, then threw her pencil on the table. None of those would do. They were all wrong, which was exactly what Chase was, and she had no idea why she kept thinking about him when she'd met a couple of great men who were almost perfect and she wasn't even dating them much less thinking about them.

Okay, she did know. Breaking up with Chase hadn't been as easy as breaking up with Owen or Evan or any of the other men she'd dated. She'd tried going out with a couple of others, but hadn't enjoyed herself. She'd even had dinner with Gerald, at a restaurant so elegant and so upscale it made Armand's look like a café. Although it was exactly the type of date she wanted, she'd been relieved when it was over.

She made a few more attempts at number fifty but none of them were decent, either, so when Stella dropped by unexpectedly, she was happier than normal to see her.

Stella, however, did not look happy. She stomped through the door, threw her coat on the sofa and glowered at the room. "Did I ever tell you that I don't like this apartment?" she asked.

"Constantly," said Tara.

"Well, I don't." Stella flopped down beside her coat. "But don't take it personally. Right now, I don't like very much."

Tara sat across from her. "What's wrong? You haven't come up with another suspect at Wutherspoon's, have you?" She crossed her fingers as she asked. She'd finished writing that piece and it was ready to send off. Another suspect would mean another delay.

"No," said Stella. "As a matter of fact, I'm giving up on my investigation. As sad as it is to say, it looks like poor Franklin died a natural death. Either that or my investigative skills aren't worth squat."

"Good," Tara muttered. Stella shot her a glare and she added, "You have to admit, it's better than finding out you've been working with a criminal all this time."

"I suppose." Stella plucked at a cushion. "I'm still disappointed, though. I thought for sure that something was going on, but I guess I just made it up. I wanted to see something, so I did." She scowled darkly. "Just like I made up Stanley."

"Stanley?"

"Yes, Stanley." Her voice rose. "I thought Stanley was interested in solving this too, but he wasn't!"

Tara shook her head. "Have I missed something somewhere?"

"No, I did." Stella folded her arms. "Do you know what Stanley did tonight? He made a pass at me!"

"That's…unfortunate."

"Tell me about it," said Stella. "Even worse, when I refused, and told him what a creep I thought he was, being engaged to Lorraine and making a pass at me, he told me that I should have been expecting it. 'Why did you think I was going along with this silly investigation of yours?' he said. I told him I thought he agreed that something sinister had happened, and he laughed!"

Tara could have cheerfully wrung Stanley's neck. "That's awful."

"I know. He said he knew all along who ordered the Volaise à la Grecque!" Stella sighed and dropped her forehead into a hand. "There I was, thinking he was such a great guy, and all the time he was trying to have a little fling on the side. How dumb can I be?"

"It wasn't your fault, Stell."

"It was my fault," said Stella, raising her head. "Now that I think about it, he did drop a few hints, but I wouldn't let myself see it. I didn't want him to be like that. I wanted him to be everything Bill wasn't, probably so I could tell myself men like that exist."

"They do," Tara assured her. "Stanley just isn't one of them."

"No, he isn't but I fooled myself into thinking he was." She shook her head. "I thought only you did that, but it turns out that I do it, too."

Tara started at her, puzzled. "You thought only I did what?"

"Fooled yourself. Ignored reality."

"I do not do that!" Tara said indignantly.

"You do so do it, Tara!" Stella gestured around. "Take this apartment. There's nothing good about it. It's two stories up, it's falling apart, it's too expensive, there isn't enough room, and you can't sit around in jeans and feel comfortable because it's so uncomfortable. But you keep telling yourself that it's perfect."

Tara squirmed. "It's not like that."

"Sure it is," said Stella, warming to the subject. "The same thing is true with this mythical man you say you want. Mr. Elegant, Debonair, Charming. You've convinced yourself that's the type of man you need, so you dumped the only man you really ever cared anything about."

Tara's mouth went dry. "You don't understand, Stella," she objected, although she had a funny feeling Stella understood all too well.

"Yes, I do." Stella got to her feet. "Matthew is sleeping over at a friend's place, so I'm going to take in a movie. Do you want to come along?"

"No," said Tara. "I need to finish this article." She looked hopefully at Stella. "I don't suppose you can think of some other quality a real man should have?"

"No," said Stella. "Unless you want to include 'Real men aren't jerks.'"

"I think I've covered that," Tara muttered. She closed the door after Stella, wandered into the living room and dropped into a chair. Stella was wrong. This was a lovely apartment and Chase was not—

A small piece of plaster came loose from the ceiling and

fell to the floor. Tara stared and gave in. Okay, maybe Stella was right about this apartment. It might look elegant, but underneath it was a mess. She wasn't wrong about Chase, though. He didn't look like her Mr. Perfect, and he didn't have the qualities that were important to her. He wasn't anywhere close to Cary Grant, and that was the type of man she wanted.

He did have some good qualities, though. He was honest and sweet, and good to his family, and a hard worker, and fun to be with, and she was crazy about him, but he wasn't sophisticated and suave and no one would ever call him debonair, and his taste in clothes was atrocious. She didn't mind those things, though. As a matter of fact, she sort of liked that about him. No, she loved that about him.

She sprang to her feet. "Oh, Tara, you are such an idiot!" She didn't care if Chase didn't have any quality on that stupid real man list. She loved him. She loved all the wrong things about him more than she would ever love the right things about anyone else.

Now what was she going to do? She could always move out of this apartment, but moving into Chase's life again might not be so easy. She'd hurt him badly, and he wasn't likely to give her another crack at it. Hadn't she written an article about this? "Perfect Prose to Plead Your Case," subtitled "How to Win Him Back." Maybe that would give her a clue.

Half an hour later, after reviewing the article on her computer, she didn't have much of a game plan. Sending him flowers would be dumb, considering he'd never sent her flowers. Romantic poetry wouldn't do much for him, which was a good thing because nothing romantic rhymed with Chase. Arriving at his door wearing black lace had possibilities, although Chase wasn't a black-lace kind of guy. He'd probably appreciate it more if she showed up in black turtleneck and leggings so they could act out the helicopter scene again, but if she did that, the neighbors would think she was robbing him.

She sat back. She was just going to have to wing it. She could use the article as an excuse. That was it. She could ask him to meet her to discuss number fifty and, well, once she got him alone, she could—

The phone rang beside her, making her jump. Be Chase, she pleaded, although there was no reason for him to call. Real men didn't read minds, even though it would be handy if they did. "Hello?"

"Tara?" It was Stella.

"Uh-huh." She sighed, disappointed. "I thought you were at the movies."

"I'm not. Listen, I've been thinking—"

"I've been thinking, too," Tara admitted. "And I've decided you're right. About everything."

"That's great," said Stella. "I've been thinking, too. If Mr. Wutherspoon died because he ate some of the shrimp dip, why did he wait until the middle of the entrée to do it? If it's that serious, wouldn't it hit you right away?"

Tara was not interested in Stella's investigation right now. "I don't know."

"Neither do I," said Stella. "I'm going to go ask Gerald right now."

"Gerald?" Tara slowly straightened. "I thought he was your chief suspect."

"He isn't. He ordered the Caesar salad, so he can't have done it. And he's allergic to fish himself. He'll know how long it takes for a reaction to start."

"He should." Why was she so uneasy about this? "But I'm not sure you should—"

"I have to. I'm going to talk to him right now. I'm only a few minutes away from the office, and I think he's still there. I'll call you from Wutherspoon's and let you know what I find out."

Tara's discomfort increased. It was after eight. There wouldn't be anyone left at the office but Gerald. "I don't think this is a good idea, Stell. Why don't I—" She stopped when she realized she was talking to dead air.

She set the phone down and got up to pace the room. This was not good. Stella shouldn't meet Gerald alone to quiz him about allergies. That was ridiculous, though. Gerald wasn't dangerous. He hadn't even had a fish dish around him. He'd just ordered Caesar salad and... What had Armand said? Everyone forgets the anchovy paste in Caesar salad.

Tara shivered. She'd forgotten about that Caesar salad, too. She hadn't even mentioned it to Stella. So what? Gerald mustn't have thought about the anchovies... No, that wasn't right. A man like Gerald was sure to know the basic ingredients of a salad! But he wouldn't have eaten it because he was allergic to fish himself. He'd told her that.

So why would a man order a salad he knew he couldn't eat?

"Stop thinking that, Tara!" Gerald probably had a good reason for ordering Caesar salad, and even if he didn't, he wouldn't hurt anyone. He was a charming man, not a murderer! She knew him. She'd even had dinner with him. He didn't looked cold-blooded. He looked like everyone else.

"Murderers don't look like murderers," Chase had told her. *"They look like everyone else."*

And Stella was going to walk into his office—his deserted office—and tell him everything she'd found out.

She flew back to the phone. No matter what, she didn't like the idea of Stella and Gerald alone together in the empty offices of Wutherspoon Outerwear. She picked up the receiver, then set it down again. Who was she going to call? The police? What would she tell them? "I think Gerald Charmichael knows there's anchovy paste in Caesar salad?'' That was hardly going to cause them to rush into action.

She'd have to do this herself. She grabbed her purse, then realized that wasn't a good idea, either. It would take her at least half an hour to reach Wutherspoon's offices, and that might be too long. Stella had told her she was only minutes away. She had to do something, but she couldn't think of what that something might be. Who would know? Cary might know, but he wasn't around. Ephram. Lowell. Nope. Not even the weatherman from Channel Three would know. She needed a real man and she needed one right now.

She headed back to the phone, tripping over a loose floorboard in her haste. She knew exactly who she needed. She took a deep breath, and called Chase.

TWO HOURS LATER, she was in Stella's apartment, drinking tea with a shaken but triumphant Stella, an undernourished-looking police detective named Frank and the realest real man she'd ever met, Chase.

''It was so weird,'' Stella was explaining. ''I told Gerald all about my investigation, and how I knew what everyone ordered, and then asked him if he could remember anything else.''

She paused to sip her tea. Tara took a look at Chase. He was sitting in a deep brown armchair, looking exactly the same as she remembered, ruffled hair, slightly bearded chin, T-shirt, khakis. She'd had a hard time taking her eyes off him, but he'd barely looked at her. Tara crossed her fingers. *Please let this work out. Please.*

''Go on,'' Frank said to Stella.

Stella continued. ''Gerald got this funny expression on his face, and the next thing I knew, he was closing the door, and—'' she shuddered ''—and then he was attacking me! Can you imagine? It was like something out of a bad movie. I was scared to death.'' She shot Frank a look of utter gratitude. "If the police hadn't arrived…''

Frank flushed. "It wasn't just the police, ma'am.'' He gestured toward Chase. "If Mr. Montgomery hadn't called us when he did, insisting that your life was in danger and we needed to take action immediately…''

"Tara was the one who called me,'' Chase put in. He glanced at Tara, then looked away. "She figured it out. I didn't even get there until it was all over.'' His wry smile didn't reach his eyes. "I was there for the arrest, so it wasn't a total loss. I got some great research notes on that part.''

Tara melted back against the arm of the sofa. What a great guy. She'd blurted out the whole story and he'd taken over. "I'll call the police. You stay there.''

"How did you know, Tara?'' asked Stella.

Tara was so distracted by him that she could barely remember. She briefly explained about the salad, and let Stella fill in Frank about the article. "You won't have any problem selling that one,'' Frank said when Stella had finished. "It was a clever piece of detective work, although next time you decide to write an investigative article, you should come to us sooner.''

"I'm never doing that again,'' said Tara. "After this, I'm sticking to fluff.''

"Sounds like a good idea to me,'' Chase grunted. He got up, thanked Stella for the tea and picked up his worn brown jacket. He was going to leave! Tara jumped to her feet then remembered her friend. "Do you want me to stay here with you tonight, Stella? Or maybe you'd feel better at my place?''

Much to her relief, Stella shook her head. "No thank you. I'll be fine. Matthew is spending the evening with a friend, and Frank's going to stay with me for a little while.''

"That's right," said Frank. "I'll make sure she's okay. Do you mind if I use your phone, though? I need to let my wife know where I am."

He emphasized the word *wife* and Stella beamed at him.

She was still beaming at him when Tara and Chase left. She gave them both big hugs and whispered, "Thank you."

The door closed behind them. Chase started down the hall and Tara hurried to keep up with him. "I, uh, want to thank you, too."

Chase opened the exit door and held it for her. "You don't have to thank me, Tara. I didn't do anything except make a phone call."

"It wasn't just a phone call! You managed to convince the police's tactical squad that a Caesar salad constituted an emergency."

He shrugged. "It wasn't that difficult, although it did help that the guy I spoke with had read all my books."

"I'm sure it did," Tara murmured.

Chase stopped behind his car. "I imagine a real man would have handled it a lot differently. He'd have smashed through the door and taken out Gerald himself."

"No, he wouldn't." The parking lot was well-lit, so she could look him straight in the eye. "A real man would have done exactly what you did. Find the best solution to the problem."

"Right," said Chase. He started to turn away.

Tara drew in a desperate breath. "I need your help with something else."

He faced her again. "What? Do you have another friend investigating a murder?"

Tara's giggle was a touch on the hysterical side. "No. No, it's nothing like that. It's the article. I'm having a little problem coming up with number fifty."

His jaw clenched. "I don't have any ideas."

"I do. I've come up with a couple I'd like to run past you."

He shrugged, loose and uncaring. "Fax them over and I'll take a look."

"I can tell you right now." Did he have to stand so far away? Tara took a few steps forward to close the distance. "How about 'Real men are tolerant'? You know, like, say, if you did something dumb, they'd understand."

His nod was slow in coming. "That's not bad."

"And then there's, um, 'Real men give you a second chance.'" She pleaded with him with her eyes. "Say you somehow screw things up between the two of you, and you'd like to give it another try, they, uh, do."

He fingered his chin, watching her. "I could go for that one, I suppose."

The slam of her heartbeat seemed to echo around the deserted lot. "This is the one I like best, though. 'A real man is the man you love. That's really all that matters.'"

Chase didn't say anything for an excruciatingly long time. When he finally spoke, his voice was hoarse and low. "Do you know anyone like that?"

"Only you," said Tara. He didn't say anything and she took one more step toward him. "Look, I'm not suggesting anything. Not really. I mean, I don't expect you to...well, you might, but...um, we could have coffee or in your case tea, and, um, go for a drive or...maybe there's a scene from your book I could help you with, just to see if maybe someday you might..."

"I already do," said Chase. He started for her, and she rushed against him, hugging him, almost weeping at how good it felt to be near him again. He nuzzled his head down against the top of her head and squeezed her, hard. "You better be sure this time," he growled into her ear. "I don't want you dumping me again. This is a lifetime kind of thing."

"I won't ever do that again," Tara promised. "And yes, it is a lifetime kind of thing." Real men were into commitment.

Chase raised his head to look into her face. "Are you positive? After all, I do eat oatmeal. Lots of oatmeal. I eat it all the time."

"I don't care. Real men eat whatever they want."

His eyes flared but there was still a touch of uncertainty there. "We're not living in your apartment no matter how great you think it is. That place is a disaster. You will move into my house, which will officially become our house."

"I don't care as long as you're there." Real men didn't all have a good sense of decor, but it wasn't important. She'd fix it up a little...get rid of some of his furniture, move in hers, ditch that picnic table...

"You'll never have dinner with an environmentalist alone again?"

"A what? Oh, sure. Whatever. I'll avoid them like the plague." She snuggled closer, smiling. Apparently, real men could be jealous.

He clamped a hand on her bottom, pressing her against him. "You'll do all the housework?"

"No," she whispered. He pulled her closer to him and the heat spread through her, but she wasn't so far gone she'd agree to that! She bit against his earlobe. "Real men like housework, Chase."

He stiffened. "I don't."

"How about if we do it together in the nude?"

Chase laughed and his grip on her tightened. "Then I'll like it."

Tara squirmed against him. "There, see. I knew all along that you were a real man."

He grinned, lighthearted, happy and easy. "You think so, do you?"

"I sure do," said Tara.

The combination of physical attraction and danger can be explosive!

Coming in July 1999
three steamy romances together in one book

HOT PURSUIT

by bestselling authors

JOAN JOHNSTON

ANNE STUART

MALLORY RUSH

Joan Johnston—A WOLF IN SHEEP'S CLOTHING
The Hazards and the Alistairs had been feuding for generations, so when Harriet Alistair laid claim to her great-uncle's ranch, Nathan Hazard was at his ornery worst. But then he saw her and figured it was time to turn on the charm, forgive, forget…and seduce?

Anne Stuart—THE SOLDIER & THE BABY
What could possibly bring together a hard-living, bare-chested soldier and a devout novice? At first, it was an innocent baby…and then it was a passion hotter than the simmering jungle they had to escape from.

Mallory Rush—LOVE SLAVE
Rand Slick hired Rachel Tinsdale to infiltrate the dark business of white slavery. It was a risky assignment, Rachel knew. But even more dangerous was her aching desire for her sexy, shadowy client….

Available at your favorite retail outlet.

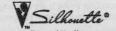

Look us up on-line at: http://www.romance.net

PSBR799

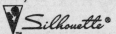

COMING NEXT MONTH

HARLEQUIN
Duets™

#7

ANNIE, GET YOUR GROOM by Kristin Gabriel

Private eye Cole Rafferty is a happily single man—despite the efforts of his matchmaking father. When Annie Bonacci turned to him for help, he made her a deal. If she played his fiancée-from-hell, he'd take her case for free. Little did he know he'd become fiancé number *three* for Annie...only soon he wanted to become husband number *one*.

TAMING LUKE by Jennifer Drew

Jane Grant's directive was simple: Transform Luke Stanton from Tarzan to tycoon...or her job was toast. So, no matter how desirable she found the enigmatic wildman, she had to make him a CEO worth his salt. Trouble was, Luke fought her every step of the way...and made her fall in love with the man it was her mission to change.

#8

THE BRIDE WORE GYM SHOES by Jacqueline Diamond

Marriage counselor Krista Lund doesn't believe in visions—especially when the prediction involved her sexy but annoying neighbor, Connor Fallon, and her wearing a wedding dress and red gym shoes! But, when Connor invited Krista on a romantic weekend to Vegas, she began to wonder if marrying this drop-dead gorgeous man *was* such a crazy idea after all....

MADDIE'S MILLIONAIRE by Tracy South

Maddie Randall was new to Ravens Gap, so how was she supposed to know that Keller Lowry was the most eligible bachelor this side of the Smokies? But after she wrecked his kitchen, renamed his dog and generally turned his life upside down, Maddie couldn't leave Keller alone until she'd set everything straight. Or lost her heart trying....